# Absent Lord

Comparative Studies in Religion and Society
Mark Juergensmeyer, editor

1. *Redemptive Encounters: Three Modern Styles in the Hindu Tradition,* by Lawrence A. Babb
2. *Saints and Virtues,* edited by John Stratton Hawley
3. *Utopias in Conflict: Religion and Nationalism in Modern India,* by Ainslie T. Embree
4. *Mama Lola: A Vodou Priestess in Brooklyn,* by Karen McCarthy Brown
5. *The New Cold War? Religious Nationalism Confronts the Secular State,* by Mark Juergensmeyer
6. *Pious Passion: The Emergence of Modern Fundamentalism in the United States and Iran,* by Martin Riesebrodt, translated by Don Reneau
7. *Devi: Goddesses of India,* edited by John Stratton Hawley and Donna Marie Wulff
8. *Absent Lord: Ascetics and Kings in a Jain Ritual Culture,* by Lawrence A. Babb

# Absent Lord

## *Ascetics and Kings in a Jain Ritual Culture*

Lawrence A. Babb

UNIVERSITY OF CALIFORNIA PRESS
*Berkeley · Los Angeles · London*

University of California Press
Berkeley and Los Angeles, California

University of California Press, Ltd.
London, England



Library of Congress Cataloging-in-Publication Data

Babb, Lawrence A.
Absent lord : ascetics and kings in a Jain ritual culture / Lawrence A. Babb.
p. cm. — (Comparative studies in religion and society ; 8)
Includes bibliographical references and index.
ISBN 0-520-20323-2 (alk. paper). —
ISBN 0-520-20324-0 (pbk.:alk. paper)
1. Jainism—Rituals. 2. Religious life—Jainism. I. Title. II. Series.
BL1376.B33 1996
294.4'92—dc20 95-35643
CIP

Printed in the United States of America
9 8 7 6 5 4 3 2 1

The paper used in this publication meets the minimum requirements of American National Standard for Information Sciences—Permanence of Paper for Printed Library Materials, ANSI Z39.48-1984.

# Contents


List of Illustrations vii

Acknowledgments ix

Note on Transliteration xi

Introduction 1

1. Victors 22
   - *The Lord's Last Life* 23
   - *The Cosmos* 38
   - *Living Ascetics* 52
2. Kings of the Gods 64
   - *The Lord's Bath* 65
   - *Reflexivity* 84
3. Magical Monks: A Ritual Subculture 102
   - *Ascetic Career as Ritual Charter* 103
   - *Dādāgurudevs* 111
   - *A Ritual Subculture* 126
4. Valor: The Transformation of Warrior-Kings 137
   - *Kings Who Give Up Meat* 138
   - *Khartar Gacch Legends* 160
   - *Warrior-Kings Transformed* 168
5. Giving and Giving Up 174
   - *Variations* 176
   - *Hot Potatoes* 186

Notes 197

Glossary 217

Bibliography 223

Index 231

# Illustrations

FIGURES


1. A *pūjā* principal holding offerings 29
2. Pārśvanāth with Dharṇendra and Padmāvatī 35
3. The Jain cosmos 39
4. Receiving a blessing from a monk 62
5. An image of Mahāvīr 67
6. Participants in a *snātra pūjā* performing *caitya vandan* 73
7. Bathing the image in *snātra pūjā* 75
8. A crowned worshiper in Ahmedabad 80
9. Diagram of rice formed in *akṣat pūjā* 89
10. Footprint image of a Dādāguru 112
11. Image of Jincandrasūri "Maṇidhārī" 113
12. Jindattsūri pointing to names of clans 162


MAP


Gujarat and Rajasthan 18

# Acknowledgments

The research on which this book is based took place at two separate times and places. I spent the summer of 1986 in Ahmedabad doing a preliminary study of Śvetāmbar Jain ritual; I was in Jaipur from August 1990 to May 1991 engaged in a more comprehensive study of Jain life. The Ahmedabad work was supported by a National Endowment for the Humanities summer stipend. My work in Jaipur was supported by a Fulbright senior research fellowship.

I would like to thank Professors D. Malvania and N. Shah of the L. D. Institute of Indology for their assistance and hospitality during my stay in Ahmedabad. I also owe special thanks to Dr. S. S. Jhaveri of Ahmedabad for his wise counsel and gracious efforts to further my understanding of the Jain tradition. I thank colleagues at the University of Rajasthan, especially in the Department of History and Indian Culture, for their generous assistance during my stay in Jaipur. I gained more than I can easily say from the intellectual stimulation of conversations with these colleagues, especially Dr. Mukund Lath. I also thank Arvind Agrawal for his generous assistance in getting me settled and started in Jaipur. I am indebted to too many members of Jaipur's Jain community to mention all of them here. I owe special thanks, however, to Mr. Rajendra Srimal and Mr. Milap Chand Jain for their extremely generous reponses to my inquiries. I would also like to express my deepest gratitude to my good friend and colleague Surendra Bothara for his companionship and guidance. There were many other good friends who made Jaipur into a second home for Nancy and me. To Daya and Francine Krishna, Mukund and Neerja Lath, Fateh and Indu Singh, Rashmi Patni, and Arun and Vijay Karki we both send our most affectionate thanks.

In response to both oral and written versions of this manuscript (or parts thereof) many colleagues have given me helpful criticism and comment. I am especially indebted to Phyllis Granoff, James Laidlaw, and John Cort. John Cort, in particular, has been an unfailing source of encouragement, an absolutely reliable critic, and a true and good mentor in all things Jain. My thanks indeed. But to all these thanks I must add that any errors of fact and interpretation are mine alone.

My wife Nancy has shared my life in India through good times and bad and has helped me in my work in ways too numerous to mention. To say that I am grateful hardly expresses what I feel, but grateful I am.

Some portions of this book consist of revised and recast material drawn from earlier articles of mine. I am grateful to *History of Religions* and the University of Chicago Press for permission to use materials from "The Great Choice: Worldly Values in a Jain Ritual Culture" (Babb 1994, © 1994 by the University of Chicago. All rights reserved), and also to the editors of *Journal of Anthropological Research* and *The Journal of Asian Studies* for permission to use materials, respectively, from "Giving and Giving Up: The Eightfold Worship among Śvetāmbar Mūrtipūjak Jains" (1988) and "Monks and Miracles: Religious Symbols and Images of Origin among Osvāl Jains" (1993).

# A Note on Transliteration

I have employed standard conventions for the romanization of words from Indian languages. Words from Indian languages have been pluralized by adding an unitalicized "s." I have used diacritics on personal names and many place names (although I have used conventional spellings for such familiar place names as Ahmedabad and Delhi). The Hindi retroflex flap and the Sanskrit vocalic "*ṛ*" are both reproduced as "*ṛ*." The soft-palatal nasal in words like *sangh* is represented by an unmarked "*n*." Many of the Indic words reproduced in this book have both Hindi and Sanskrit forms, with the Hindi form dropping the final "*a*" (*dāna* thus becoming *dān*). In keeping with the vernacular milieu of the study, I have privileged the Hindi forms throughout most of the book (Mahāvīra therefore appearing as Mahāvīr). In some cases, however, I have bowed to conventions employed by secondary sources on which I rely heavily and have given the more familiar Sanskrit versions (for example, Śaiva and Vaiṣṇava). Occasionally, moreover, context or common practice has made it seem desirable to give the word in question in its Sanskrit form even though it has been given in its Hindi form elsewhere in the book. When this has been done, both forms are included in the glossary. Recurrent and important terms, but not all Indic terms, are included in the glossary; Hindi glosses given in the text are not given in the glossary.

# Introduction

What does it mean to worship beings that one believes are completely indifferent to, and entirely beyond the reach of, any form of worship whatsoever? What are the implications of such a relationship with sacred beings for the religious life of a community? These turn out to be questions that can be investigated and answered, for a very close approximation of such a state of affairs can be found in the South Asian religious traditions known collectively in English as Jainism. This book is an exploration of one of Jainism's several branches from the standpoint of the interactions—real, putative, or lacking altogether—between human beings and the sacred entities with which they attempt to build ritual relationships.

The book deals with these issues at two levels. Most of the book is a consideration of a specific Jain tradition on its own terms. As readers will come to see, to worship entities such as those worshiped by the Jains is to possess a very specific understanding of the nature and meaning of ritual. My goal is to characterize this understanding and to trace its implications for other areas of Jain religious life. My readers will, I hope, come to see that divine "absence" can be as rich as divine "presence" in its possibilities for informing a religious response to the cosmos. At the same time, however, Jain traditions exist as part of a wider South Asian religious universe. At the end of the book I place Jain traditions in a broader context by showing how they relate to ritual patterns found in other Indic traditions.

## THE JAINS

Jainism is Buddhism's lesser-known cousin; although their belief systems are in some ways radically different, they are together the only surviving examples of India's ancient non-Vedic religious traditions. Jainism is above all, and justly, celebrated for its systematic practice of nonviolence (*ahiṃsā*) and for the rigor of the asceticism it promotes. Jainism is sometimes said to have been founded by Mahāvīra in the sixth century B.C.E. In reality, however, Jain traditions are much older than this, dating back in all probability to the teachings of Pārśvanāth, who lived in the ninth century B.C.E. Unlike Buddhism, Jainism never (until quite recently) spread beyond India; but also unlike Buddhism, it did not die out in India, and it continues to be an important element in India's contemporary religious life. Although the Jains are relatively few (currently they probably number around four million), many among them enjoy positions of great power and influence in modern Indian society. In northern India the Jains are concentrated mainly in Gujarat, Madhya Pradesh, and Rajasthan; farther south they are found mainly in Maharashtra and Karnataka. Jains, however, live everywhere in India, and significant numbers of Jains also live in Europe and North America.

Jains have a strong and conspicuous religious identity in India. Their monks and nuns are frequently seen in India's urban centers, and are readily identifiable as Jain mendicants. The rigor of both monastic and lay Jain ascetic praxis is widely known and admired. This asceticism is manifested in many ways, but emblematic of its uncompromising severity—in the public eye and in reality—is the fact that death by self-starvation (*sallekhanā*) is enshrined as one of Jainism's highest ideals. Jains are also widely known to place great emphasis on the principle of nonviolence. For non-Jain observers this is dramatized by the brooms carried by Jain mendicants for the purpose of removing small forms of life before sitting or lying down, and by the practice of some Jain mendicants of donning masks to prevent the wearer's breath from harming microscopic forms of life in the atmosphere. The commitment to nonviolence is also publicly manifested in the generous support lay Jains give to animal welfare organizations and to organizations promoting vegetarianism. Few visitors to Delhi fail to notice the Jain Birds' Hospital, conspicuously located at Chandi Chawk in one of the busiest concourses of the city.

Lay Jains also bear a stereotypical social identity as wealthy traders.

However, this element of Jain identity requires qualification. It is not true that all Jains are traders; Jains are found in diverse occupations, and in fact in the south some Jains are farmers. Nor is it the case that all Jains are wealthy, although many undeniably are. Nonetheless, for centuries the Jains have been strongly identified with trade, and in the north Indian region—which is the cultural locale of this study—they are predominantly a merchant community. It should also be said that business in general tends to be the most admired occupation among the Jains of this region. Jains are renowned for the munificence of the monetary donations they provide for the upkeep of their temples and other religious institutions. Their temples are famous for their lavishness and also for their cleanliness.

In North India the general social category to which Jains are assigned by others carries the label *Baniyā,* which is an all-purpose term for traders and moneylenders. It is not a term that applies specifically to Jains, for various Hindu groups belong to this category as well. Most groups belonging to the Baniyā category—Jains or not—share a generally similar lifestyle and social persona. Probably the most important of their shared characteristics is a strict vegetarianism, which in fact is a strong social marker of Baniyā status. The term *Baniyā* is also a word with definite negative connotations of miserliness and shady dealing. To note this is, of course, not to endorse such a judgment. Most non-Jains refer to Jains more or less automatically as Baniyās, but because of the unfortunate associations of the term, many Jains (and non-Jain Baniyās as well) do not use this term in self-reference (on these points, see Ellis 1991 and Laidlaw 1995:Ch. 5). The preferred term is *Mahājan,* which literally means "great person." This word lacks the negative connotations of Baniyā, and is generally seen as referring to the category of merchants and traders, both Jain and non-Jain.

To what degree do the Jains see themselves as an actual community of co-religionists? The question of Jain identity in relation to other religious identities is a complicated matter. For present purposes let it suffice to say that this remains an ambiguous issue and that Jains are continuing to negotiate their identities—religious and social—to the present day. A heightening of Jain self-identification as a discrete religious community seems to be a relatively recent development. As Paul Dundas points out (1992: 3–6), Jains often reported themselves as "Hindu" in the early British censuses, and even today Jains see this question in more than one way. Some Jains accept the label *Hindu,* understanding the term in its most inclusive sense, while others are more adamant in the claim to a completely separate Jain identity. Many Jains worship at Hindu temples and participate in Hindu festivals. These issues are, of course, greatly complicated by the fact that the status of "Hinduism" as a unified religious tradition is itself doubtful and contested, and that "Hindu identity" is a historically recent phenomenon. The modern tendency is probably in the direction of a Jain identity separate from that of Hindus, but this transformation is far from complete and will probably never be completed. There appear to be, moreover, countervailing forces. For example, my own general observation is that, as religious politics has become increasingly important in India, large numbers of Jains have identified with the Hindu nationalist viewpoint with hardly a second thought.

Within the Jain community—if it is a community—there are many fissures and cleavages. The most important division is the sectarian divide (and rivalry) between the Śvetāmbars and the Digambars. The term *Śvetāmbar* means "white clad" in reference to the fact that mendicants of this branch of Jainism wear white garments. Digambar means "space clad," which is to say unclad, and the term refers to the fact that male mendicants of this branch wear nothing. These two great branches of Jainism possess different bodies of sacred writings and are also radically distinct socially. Even when they live in the same locality, their adherents are drawn from totally different castes. In Jaipur—one of the principal sources of material for this book—most Digambar Jains (sometimes collectively called Sarāvgīs)[1] belong to either the Khaṇḍelvāl or the Agravāl caste, with the former predominating. The Śvetāmbars mostly belong to the Osvāl and Śrīmāl castes, a point to which we shall return later.[2] These caste differences mean that there are few social fields, such as marriage, within which sustained and intimate interaction can take place. The only occasion in which I ever saw significant interaction between Digambar and Śvetāmbar Jains was in connection with the pan-Jain festival (and Indian national holiday) of Mahāvīr Jayantī (Lord Mahāvīra's birthday). For all practical purposes, they exist in totally different worlds.

This book is mainly concerned with a subbranch of the Śvetāmbar Jains. The Śvetāmbar branch of Jainism is (as is the Digambar branch as well) divided into sects and subsects. The principal division is between those who worship images in temples and those who do not. Image-worshipers are known as Mūrtipūjak (image-worshiping) or Mandirmārgī (temple-going). The practice of image-worship is opposed by two reformist sects, the Sthānakvāsīs and the Terāpanthīs. I am concerned here entirely with the image-worshiping group. The image-worshipers are further subdivided by caste and by affiliation with differing ascetic orders. These divisions will be discussed in greater detail later.

## JAIN BASICS

Despite major sectarian differences there is enough common ground among Jain groups that one may legitimately speak of "Jainism," a Jain religious tradition in a general and inclusive sense. Who, in this sense, is a Jain? The answer is in part supplied by etymology. "Jain" means "a follower of a Jina." The term *Jina,* in turn, means "victor" or "conqueror," by which is meant one who has achieved complete victory over attachments and aversions. A Jain is someone who reveres and follows these personages and regards their teachings as authoritative. This is the sine qua non of all forms of Jainism.

The term *Jina* itself tells us something of great importance about Jainism. Jainism's emphasis on nonviolence might foster the impression that this is a tradition that emphasizes mere meekness or docility. Such an impression, however, would be quite mistaken. Martial values, albeit in transmuted form, are crucial to Jainism's message and to its understanding of itself. The Jina is a conqueror. As we shall see later, he is also one who might have been—had he so chosen to be—a worldly king and a conqueror of the world. But instead the Jina becomes a spiritual king and transposes the venue of war from the outer field of battle to an inner one. As I shall show, the metaphor of transmuted martial valor is basic to the tradition's outlook and integration.

The Jinas are also called Tīrthankaras (in Hindi, Tīrthankars, which form I use from this point on). This term means "one who establishes a *tīrth.*" The word *tīrth* has two meanings. Its primary meaning is "ford" or "crossing place." In this sense, the Tīrthankar is one who establishes a ford across what is often called (by Hindus as well as Jains) "the ocean of existence." The term also refers to the community, established by the Tīrthankar, of ascetics and laity who put his teachings into practice; such a community is itself a kind of crossing place to liberation. A Tīrthankar is a human being. He is, however, an extraordinary human being who has conquered the attachments and aversions that stand in the way of liberation from worldly bondage. By means of his own efforts, and entirely without the benefit of being taught by others, he has achieved that state of omniscience in which all things are known to him—past, present, and future. But, before final attainment of his own liberation, the Tīrthankar imparts his self-gained liberating knowledge to others so that they might become victors too. Thus, he establishes a crossing place for other beings.

By either name—Jina or Tīrthankar—these great personages are the core figures of all forms of Jainism. Not only are their teachings central to Jainism but they themselves are also Jainism's principal objects of veneration, and this is true whether or not they are actually represented by images in temples. However—and this is a fact crucial to this study—they are not believed actually to interact with their worshipers. This is because they are no longer present in our part of the cosmos. They came, achieved omniscience, imparted their teachings, and then they departed. And when they departed they became completely liberated beings. In this condition they have withdrawn entirely from any interaction whatsoever with the world of action and attachment. They dwell forever at the apex of the cosmos in a condition of omniscient and totally isolated bliss. Their former presence, however, has left strong traces in the world. They left their teachings behind, and also a social order (called the *caturvidh sangh*) consisting of four great categories: *sādhu*s (monks), *sādhvī*s (nuns), *śrāvak*s (laymen), and *śrāvikā*s (laywomen). The monks and nuns are those who most directly exemplify the Tīrthankars' teachings in their manner of life. The term *śrāvak* and its feminine counterpart, *śrāvikā,* mean "listener." The *śrāvak*s and *śrāvikā*s, that is, are those who hear the Tīrthankars' teachings. The Tīrthankars also left behind them a kind of metaphysical echo of the welfare (*kalyāṇ*) generated by their presence that continues to reverberate in the cosmos and that can be mobilized by rituals and in other ways at the present time (Cort 1989: 421–22).

An infinity of Tīrthankars has already come and gone in the universe, and indeed there are Tīrthankars teaching at the present time in regions of the cosmos other than ours.[3] In our region, twenty-four Tīrthankars have appeared over the course of the current cosmic period. The last of these was Lord Mahāvīra (hereafter I shall use the Hindi form, Mahāvīr), who lived, taught, and achieved liberation some 2,500 years ago. In our sector of the world there will be no more Tīrthankars until after the next cosmic time-cycle has begun. The twenty-four Tīrthankars who have come and gone in our region are the principal beings represented by images and worshiped by image-worshiping Jains. It is true that Jains also worship deities who are not Tīrthankars. But as we shall see, the worship of such beings—if, indeed, it is worship at all—is seen as entirely subordinate to the worship of the Tīrthankars themselves.

It should be clearly understood that, from the standpoint of the Jain tradition itself, the Tīrthankars were in no sense the creators of Jainism. From an outsider's point of view, Mahāvīr can be seen as someone whose teachings drew upon traditions existing at the time, and who probably elaborated on those teachings in his own distinctive way.[4] From the Jain point of view, however, Mahāvīr created nothing, for the teachings of Jainism have existed from beginningless time and will never cease to exist.[5] It would be a major mistake, moreover, to think of Jain teachings as resembling speculative philosophy in any way. From the tradition's standpoint, Jain teachings do not stand or fall on rational arguments; rather, the sole and sufficient guarantee of their validity is the Tīrthankars' omniscience. These teachings are not only regarded as unconditionally true; they are also enunciated for one specific purpose and for no other reason. That purpose is the attainment of liberation from the world's bondage.

In common with other South Asian religious traditions, Jainism teaches that the self or soul is ensnared in repeating cycles of death and rebirth. Liberation is escape from this cycle. The Jains believe that the cycle is without beginning or end; neither the cosmos nor the souls that inhabit it were ever created, nor will they ever cease to be. Each soul has therefore already been wandering from birth to death to birth again from beginningless time, and unless liberation is attained, the soul will continue so to wander for all of infinite time to come. Thus, the stakes are high indeed. As a Jain friend once put it to me, "Bondage is *anādi* (beginingless) but not necessarily *anant* (endless)." But whether one leaves the cycle or not depends entirely on one's own efforts, and what is required is not easy.

Central to the Jain view of the predicament of the soul is the distinctive Jain theory of *karma*. The concept of *karma* is basic to all South Asian religious systems, but the Jains have given it a unique twist. In general, the term refers to actions and their results. We act and experience the results of our acts; that is, we consume (and *must* consume) the fruit (*phal*) of our actions (*karmas*). Because actions inevitably have consequences, our actions and their results constitute a self-replicating concatenation that pulls the soul through the endless cycle of birth, death, and rebirth. The Jains share this general view with other South Asian systems, but they also—as others do not—maintain that *karma* is an actual physical matter that is attracted to the soul by an individual's actions and adheres to the soul because of the individual's desires and aversions (*rāg* and *dveṣ*). This view is one of the most distinctive features of the Jain belief system.

The accumulations of *karma* on the soul are responsible for the soul's bondage. This is because they cover the soul and occlude its true nature, which is omniscient bliss. The keys to liberation, therefore, are two. First, one must avoid the accumulation of further *karma*. Violent actions are particularly potent sources of karmic accumulation, and this is the foundation of the tradition's extraordinary emphasis on nonviolence. Second, one must eliminate the *karma* already adhering to the soul. The fact that *karma* is viewed as an actual physical substance means that the most radical measure will be required for its removal. This radical measure is ascetic practice of great severity. The tradition's recurrent image is that of asceticism as a kind of fire that burns away the soul's karmic imprisonment; hence, ascetic values are central to the tradition's highest aspirations.

The Jains visualize the attainment of liberation (*mokṣ, nirvāṇ*) as a process that occurs in stages (called *guṇasthān*s), although it can occur very quickly in the case of certain extraordinary individuals. Liberation is preceded by the attainment of omniscience (*kevaljñān*), which is an innate quality of the soul that becomes manifest when certain occluding *karma*s are removed. After a period of time (which may be quite lengthy) during which certain remaining karmic matter is removed, the body ceases to function; then, after the last karmic vestiges are shed, the soul rises to the abode of the liberated (*siddh śilā*) at the very top of the cosmos. There it abides in omniscient bliss for all of infinite time. The liberated beings are known as *siddh*s, and are infinite in number. Among them are the liberated souls of the Tīrthankars and also the liberated souls of others who did not, as did the Tīrthankars, find the path to liberation on their own and teach it to others.

## THE PROBLEM

I have provided the foregoing brief sketch of Jain doctrine in order to introduce what seems to me to be the central analytical problem presented by Jainism to the student of religious culture. At Jainism's highest levels, by which I mean Jainism as embodied in its most important sacred writings, we are dealing with a soteriology, not a way of life. The question is, how can such a soteriology be woven into a way of life? This question is given special force and interest because of this tradition's extreme emphasis on nonviolence and asceticism.

It is clear that faithful adherence to Jainism's highest ethic, which is nonviolence, necessarily means a radical attenuation of interactions with the world, and in this sense nonviolence and asceticism can be seen as two sides of the same coin.[6] In the last analysis, all actions—eating, movement, whatever—inevitably result in harm to other beings. The behavior of men and women who are not Jains creates the most damage. The meat eaters of this world, the fighters of wars, the butchers, the choppers of trees, and so on leave a vast trail of carnage wherever they go. Observant lay Jains create havoc, but less havoc. Restrictions apply to them—restrictions of diet, occupation, and other kinds too. As a result, they, at least, confine the harm they do to the smaller and less highly organized forms of life, as will be seen in Chapter One. Jain ascetics create the least harm of all. Theirs is a manner of life maximally governed and restricted—or, to put it in the obverse, minimally free. The many rules and regulations that govern their lives ensure that minimal harm is done to other beings, even the most microscopic.

Given all this, it is clear that from the standpoint of Jain teachings the more restrictions to which conduct is subject the better. Moreover, it is also clear that to the degree that such restrictions are applied, the individual's sphere of activity becomes limited and his or her aperture of interaction with the world and other beings becomes closed. At the ideal limit of the application of this principle we find a complete cessation of all activity and of interactions with matter and other beings. This is in fact what liberation is. Liberated beings are entirely devoid of attachments and aversions (that is, they are what Jains call *vītrāg*) and exist in a state of total isolation. In their turn, those who *seek* liberation—that is, those who are followers of the Jinas—should try to approximate this state of affairs as best they can, given the many existing limitations of their power to do so.

What place can there be for such a radically world-rejecting vision of the world in the lives of ordinary men and women? This is the crucial question in the study of Jainism as a cultural entity as opposed to a strategy for attaining liberation. For any radically world-rejecting religious tradition to succeed in the midst of the world's endeavors—that is, for it to exist as a reproducible social institution—there must be points of connection between the central values it affirms and the ends pursued by adherents who make their way in the world. Ascetics require the support and protection of those who are not ascetics, and this means that nonascetics must somehow be brought into the ambit of a wider tradition that encompasses the religious interests of those who do and those who do not renounce the world. In the particular case of Jainism, the tradition's highest values define a way of life suitable only for a mendicant elite—the monks and nuns—but at the same time this elite cannot exist without the support of lay communities. One of the most striking features of Jainism, as we shall see, is that the monastic elite is *utterly* dependent on the laity. Therefore, a Jain tradition in the fullest sense, as opposed to a mere soteriology, cannot be for mendicants alone; it must bring ascetics and their followers into a system of belief and practice that serves the religious interests of both. How can such a religious system "work" when asceticism is so central a value?

This book addresses this general problem.[7] It does so, however, within a special frame of reference. Our attention will be directed mainly to ritual, and especially to rituals of worship.[8] The advantage of this approach is that rites of worship provide a lens through which the very large question of worldly and otherworldly values in Jainism can be brought into a precise and manageable focus. It should not be imagined, moreover, that ritual is a peripheral aspect of the Jain traditions with which we shall be concerned. Rites of worship define one of the principal venues within which lay Jains of the image-worshiping groups actually come into contact with their religion. This being so, a focus on such ritual is one good way (certainly not the only way) to understand Jainism as a living tradition.

At the level of ritual the Śvetāmbar Mūrtipūjak tradition's commitment to otherworldly values is manifested in the form of a particular ritual pattern, namely, the veneration of ascetics. Above all else, as we shall learn, Jains worship ascetics. But to be committed to the worship of ascetics is to confront an inherent contradiction. The greater the ascetic's asceticism, the more worthy of worship he or she becomes. But the greater the asceticism, the less accessible is he or she to interaction with worshipers. The logic of the situation drives ineluctably toward the paradox that the most worshipable of beings is inaccessible to worship by, or to any other form of interaction with, beings remaining in the world. This is the problem of reconciling worldly and otherworldly values in Jainism as it is manifested in the ritual sphere.

As noted already, the Tīrthankars are the supreme embodiment of Jain ideals. Because of this, they are the principal objects of worship in Jainism. But precisely because they exemplify the tradition's highest values—ascetic values—in the highest degree, they are, in the world of ritual logic, inaccessible to worship. Hence, the question with which this book began: What does it mean to worship entities of this sort? How, to expand on the question, does one deal with them in ritual? What can one gain by doing so? And what implications does worshiping such beings have for the worshiper's relations with the world? These are the questions addressed in the chapters to follow.

As we shall see, this approach is not as narrow as it might appear to be at first. It will lead us to the most general issues concerning the religious and also the social identities of lay Jains. Moreover, it will propel us beyond the boundaries of Jainism to questions concerning Jainism's place in the Indic religious world.

## RITUAL CULTURE AND RITUAL ROLES

In this book I frequently use the expression "ritual culture." In doing so I have more in mind than the scarcely controversial notion that rituals are manifestations of culture. Rather, I want to suggest that rituals actually occur within a cultural mini-milieu, a cultural domain associated specifically with rituals. I want to suggest further that this domain can be treated as a partly autonomous context of investigation. Ritual culture in the sense I have in mind is not just a bundle of recipes for the performance of rites of worship. Nor is it merely an ideology that justifies or rationalizes ritual activities. Rather, it is an internally coherent body of skills, kinetic habits (such as patterned physical gestures expressive of deference), conventions, expectations, beliefs, procedures, and sanctioned interpretations of the meaning of ritual acts. It is, one might say, an entire symbolic and behavioral medium within which ritual acts are invested with cognitive, affective, and moral "sense."

Ritual culture, thus defined, is carried—in part—as a component of the general cultural repertoire of those who perform rituals. It also forms a sort of peninsula of what might be called "religious culture," although for those whose contact with a religious system is primarily in the sphere of ritual, ritual culture may indeed be the continent and not the appendage. Its boundaries are thus always a bit hazy. It is never a closed system. But it can nevertheless be seen as a partly independent reality—independent in the same sense, let us say, that "political culture" can be treated as a cultural subsystem. In traditions that have them, ritual specialists can act as special repositories and transmitters of ritual culture. To some extent, laymen who have acquired special ritual expertise play this role in Śvetāmbar Jainism, as do some monks, although the latter are not seen as ritual specialists. Ritual culture is also deposited in, and transmitted by, certain kinds of writings. These may be writings that instruct people about how to perform rituals, texts sung or recited in rituals, or texts of other kinds; the important thing is that they are part of the immediate surround in which rituals are performed. Writings of this sort, mostly authored by monks or nuns, are a very important aspect of the ritual culture of temple-going Śvetāmbar Jains. Ritual culture is also embodied in, and transmitted by, the ongoing talk about ritual—instruction, rationalization, interpretation, whatever—that takes place in a given community of co-ritualists. But although ritual culture is carried in a variety of media—writing, talk, even emotional and motor habit—it becomes visible mainly in actual ritual performances.

The allusion to "performance" is not accidental and brings us to an important point. The rituals discussed in this book are excellent examples of what Milton Singer has called "cultural performances"—performances that encapsulate culture in such a way that it can be exhibited to the performers themselves and also to outside observers (1972: 71). In fact, the dramaturgic comparison can be pressed even further than this. As readers will see, the rituals discussed in this book bear a close resemblance to actual theatrical performances. But they are not just the same as theatrical performances, and the difference is important.

As Richard Schechner has pointed out (1988, esp. Ch. 4), theater and ritual belong on the same general continuum of "performance," and whether a given performance is theater—in the strict sense—or ritual depends mainly on its context and ostensible function. The real essence of what we normally consider theater is its function as entertainment. Ritual, on the other hand, is supposed to be efficacious, by which we mean that it is supposed to bring about transformations of some kind or another. Associated with this difference, in turn, are others, and perhaps the most important of these has to do with the relationship between performers and audience. Where entertainment prevails—that is, in theater—the audience and performers are separated. To be a member of the audience in theater is to be "out of the action," a spectator and a potential critic. To the degree that a performance belongs to the ritual category, on the other hand, audience and performers are one and the same.

These insights provide us with a useful way to view Jain ritual. Jain rites of worship are certainly theater-like performances, but at the same time they are not quite theater in the usual sense of the English word. As we shall see, the question of what actually constitutes the "efficacy" of ritual is one of the central problematics of Jain religious life. Nonetheless, in Schechner's terms, efficacy, not entertainment, is what Jain rites are basically about, although this certainly does not preclude individuals from taking pleasure in the spectacle of their own performances or of those of others. Moreover, this is theater in which the players are largely their own audience. It is true that groups of participants sometimes assume a spectator-like stance in some Jain rituals, but the general principle still holds that the audience is part of the action. The principle finds its logical limiting case in one of the most important Jain rites of worship—the eightfold worship (*aṣṭprakārī pūjā*)—in which the performer and audience can be said to be a single person.

Where there is theater, of course, there are performers playing in roles, and this brings us back to the matter of ritual culture. As is true of the larger stage of social life, the roles played by actors in the theater-like performances of ritual are manifested in interactions with the occupants of other roles. In this sense, rituals can be understood not only as performances but as minute and ephemeral social systems. *Ritual culture* is the environment—cognitive, affective, and even motor-habitual—that supplies much of the content of such role-governed interaction and also the wider frame of reference within which that content is meaningful to ritual performers.[9] Ritual roles and ritual culture are thus mutually dependent. Ritual roles may be said to express ritual culture; ritual culture in turn shapes ritual roles.

These ideas are unremarkable, but to them I add what may strike some readers as an unusual twist. To assert that human participants in rituals play roles is uncontroversial. They walk on the ritual stage as supplicants, offerers, experts, interested onlookers, or whatever—the list is potentially long. Here, however, I shall interpret the entities who are *objects of worship* as also "playing" a role. I shall say further that such entities are, from an analytical standpoint, role players whether or not they are living persons.

Moreover, I shall say this role—that of object of worship—is one of the two basic constituent features of any rite of worship. That is, in the simplest instance a rite of worship necessarily encompasses two elementary roles. There is, first, the role (which may be differentiated into subroles) of those who worship; these are the human performers of ritual acts. They initiate ritual performances, set the stage, make offerings and direct other kinds of honorific attentions to the object or objects of worship, and bring matters to a conclusion. They typically expect results (Schechner's efficacy) to flow from what they have done. They may play differently scripted parts in the performance, but in the widest frame of reference they may all be considered "worshipers." Second is the role occupied by certain very special others, the objects of worship. From the standpoint of our model, worshipers and objects of worship may be considered ritual/social "alters" of each other.

The possible objection that, in rites of worship, the worshiper's alter—the object of worship—is not "real" is irrelevant to this formulation. In the first place, the role of object of worship is often occupied by living human persons. This is frequently true in Jainism as well as in other South Asian religious traditions. But even more important, whether this role is occupied by a living (and thus kinetically and verbally interacting) person or an (apparently) lifeless image, or even a completely disembodied or disengaged being, the crucial thing for the worshiper is how he or she *thinks* the ritual other reacts (or does not react) to ritual acts, and this is *always* imaginary from the worshiper's perspective. This is true whether or not the alter is a living person. It is enough that the act of worship takes place; if it does, then from the standpoint of the worshiper an interaction has occurred, and the ritual alter may be said to be as real as the interaction itself is *felt* to be real.

To push matters slightly further, I shall also say that the roles of worshiper and object of worship must be seen as reflexes of each other. This is because both roles are shaped by their mutual interaction; they are the "others" of each other, and thus each is—in part at least—a product of the other. It is, moreover, precisely in this mutually creative relationship that the behavioral characteristics of ritual roles and the content of ritual culture most dramatically intersect. What worshiper and worshiped actually *are* to each other depends on ambient habits of thought, emotion, evaluation, as well as on prevailing assumptions about the nature of the world and the nature of persons or beings in the world. That is, it depends on the general cultural background of ritualists and, more immediately, on their ritual culture. In turn, this ambient atmosphere, having been given embodiment in the form of ritual acts (whether or not the occupants of all roles act in the kinetic sense) of a particular kind, is thereby supported and regenerated. For example, a conception of the object of worship as lofty and remote fits well with a worshiper's ritually enacted attitude of humility. This relationship, in turn, is deeply resonant with a more general notion of the worshiper as slavelike and dependent on an all-powerful other, and these notions, in turn, can open out into a complex theology of divine majesty and power. All this can and does come together in crystallized form in ritual interactions. By contrast—and as one sees especially in some subtraditions of the worship of the Hindu deity Kṛṣṇa—a portrayal of the object of worship as childlike meshes with a worshiper's role defined as nurturant and maternal. This, in turn, supports, and is supported by, a very different vision of the world and the worshiper's place in it: a theology of reciprocated parental and filial devotion. All this, too, can be distilled in ritualized interactions between devotees and the objects of worship.

But what if, as in Jainism, the principal object of worship is *absent*? What implications would this have for the worshiper's identity and for the cultural surround of these ritual roles? These issues provide the basic point of departure of this book. What kind of a ritual system results, we wish to know, when a commitment to asceticism as a value is so powerful as to push objects of worship into a condition of transactional nonexistence?

There is one final point to be made about ritual roles. For human worshipers—the self-audiences of this particular kind of theater—playing such roles leaves deposits of feeling and conviction that can outlast the ritual situation, augmenting a worshiper's sense of identity on both the personal and social planes.[10] The ritual setting is extraordinary, a special time and place set apart from all mundane times and places. Given this extraordinary context, the object of worship is not only a social alter of the worshiper but an alter quite unlike any other—a hypersignificant other in a hypersignificant situation. When the worshiper enters a relationship with such a being, he or she is thrust into a defined role in relation to this being. Depending on how the ambient ritual culture characterizes the situation, this role can impart to the worshiper a sense of extramundane personal identity—as one who is powerful in some special way, or beloved of God, or redeemed, or on the road to liberation. Moreover, and as this book will show, it can also—and at the same time—impart a special kind of significance and energy to a worshiper's social identity, in the present case that of clan and caste. In the materials to be presented here, ritual emerges not just as theater-like, but as a theater of soteriological and social identities.

The concepts of ritual culture and role constitute the basic frame of reference within which Jain materials are interpreted in this book. One important consequence of this approach is the manner in which materials are presented here. Religious traditions are often described and analyzed as "systems of belief." An account based on this idea typically describes religious ideas and values first, with ritual coming only later. The basic (though usually unstated) idea is that ritual is a kind of behavior that is somehow deductively related to beliefs. In this book, however, I take the opposite approach. Instead of treating ritual as a behavioral surface of beliefs, I treat the entire domain of ritual as an analytical shell within which matters of belief are (sometimes) best understood. In my view, this is far closer than the conventional approach to the tradition's experiential reality for most Jains. As a practical matter this means that in this study we begin with rituals instead of ending with them, and what we learn of beliefs we learn from rituals and the texts associated with rituals.

A second consequence of this approach is that this book stresses ritual roles and interactions, and indeed is organized around these concepts. In this sense the book might be understood as an attempt to push social concepts to the center of the analysis of religious symbolism. Who are the dramatis personae in ritual performances? Who is worshiped? Who does the worshiping? How do these roles interact in ritual settings, and what significance do these patterns have for the overarching question of how Jainism (or one variety of Jainism) deals with the tensions between otherworldly values and the requirements of life in the physical and social worlds? These are the guiding questions taken up here.

In approaching these questions, moreover, we shall give special attention to the kinds of exchanges and transactions that are engaged in, or are not engaged in, by occupants of ritual roles. This connects the study with a tradition of social analysis that can be said to have begun with Marcel Mauss (1967; orig. 1924) and that more recently has—especially in the work of McKim Marriott (1976, 1990), Jonathan Parry (1986, 1994), Gloria Raheja (1988), and Thomas Trautmann (1981)—produced major advances in social scientific understanding of ritual gifting in South Asia. These new insights will play an important part in the book's final chapter in which Jain ritual patterns are compared with other South Asian ritual cultures.

## TWO CITIES

My materials are drawn from two periods of field research. I spent the summer of 1986 in the Gujarati city of Ahmedabad. Here my work was quite narrowly focused on the structure of the principal Śvetāmbar rite of temple worship (the eightfold worship or *aṣṭprakārī pūjā*). This initial investigation was followed by a stay of several months in Jaipur, the capital city of Rajasthan, in 1990–91 (see map of Gujarat and Rajasthan). This time my research was much more broadly based. Ahmedabad is a major Jain center and is dominated by the Śvetāmbar sect; my work in this city was entirely with Śvetāmbar Jains. Jaipur also has a large Jain population, but its composition is very different from Ahmedabad's. Most Jaipur Jains are Digambars, but there is also a relatively small but flourishing Śvetāmbar community, mainly supported by the gemstone business.[11] In general, Jaipur's Śvetāmbar community has been a business community, whereas the Digambars have been more prominent in service occupations. As in Ahmedabad, my work in Jaipur was focused mainly on the Śvetāmbars, but I was also able to learn something about Digambar traditions during my stay in this city.

An important difference in my work in these two cities has to do with caste.[12] Caste was hardly relevant at all to my work in Ahmedabad, but it became a significant element in my investigations in Jaipur. Here the principal Śvetāmbar castes are only two, the Osvāls and the Śrīmāls, who are more or less equal in status but with the Osvāls the larger of the pair. In Jaipur the division between superior *bisā* and inferior *dasā* sections, so important to intracaste stratification among Osvāls and Śrīmāls elsewhere, seems to have fallen into desuetude, and intermarriage between Osvāls and Śrīmāls is not uncommon. My concern was primarily with the Osvāls of Jaipur, and particularly with the relationship in this caste between Jainism and clan and caste identity.

The image-worshiping Śvetāmbar communities in Ahmedabad and Jaipur are very similar in most ways. The principal difference is that in Ahmedabad (and in Gujarat generally) most temple-going Śvetāmbar Jains are linked with a particular ascetic lineage—that is, a lineage of monks and nuns based on disciplic succession—called the Tapā Gacch, whereas in Jaipur the dominant ascetic lineage is the Khartar Gacch. This in itself is a highly significant fact about the two communities. The Tapā Gacch is currently in a flourishing state, with large numbers of monks and nuns. The Khartar Gacch is much smaller and

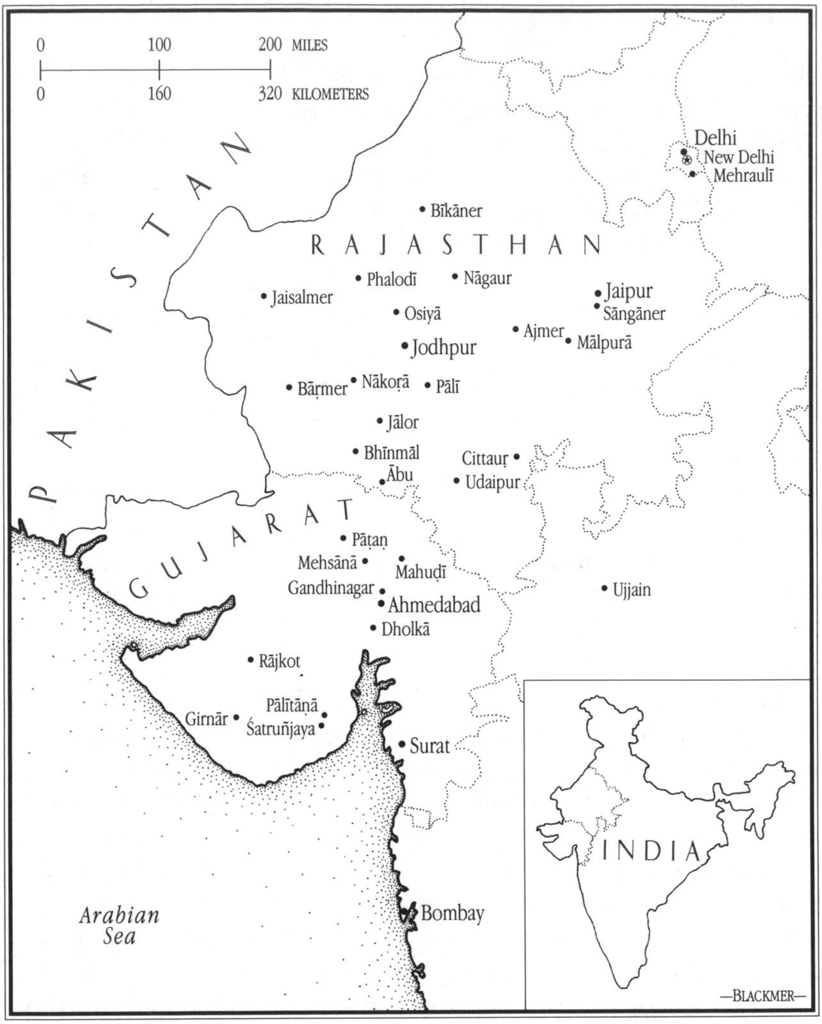


Gujarat and Rajasthan with selected locations

seems to be languishing at the present time. This means that the lay Śvetāmbar Jains of Ahmedabad enjoy much more sustained contact with monks and nuns—especially monks—than do their co-religionists in Jaipur. Khartar Gacch nuns are almost always present in Jaipur, but monks visit only from time to time. This issue aside, however, the ritual practices of the two communities are very similar in most ways. Accordingly, my treatment of general ritual idioms—by which I mean those associated with the worship of the Tīrthankars—is based on materials drawn from observations in both cities.

At another level, however, there are certain special features of the Jaipur scene to which I shall give very close attention. Associated with the Khartar Gacch is a complex of ritual and belief—a "ritual subculture," as I call it—based on the veneration of certain deceased monks known as Dādāgurus or Dādāgurudevs. The cult of the Dādāgurus is central to the ritual pursuit of worldly success among the Śvetāmbar Jains of Jaipur, and it is also linked to the origin mythology of clans belonging to the Osvāl caste. This is where caste becomes relevant in the Jaipur context. An extended discussion of the cult of the Dādāgurus will enable us to see how, in one Śvetāmbar community, the tension between ascetic and worldly values (including social values) is dealt with and mitigated.

• • •

This book is an interpretation of a Śvetāmbar Jain tradition from the standpoint of the theoretical ideas sketched out earlier. I use the term *interpretation* deliberately. I wish to emphasize the fact that I have not attempted to write anything resembling a complete ethnography of either a religious way of life or of the way of life of a localized religious community. Instead, I have concentrated on a particular analytical problem and have pursued it wherever it has taken me. The trail I followed led me to discussions of Jainism and Jain affairs with many individuals, to ritual performances, to texts and other writings, and to various temples and sacred centers. But there are important areas of Jain life to which it did not lead me, and which are therefore not treated—or are not fully treated—in this book. For example, lay and mendicant ascetic praxis is only touched upon. In this respect the present study is a narrow one. I believe that my findings are certainly relevant to any general understanding of Jain life, but I do not present them as constituting such an understanding.

The materials on which the book is based were obtained by means of observations of rituals and other aspects of Jain life, from formal and informal interviews, and also from a wide variety of writings. My use of written sources is, in fact, a good deal more extensive than is common in ethnographies. It needs to be stressed that the conventional model of ethnographic research—participant observation and conversation—is not fully adequate in the case of the Jains. The level of education and intellectual sophistication in Jain communities is high. Jain traditions have always been productive of written materials, and this includes not only texts in classical languages but currently many works in modern Indian languages and even English. The books I encountered in the homes of my respondents were often well thumbed, suggesting that they are indeed read. Anyone who would understand Jain life must read what Jains themselves read.

My contact with written materials developed as a natural consequence of following the trail of my inquiry wherever it might lead. In the course of my inquiries individuals would place books and other written materials in my hands as relevant to my questions, and in this sense my interest in literature emerged from the fieldwork situation itself. The writings in question included ritual manuals, texts designed to be recited or sung in rituals, published discourses of ascetics, and compilations of caste and clan histories. These materials, mostly written in Hindi, played a part in my investigation somewhat like that of passive "informants." To the extent that I used these writings, one might say that the vantage point of this study hovers somewhere between the informant-oriented, ground-level ethnographic study and the loftier bird's-eye view of some textual scholarship.

The book starts with an analysis of basic ritual roles. Chapter One utilizes a detailed account of a complex rite of worship as a way of introducing the Jain concept of what constitutes a proper object of worship. This rite tells a story, and the story it tells defines with special clarity what it means to be worthy of worship in the Jain sense. To be worthy of worship is to be an ascetic, and the Tīrthankar's life—which is what the text of the rite is about—epitomizes ascetic values. The chapter then turns to an account of Jain cosmography, cosmology, and biology; here we see a world portrayed in which only the most radical asceticism makes intellectual and moral sense. The chapter concludes with a brief discussion of living ascetics, that is, the monks and nuns who most directly exemplify Jainism's ascetic values.

Chapter Two turns Chapter One around; now our concern is the role of the worshiper, as opposed to the object of worship. The chapter begins with an account of a ritual that illustrates the role of the worshiper; this leads to a discussion of the nature of Jain deities—as opposed to Tīrthankars—and also to the metaphor of kingship, which emerges as a central feature of this Jain tradition. A Tīrthankar is someone who might have been a worldly king but who became an ascetic and spiritual king instead. A Jain layperson is someone who venerates ascetics, and who, in so doing, becomes a kind of king. But because of the tradition's unrelenting commitment to ascetic values, this metaphor proves unstable. When the Tīrthankars are worshiped there is an inherent and apparently unresolvable tension between otherworldly and worldly values, and worldly values must always give way in the end.

Chapter Three narrows the book's focus to Jaipur and those Śvetāmbar Jains who are associated with the ascetic lineage known as the Khartar Gacch. The chapter introduces the cult of the Dādāgurus. In this cult the dominant image of the relationship between worshiper and object of worship is redefined and given a somewhat different symbolic surround. It is certainly a form of worship that is attuned to Jainism's central values, for the objects of worship are Jain ascetics; but in this cult asceticism supports, instead of challenging, the worldly aspirations of devotees. I characterize this cult as a ritual subculture because, although the ritual patterns it employs are distinctively and recognizably Jain, it nonetheless differs in significant ways from the dominant ritual culture focused on worship of the Tīrthankars.

The Dādāgurus not only serve as a connecting point between the worldly aspirations of lay worshipers and ascetic powers associated ultimately with the Tīrthankars, but they also provide a link between religious values and the structure of the contemporary Jain community. The link is seen in the origin mythology of Jain clans, and this is the principal concern of Chapter Four. The metaphor of kingship is again central; most of the Jains we see in Jaipur today are believed to be the descendants of warrior-kings who were tamed and vegetarianized by great ascetics of the past.

Chapter Five places Jain ritual culture in a wider South Asian context. The focus of this chapter is on patterns of religious gifting, and we learn that from this standpoint Jain ritual culture is not truly distinctive. Although some Hindu ritual cultures exhibit striking differences from Jain patterns, at least one Hindu ritual culture seems very similar to that of the Jains. Among other things, this discovery raises serious questions about conventional methods used in classifying South Asian religions. The materials surveyed suggest that, from the standpoint of ritual culture, there is no clear boundary between Jain and Hindu traditions. Instead, we are dealing with a series of logical permutations of the relationship between the roles of those who worship and those who are worshiped in South Asia.

CHAPTER ONE

# Victors

We begin with the *namaskār mantra*. This utterance, also known as the *mahāmantra* or the *navkār mantra,* is Jainism's universal prayer and all-purpose ritual formula. It is hardly possible to exaggerate its importance. It is repeated on most ritual occasions, and many Jains believe it to contain an inherent power which, among other things, can protect the utterer in times of danger. When, in the summer of 1986, I arrived in Ahmedabad to study Jain rituals, a Jain friend who was assisting me in my research insisted that my first order of business should be to commit the *namaskār mantra* to memory. One of my most pleasant memories of Jaipur is of an elderly friend pointing with pride to his small grandson who, hardly yet able to talk, had memorized the *mantra*. A somewhat more disquieting memory is of yet another friend who responded to an allusion to my own nonvegetarian background by hastily mumbling the *mantra* under his breath.

In essence it is a salutation (*namaskār*) to entities known as the five *parameṣṭhin*s, the five supreme deities.[1] These beings are worthy of worship, and it is crucial to note that these are the *only* entities the tradition deems fully worthy of worship. They are, in order, the *arhat*s ("worthy ones" who have attained omniscience; the Tīrthankars), the *siddha*s (the liberated), the *ācārya*s (ascetic leaders), the *upādhyāya*s (ascetic preceptors), and the *sādhu*s (ordinary ascetics). The *mantra*'s importance to us is that it is a charter for a type of ritual, singling out a certain class of beings as proper objects of worship. These beings, we see, are all ascetics.[2] This is the fundamental matter: Jains worship ascetics, and this is the most important single fact about Jain ritual culture.

This chapter deals with ascetics as objects of worship among the Jains. Who are they? What qualities single them out from other beings? What makes them worthy of worship? We begin addressing these questions by examining the text of an important ritual. The *namaskār mantra* lists the *arhats*, by which is meant the Tīrthankars, as foremost among those who are worthy of worship. The ritual with which this chapter begins is itself an example of Tīrthankar-worship. Its text, moreover, tells us something of *why* the Tīrthankar is worthy of worship. After examining this rite, we will consider ideas about the cosmos that inform the rite, and move finally to a discussion of living ascetics as objects of worship.

## THE LORD'S LAST LIFE

Most of my Jain friends and acquaintances in Jaipur were businessmen, many in the gemstone trade. These men were not, by and large, sophisticated about religious matters and did not pretend to be. They were men of business and masters of their craft. They had little time or inclination to worry about or debate the fine points of Jainism.

Nor were they usually very observant beyond a certain minimum. Of course they were all vegetarians. Although I frequently heard the allegation that many men of their sort ate meat on the sly, I saw absolutely no evidence of this. Nonetheless, despite the constant exhortations of ascetics, most did not strictly adhere to such rules as the avoidance of potatoes, and few indeed avoided eating at night. Avoiding vegetables that grow underground (which are believed to be teeming with life-forms) and not eating at night (so as not to harm creatures that might fall into the food) are generally regarded as indices of serious Jain praxis. Most were not daily temple-goers, although I believe most of them knew at least the rudiments of temple procedures. But in spite of a certain amount of behavioral and ritual corner-cutting, by any reasonable standard these men were serious Jains.

One good friend, then a youngish bachelor in whose gem-polishing establishment I spent many an hour, is exemplary of this whole class of men. He knows how to perform the basic Jain rite of worship (the eightfold worship, to be discussed in Chapter Two). He visits a temple about once a week. He usually does so for *darśan,* for a sacred viewing of the images, not to perform a full rite of worship. He used to go to an important regional pilgrimage site (at Mālpurā near Jaipur) every month on full moon days, although this has dropped off because of the pressures of business. He fasts only once a year on the last day of Paryuṣaṇ, the eight-day period that is the most sacred time of the year for Jains. He performs the expiatory rite of *pratikramaṇ* on this day also. He certainly does not pretend to live the life of an ideal Jain layman, but he nevertheless identifies strongly with Jainism and holds its values and beliefs in the highest possible esteem.

As do many other men of his general class, condition, and age, he comes from a family in which women are highly observant and usually far more so than the men. His mother performs the forty-eight-minute contemplative exercise called *sāmāyik* and visits a temple daily. She fasts four times a month, and on fasting days she performs the rite of *pratikramaṇ*. She has not eaten root vegetables from the time of her birth, and for at least thirty years has not taken food at night. The wife of one of his six brothers follows the same strict pattern as her mother-in-law. His other sisters-in-law visit the temple once or twice a week and fast approximately once a month; they would probably do more, he said, were it not for the responsibility of young children.

And here is the mystery. Even in this rather observant family, my friend told me, the topic of liberation (*mokṣ*) from the world's bondage simply never comes up. He added that he does not even remember anyone ever mentioning the word; it just was not part of the family discourse. He himself hardly gives any thought to liberation. Indeed, in response to my queries he ventured the opinion that liberation is really "not possible" at all (meaning, I believe, for people in his own position). In order to attain liberation, he said, you have to renounce the world and devote yourself to spiritual endeavors. "But we," he said, "have our businesses to attend to." He went on to state that most Jains do not actually know what liberation is, and visit temples solely for the purpose of advancing their worldly affairs.

The matter, however, is more complex than my friend's remarks might suggest. Let me say at once that to some degree he was exaggerating, probably for pedagogical effect. For example, the issue of liberation would not normally arise in a family context, but the same individuals might well speak of liberation in more specifically religious contexts. Still, it remains true that the religious lives of most ordinary lay-Jains are not liberation-oriented. Even women's fasting—which is often spectacular and certainly evokes the image of the *mokṣ mārg* (the path to liberation)—seems often, and perhaps mostly, to be motivated by the desire to protect families, to achieve favorable rebirth, or even to gain social prestige.[3] I found a general awareness and understanding of the goal of liberation among Jains with whom I discussed the matter, but liberation tends to be seen as a very remote goal—not for now, not for any time soon.

But at the same time, it is also generally understood that although rituals, fasting, and other such religious activities generate merit (*puṇya*) that will lead to worldly felicity, the goal *should* be liberation. This is certainly the view promoted by Jain ascetics in their sermons, and it is reasonably well understood by the laity. Many Jains say, as my friend does, that other Jains engage in ritual purely to advance their worldly affairs. But the point, of course, is that one should not be so motivated; one should really be seeking liberation. Given all this, we are presented with a puzzle. Just what is the relationship between liberation and the lives and aspirations of lay Jains?

This puzzle is perhaps nowhere more evident than in the major periodic rites of worship. These rites are, in fact, a vital domain of religious activity for men such as my friend. As Josephine Reynell points out (esp. 1987; see also Laidlaw 1995: Chs. 15–16), there is a basic division of ritual labor among temple-going Śvetāmbar Jains: women fast, while men—too immersed in their affairs to do serious fasting—make religious donations (*dāna;* in Hindi, *dān*). A major field for religious donations is the support of important periodic rites. These are often held in conjunction with calendrical festivals and also on the founding anniversaries of temples. They are frequently occasions for the display of great wealth. Truly startling sums are often paid in the auctions held to determine who will have the honor of supporting particular parts of the ceremony or of assuming specific ceremonial roles. This aspect of sponsorship seems to function as a public validation of who's who in the wealth and power hierarchies of the Jain community. The ceremonies supported by this cascade of wealth are typically sumptuous, lavish occasions—full of color and suggestions of the abundant wealth of the supporters. They seem to have little to do with liberation from the world's bondage.

And yet here is the paradox. If we peel away the opulence and glitter from these occasions we discover that liberation is there, right at their heart. At the center of all the spending, the celebration, the display, the stir, is the figure of the Tīrthankar. He[4] represents everything that the celebration is apparently not, for he is, above all else, an ascetic. His asceticism, moreover, has gained him liberation from the very world of flowing wealth of which the rite seems so much a part. Liberation and the asceticism that leads to liberation are thus finally the central values, despite the context of opulence. Wealth is not worshiped; wealth is *used* to worship the wealthless.

We now look more closely at an example of such a rite. The example I have chosen is not only a rite of which the Tīrthankar is the object; it is also a rite that, in a kind of doubleness of purpose, explains *why* the Tīrthankar is an object of worship.

## A MAJOR RITE

The end of the year 1990 was a troubled time in Jaipur. In many north Indian cities the autumn months had been marred by agitations against the national government's decision to implement a far-reaching policy of job reservations for lower castes. In Rajasthan these same months had seen a lengthy and exasperating bus strike. Then, in late October, there were deadly communal clashes between Hindus and Muslims in Jaipur provoked by the efforts of Hindu nationalists to demolish a mosque in Ayodhya, one supposedly built on the site of Lord Rāma's[5] birth, and to replace it with a Hindu temple. By December, Jaipur was still a very uneasy city, and for this reason the Jain festival of Pauṣ Daśmī was not celebrated with the usual éclat.

Pauṣ Daśmī is an annual festival celebrated by Śvetāmbar Jains in commemoration of the birth date of Pārśvanāth. Pārśvanāth is the twenty-third Tīrthankar of our region of the cosmos and era, and is one of the most greatly revered of the Tīrthankars. He was born on the tenth day (Daśmī) of the dark fortnight of the lunar month of Pauṣ (December/January), which is why the festival is called Pauṣ Daśmī. In 1990 this day occurred on December 11. In Jaipur this festival is normally the occasion for a major public display of religious symbols. In ordinary years, on the day before Pauṣ Daśmī a portable image of the Tīrthankar is taken in public procession from a large temple in Jaipur's walled city to a temple complex at a place called Mohan Bāṛī on Galta Road.[6] There, on the morning of the birthday itself, the image is worshiped, and then on the afternoon of the same day the image is returned to its original temple in another public procession. But in December of 1990 this was not to be. Because of the city's troubles, no permit for the procession could be obtained. Still, at least the basic rite of worship could be performed, and it is this performance that is described in what follows. It was perhaps fortunate for me that it was celebrated in a relatively small way, for this gave me a chance to observe its performance with special closeness.

The rite is an example of a type of congregational worship commonly known as *mahāpūjā,* a "great" or "major" (*mahā*) "rite of worship" (*pūjā*). Such rites, which come in several varieties, are commonly performed by Śvetāmbar Jains on special occasions in both Ahmedabad and Jaipur. Most of them are directed at the Tīrthankars, but I once witnessed a *mahāpūjā* for the goddess Padmāvatī (a guardian deity, not a Tīrthankar) in Ahmedabad, and the congregational worship of certain deceased ascetics who are not Tīrthankars, figures known as Dādāgurus, is central to Śvetāmbar Jainism in Jaipur. The occasions for these rites are quite various. Sometimes, as in the present case, they are performed in conjunction with calendrical festivals. The consecration anniversaries of temples are celebrated by means of these rites, and they are sometimes held to inaugurate new dwellings or businesses. Congregational worship of the Dādāgurus is often held in fulfillment of a vow (see Chapter Three). A rite called the *antarāy nivāraṇ pūjā* (the *pūjā* to "remove obstructive *karmas*") is frequently performed on the thirteenth day after a death.

The specific rite to be discussed here belongs to a class of rites known as *pañc kalyāṇak pūjās*. The expression *pañc kalyāṇak* means "five welfare-producing events," and refers to five events that are definitive of the lives of the Tīrthankars. Although the Tīrthankars have different individual biographies, the truly significant events in the lifetime of each and every Tīrthankar are exactly five in number and are always precisely the same.[7] They are: 1) the descent of the Tīrthankar-to-be into a human womb (*cyavan*),[8] 2) his birth (*janam*), 3) his initiation as an ascetic (*dīkṣā*), 4) his attainment of omniscience (*kevaljñān*), and 5) his final liberation (*nirvāṇ*). A *pañc kalyāṇak pūjā* is a rite of worship celebrating the five welfare-producing events—the five *kalyāṇaks*—in the life of a particular Tīrthankar.[9] Five-*kalyāṇak pūjās* are very important as a class of rites, a fact that reflects the importance of the *kalyāṇaks* as cosmic events. Five-*kalyāṇak pūjās* are often performed as part of the ceremony that empowers the images in Jain temples, and this suggests that the Tīrthankars' *kalyāṇaks* have left a residue of welfare (*kalyāṇ*) in the cosmos that can be focused in images and mobilized by rituals in the service of worshipers.

Every major Jain rite of worship is based on a specific text that carries its distinctive story line or rationale. In the case of a *pañc kalyāṇak pūjā* of the sort to be described here, the story line recounts the five *kalyāṇaks* as the key episodes in the biography of a specific Tīrthankar. Such texts are always authored by ascetics. The text of the present rite was written by a Khartar Gacch monk named Kavīndrasāgar (1905–1960) whose chief works include a number of well known *pūjās*. The type of Hindi in which the text is written is easy for participants to understand.

The particular rite performed on Pauṣ Daśmī celebrates the five *kalyāṇaks* of Pārśvanāth. It is, accordingly, called the *pārśvanāth panc kalyāṇak pūjā,* and its story line is an account of the five *kalyāṇaks* as they occurred in Pārśvanāth's own particular career. Participants sing songs from the text that recount and praise each of Pārśvanāth's five *kalyāṇaks*, and at the conclusion of each set of songs certain prescribed ritual acts occur.[10] Sometimes favorite devotional songs not in the text are added. The rite thus consists of five separate groups of ritual acts, each preceded by a group of songs. It should be understood that most participants in such rites are at least minimally conversant with these songs, and some will know some of them or parts of them by heart. The text is as central to the rite as the ritual acts that accompany its singing. The ritual acts (to be described below) are completely standard in the sense that more or less the same ones occur in all rites of this sort. It is the text that embeds the ritual acts in a narrative that differentiates the significance of one type of rite (in this case the *pārśvanāth pañc kalyāṇak pūjā*) from others.

The spirit in which the songs are sung is also very important. The rite is seen as an expression of devotion (*bhakti*). For a rite of this sort to be successful, the songs should be sung with gusto and feeling; they should express, that is, the proper spirit (*bhāv*). Typically, rites of this kind start slowly with a limited number of participants. As time passes, more participants arrive, and at the end—if all is well—the site of the ceremony will be packed with lustily singing devotees. In the case of the particular rite described here, the troubled context kept attendance down, but the singing was spirited.

The ritual acts are the responsibility of a limited number of individuals who are bathed and wearing clothing appropriate for touching sacred images (see Chapter Two). These I call "*pūjā* principals." They stand, often in husband-wife pairs, holding a platter containing offerings while the songs appropriate to a given segment of the rite are sung; when the appropriate moment comes they perform the required actions

Figure 1. A *pūjā* principal holding offerings in Jaipur. Note the mouth-cloth designed to prevent impurities from being breathed on the image.

(see Figure 1). Because of the troubled atmosphere in the city, in this case the temple's *pujārī* (ritual assistant) was the sole *pūjā* principal; normally there would have been several drawn from the city's lay community. The other participants serve as both singers and as a sort of audience (though they are not pure spectators). Remaining seated, they sing the *pūjā*'s verses and witness the *pūjā* principals' acts. In the case in question about a hundred participants of this sort were on the scene by the ceremony's end.

We thus see that the role of worshiper is actually manifested in two ways in rites of this sort. The *pūjā* principals are in physical contact with the image; others are at an audience-like distance. In a sense the *pūjā* principals "do," while the others felicitate what is "being done." Jains believe that one's approval (*anumodan*) of another's good deed is spiritually and karmically beneficial, and the division of ritual labor seems to capitalize on this concept; by means of vocal participation an indefinite number of individuals can partake of the benefits of the rite.[11] Śvetāmbar Jain ritual culture is of the do-it-yourself sort; there is no role for priestly mediators, and this would seem to inhibit any sort of congregationalism. We see, however, that the differentiation of the worshiper's role into two modes allows for a strong congregational emphasis.

What follows is an abstracted account of the rite as I saw it performed in 1990 with a special emphasis on the text. The focus of worship was a small metal image of the Tīrthankar and a metal disc on which the *siddhcakra* had been inscribed.[12] These items were placed atop a stand that was stationed at the entrance to the main shrine at Mohan Bāṛī. Participants sat in the temple's courtyard, with men to one side and women to the other (the standard arrangement). In front of this stand with the image was a low table on which five small flags had been placed in a row. *Svastik*s (executed in sandalwood paste) marked the positions at the foot of each flag where offerings were deposited as the ceremony progressed.

## PĀRŚVANĀTH'S STORY

The *pūjā* of Pārśvanāth's five *kalyāṇak*s begins with the *cyavan kalyāṇak,* his descent from his previous existence as a god into a human womb.[13] The text for this sequence consists of three songs that recount Pārśvanāth's nine births prior to his final lifetime. This narrative centers on Pārśvanāth's relationship with Kamaṭh, who is Pārśvanāth's transmigratory moral alter. Kamaṭh's defects reverse Pārśvanāth's virtues, and Pārśvanāth's virtues provoke Kamaṭh again and again into the gravest sins. The story of how this fateful relationship began is not covered in the text, but is well known to the rite's participants. Marubhūti (who will become Pārśvanāth in a later birth) and Kamaṭh were once Brāhmaṇ brothers. Marubhūti was a paragon of virtue who had accepted Jainism and spent his time in meditation and fasting. Kamaṭh, much given to sensual pleasures, committed adultery with Marubhūti's wife. Marubhūti spied on the couple and reported Kamaṭh's misdeed to the king. Kamaṭh was punished, and Marubhūti was filled with regret. Marubhūti came to Kamaṭh to beg forgiveness, and, while he was bowing, Kamaṭh killed him with a stone.

It is at this point that the narrative begins. "Crooked Kamaṭh was attached to sensual vices," says the opening verse, "he killed his brother Marubhūti." As the text (which I summarize) continues, we learn how Marubhūti took his next birth as an elephant and was returned to the piety of his previous life by the king, who in the meantime had become an ascetic. Taking the form of a *kukurṭ* serpent (part snake, part cock), Kamaṭh then murdered him again. Marubhūti was reborn as a god, while Kamaṭh went to hell. In his next birth Marubhūti became a king named Kiraṇveg. He renounced the world, only to be murdered again by Kamaṭh in the form of a snake. Marubhūti now became a god in the twelfth heaven, while Kamaṭh descended to the fifth hell. In his next birth Marubhūti was a king named Vajnābh. He again renounced the world, and Kamaṭh, in the form of a Bhīl (a member of a particular tribe), killed him with an arrow. Marubhūti then became a god in one of the highest heavens, and Kamaṭh descended to the seventh hell.

Marubhūti's eighth birth was announced by the fourteen dreams that herald the birth of a *cakravartin* (or a Tīrthankar), and he became an emperor named Svarṇbāhu. This birth was decisive, for after renouncing the world and performing the *bīs sthānak tapasyā*[14] he acquired the *karma* that would result in a future birth as a Tīrthankar (*tīrthankar pad nām-karm*). Wicked Kamaṭh, this time in the form of a lion, murdered him again. In his next birth Marubhūti became a god in the tenth heaven, and Kamaṭh fell once again to hell. As a god, Marubhūti worshiped Tīrthankar images in Nandīśvar Dvīp (a continent, inaccessible to humans, where there are temples in which the gods worship Tīrthankar images) and served ascetics. Although he experienced enjoyment, his mind remained detached; he was like the lotus, says the text, that remains separate from the slime in which it grows. Unlike other gods, the text observes, a Tīrthankar-to-be does not grieve when he learns of his death six months before. He rejoices because he knows that after his human rebirth will come liberation. The narrative pauses here. It is time for the first offerings.

Meritorious action (*puṇya*) and sin (*pāp*) are important themes in the story thus far. Virtue is rewarded by rebirth in heaven; sin brings the miseries of hell. The wretched Kamaṭh's career is the mirror opposite of Marubhūti's. Drawn by his hatred into a transmigratory career of crime (of which we have not yet seen the end), Kamaṭh repeatedly falls into hell. It should be noted, however, that even Tīrthankars-to-be can suffer the pains of hell. During the twenty-seven births leading up to his Tīrthankarhood, Mahāvīr did two terms in hell, one in the seventh hell. There is, therefore, a higher point to the tale, which is that the value of world renunciation transcends mere questions of sin and virtue. Heaven's joys are transient (as are hell's agonies). Although his virtues bring him stupendous worldly and heavenly enjoyments, wise Marubhūti remains indifferent, and this is what brings him to final victory.

The text thus introduces us to a central problematic in the Jain view of things. Religious practice (such as this rite itself) generates that "good *karma*" known as "merit" (*puṇya*). Merit brings worldly rewards (the world, of course, includes heaven). But no *karma* is ever really "good," and these rewards are of no ultimate value. Thus one must—even in their midst—strive to aim beyond them. The Tīrthankar exemplifies what it means to succeed in this endeavor. This is a theme that we will encounter repeatedly in this book.

At the end of these verses comes the poet's signature line, and a short Sanskrit verse recapitulating the main themes of the preceding text, followed by a formula (a Sanskrit *mantra*) of offering. The recapitulative Sanskrit verse and the offering formula are standard preliminaries to the offering itself. At this point a gong is sounded, and the required ritual actions are then performed by the *pūjā* principal or principals (in the observed case, a single individual). A small amount of water is poured on a folded cloth: this is an abbreviated bathing of the image. The image is then anointed with sandalwood paste. The leftmost flag is garlanded, and incense and a lamp are proffered. A *svastik* is formed from rice (taken from the platter) atop the one already drawn on the table's surface in front of the flag. On this is placed a coconut to which a cloth and a currency note have been tied with a ceremonial string. In this context the coconut is called "*śrīphal,*" and, according to informants, it stands for auspiciousness, for good results. Sweets and fruits are then arranged around the coconut. With this the *cyavan kalyāṇak* is complete.

Before resuming, it should be noted that the edibles and other offerings made in these sequences are never returned to the offerers. This point is exceedingly important and will be explored in greater detail later.

Next comes the *janam kalyāṇak,* the Lord's birth. The text resumes. Parśvanāth is born in Banaras; his mother is Queen Vāmā, his father King Aśvasen. "Blessed is the city of Banaras," the opening couplet proclaims; "blessed is king Aśvasen / Blessed is the virtuous Queen Vāmā, because they obtained the Lord." The text then tells of how the queen experienced the fourteen auspicious dreams that always precede the birth of a Tīrthankar: first an elephant, then a bull, a lion, the goddess Śrī, and ten other highly auspicious visions.[15] A reader of dreams pronounced that they heralded wonderful things to come.

These dreams are of crucial importance. Although the text does not elaborate the point, it is well understood that they have a double meaning. They indicate that the child-to-be will become a *cakravartin,* a universal emperor, but they also can be taken to mean that he will be a Tīrthankar. This is a matter to which we shall return.

Lord Indra (one of the sixty-four kings of the gods, in this case the ruler of the first Jain heaven) then rose from his lion-throne and saluted the child-to-be as the "self-enlightened Lord, light and benefactor of the world." The Lord was born, the text says, on the tenth day of the dark fortnight of Pauṣ. The fifty-six goddesses known as Dikkumārīs performed chores associated with childbirth. The sixty-four Indras then took the infant to Mount Meru and there performed his birth ablution (*abhiṣek*). At this point this portion of the text ends. The usual Sanskrit verse and formula of offering are repeated, and the gong is sounded. The ritual acts are performed exactly as before, but this time the garland, lamp, and other items are offered at the position of the second flag from the left.

The Lord's *dīkṣā,* his initiation as an ascetic, comes next. The text continues, and the narrative now shifts to Pārśvanāth's childhood. He was beloved by the people. He possessed the three *jñān*s of *mati, śrut,* and *avadhi.*[16] He sucked nectar from his thumb. Youth and adolescence passed, and he married the princess Prabhāvatī. Wicked Kamaṭh appeared again, this time as a fraudulent Brāhmaṇ ascetic performing the five-fire penance. Having arrived at the scene with his mother, Pārśvanāth saw a cobra hiding in one of the pieces of burning wood. "Tell me how," he asked the ascetic, "austerities accompanied by violence can be fruitful?" He then removed a pair of half-burnt cobras from the wood (in other accounts only one snake is removed). He repeated the *namaskār mantra,* and the now-enlightened cobras became the guardian deities Dharṇendra and Padmāvatī.[17] Kamaṭh fled, died, and became a demonlike being named Meghmālin.

The text now turns to the initiation. One spring season Pārśvanāth saw a picture of Nemināth's wedding party, and his mind turned to thoughts of world renunciation.[18] The Lokāntik gods urged him to renounce the world, to teach, and to redeem those who were capable of liberation. He gave gifts for a year. The gods and kings then took him to the garden named Āśrampad, and there he fasted for three days and obtained the fourth *jñān* (the mind-reading ability acquired by all *arhats* at the time of initiation). With three hundred men he took initiation, and the gods gave him his ascetic garb.[19] The gods celebrated the initiation *kalyāṇak* and went to Nandīśvar to worship the eternal Tīrthankar images there. The signature line is followed by the Sanskrit stanza and offering formula. The ritual actions are performed as before, but this time at the position of the third flag from the left.

Next is *kevaljñān,* the Lord's achievement of omniscience. The text resumes. The Lord wandered from place to place, totally devoid of attachments, and took his first post-fast meal in the house of a rich man named Dhan. He came one day to the forest named Kadambri, and there once again met Kamaṭh, now Meghmālin. Meghmālin tried to break his concentration. He conjured up the forms of a lion and a snake, but the Lord was undisturbed. Clouds then thickened and surged, lightning cracked, rain fell like missiles, and the world began to flood. The water rose to Pārśvanāth's nose, but his concentration was still unshaken. The throne of Dharṇendra began to shake, and by means of *avadhijñān* (clairvoyant knowledge) he saw his Lord's danger. He and Padmāvatī then saved Pārśvanāth from the flood. Here the text is referring to the famous incident, known to virtually all Jains, in which Dharṇendra, aided by Padmāvatī, rescues the Tīrthankar by raising him from the water on a lotus and protecting him from the pelting rainfall with his multiple cobra hoods (see Figure 2). Dharṇendra then rebuked Kamaṭh. Humbled at last, Kamaṭh "took the shelter of Pārśvanāth's feet"; that is, he became Pārśvanāth's devotee.

The text continues. For eighty-four days the Lord remained an ascetic; on the fourth of the dark fortnight of the lunar month of Caitra (March/April), while under the *dhātaki* tree, he obtained *kevaljñān.* He advanced through the *guṇasthān*s and cut the *ghāti karma*s. He manifested the eight *prātihārya*s (miraculous signs of Tīrthankarhood). After the signature line of the final hymn come the Sanskrit verse and formula of offering. The ritual acts are performed, this time at the position of the fourth flag.

Fifth and last is the *nirvāṇ kalyāṇak,* the Lord's liberation (*nirvāṇ*). The previous *kalyāṇak*s have all had three songs; this time there are only two. The text resumes. The Lord sat and preached in the place of assembly of humans, gods, and animals (*samvasaraṇ*). His parents came to hear his teachings and took initiation themselves. Śubh (Śubhdatt) and his other chief disciples appeared. The Lord brought enlightenment to ascetics and nonascetics, men and women. The text now reiterates

Figure 2. Pārśvanāth with Dharṇendra and Padmāvatī. From a framing picture obtained in Ahmedabad. Courtesy of Premchand P. Goliya.

the story of his last lifetime: for thirty years he was a householder, and an ascetic for eighty-three days; he spent sixty-nine years, nine months, and seven days in the condition of *kevaljñān*. He knew he would live one hundred years. He spent his last rainy season retreat (*cāturmās*) on the peak of Samet mountain. Thirty-three ascetics were with the Lord; together they fasted for one month. On the eighth of the bright half of the lunar month of Śrāvan (July/August) he attained liberation. The gods came, their hearts filled with joy and sorrow; they celebrated the *kalyāṇak* with cries of victory.

The author signs, the usual verse and offering formula are repeated, and the ritual actions are performed, this time at the position of the fifth flag. This is the conclusion of the ceremony, except for a final sequence called *kalaś* (in which participants toss colored rice and flower petals at the image and water is poured at the four corners of the ceremony's site) and two lamp offerings (*āratī* and *mangal dīp*), which are standard exit-acts for all important rites of worship.

## THE IDEAL LIFE

What is this rite about? Its performance is, in part, seen as a source of auspiciousness and benefit to those who participate in it. This is a theme to which we shall return in the next chapter. In its narrative dimension, however, it is concerned with the nature of worship-worthiness. The most worship-worthy of all beings is the Tīrthankar. This is because he leads the ideal life, and Pārśvanāth's five-*kalyāṇak pūjā* is, at its textual core, a celebration of such a life.

The rite tells us first of all that the ideal life has a transmigratory context. This is a point often missed in English-language accounts of Jainism in which attention is usually focused entirely on the Tīrthankars' final lifetimes. To Jains, however, one of the crucial things about a Tīrthankar is that his final lifetime is indeed his *final* lifetime, the last of a beginningless series of rebirths. It must be stressed that, from the Jain point of view, a lifetime considered outside the context of the individual's transmigratory career is meaningless. We shall consider this point in greater detail later in this chapter.

In conformity with hagiographic convention, the text recounts Pārśvanāth's previous births beginning with the lifetime in which he obtained "right belief" (*samyaktva*). This is a crucial idea in Jainism. Jains say that once the seeds of righteousness have been planted, progress is always possible, no matter what the ups and downs in the meantime. An Ahmedabad friend once told me that if you possess right belief for as little time as a grain of rice can be balanced on the tip of the horn of a cow, you will obtain liberation sooner or later.[20] Therefore, even if one has little immediate interest in the ultimate goal of liberation or little sense of its personal gainability—which is in fact true of many ordinary Jains—one can still believe that one is on the right road if one has been touched by Jain teachings and if one has the necessary "capability" (*bhavyatva*). How does one know who is on this path and who has this capacity? Such persons are, surely, among those who celebrate the Lord's *kalyāṇaks* and who do so in the proper spirit of devotion and detachment from worldly desires.

Pārśvanāth's transmigratory career then takes a decisive turn. His destiny is fixed when he acquires the *karma* of a future Tīrthankar two births before his final one. He has reaped the rewards of his virtues, but these he sees in the perspective of a fully realized detachment. The rite then draws our attention to his penultimate existence as a god. Other gods mourn their impending earthly rebirths. Not so the Tīrthankar-to-be, for he regards the fall into a human body as an opportunity. This is a crucial matter, for it marks the separation of two possible paths. Divine and earthly happiness is the inevitable reward of virtuous action. This the Tīrthankar-to-be achieves in abundance, but he is completely indifferent to it. His is another goal. Felicity is a shackle, albeit (as Jains frequently say) one of gold.

The text thus illustrates a choice, and in theory Pārśvanāth might have chosen differently. His virtues bear the fruit of material rewards. The highest of these is rebirth as a deity. But this he rejects. Pārśvanāth-to-be *does not regret,* as do others, his loss of this status and condition. By the time of his descent into Queen Vāmā's womb he has already attenuated his attachments to the world and his basic detachment is secure.

The fourteen dreams that precede his birth are emblematic of the parting of the two ways. As noted, the dreams can be interpreted as foretelling the birth either of a universal emperor or of a Tīrthankar (Dundas 1992: 31–32; Jaini 1979: 7). A universal emperor embraces the entire world—one might even say devours it. The Tīrthankar rejects it utterly; the potential conqueror of all thus becomes the renouncer of all. The rejection occurs with his initiation, and it is significant that before initiation he gives (as do all Tīrthankars) gifts for a year—a dramatic and complete shedding of his wealth and of the world. Kingly largess and the ascetic's giving up are, at this moment, different aspects of the same thing. This idea is basic to Jain ritual culture, as we shall see. Then follow omniscience and the inception of his teaching mission. Unlike others who attain liberation, the Tīrthankar, as the text tells us, is self-enlightened; he assists others on the road to liberation, but requires no assistance himself.

Having taught, he attains final liberation. His links with the world are severed entirely. Now, in completely isolated and omniscient bliss, he abides eternally in the abode of the liberated at the top of the universe.

## THE COSMOS

We have seen that the text of Pārśvanāth's five-*kalyāṇak pūjā* places great emphasis on the wider transmigratory context of Pārśvanāth's Tīrthankarhood—his journey through different states of existence in different regions of the universe. This is one of the most obvious facts about the rite: that it situates itself in relation to a cosmos far wider than the place and time of Pārśvanāth's last birth. Within the framework of the rite, it is his cosmic situation that renders his final lifetime intelligible. A certain vision of the cosmos is therefore an element in the ritual culture within which the rite occurs. This is a vision in which the radical asceticism represented by the Tīrthankar—asceticism that culminates in his complete disappearance from the world of acts and consequences—is a reasonable response to existence.

The key to this vision is magnitude. If we supplement the rite's text with other sources, as I now propose to do, we discover that the Jain cosmos is a place of very large numbers. It is a stupendous vision in which, some would say, we see the numerical and metrical imagination run riot. The point of the vision, however, is not simply metrical; rather, its purpose is to illustrate the difficulty of attaining liberation. The cosmos, enormous in extent, swarms with forms of life, most of which are highly vulnerable to inadvertant or deliberate violence. Within this vast system, the opportunity to acquire a human body, which is the only body in which liberation is possible, is vanishingly small. The numbers in question are deployed in three domains: space, time, and biology.[21]

### SPACE

The Jain cosmos is a multi-tiered structure divided into three "worlds" (*lok*s): a world of the gods above, a hell below, and between them a thin terrestrial world where (among others) human beings dwell (Figure 3). At the very top is a small fourth region, resembling a shallow depression, which is the abode of liberated souls (*siddh śilā*). Running like a shaft from top to bottom is a zone called the *tras nāḍī,* so named because multisensed beings (*tras*) cannot exist outside it. The entire structure is fourteen *rajjūs* high. The standard unit of distance in Jain cosmography is the *yojan,* which equals about eight miles. A *rajjū* (rope) is equal to "uncountable" *yojan*s.[22] Mt. Meru, which is 100,000 *yojan*s (800,000 miles) high, is depicted on Jain maps as the merest bump in comparison with the whole structure. This vast cosmos, with its multiple layers and enormous internal volume, is the venue of the

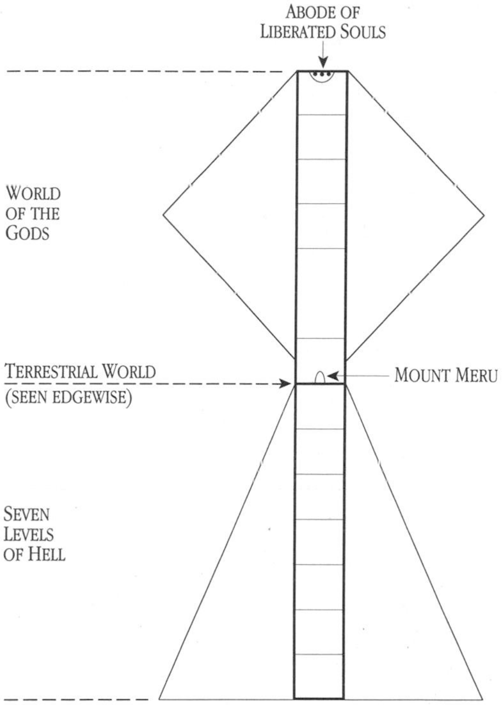


Figure 3. The Jain cosmos. A simplified version of a book illustration (Śāntisūri 1949: unnumbered page). Note the shaft-like *tras nāḍī* extending from top to bottom. The horizontal lines mark the fourteen *rajjūs* of the structure's height. The levels of hell correspond to the *rajjū* lines below the terrestrial world; the various heavens are distributed within the upper half of the *tras nāḍī*.

drama of the soul's bondage and liberation. Like a gigantic sealed aquarium, it is completely self-contained: Nothing enters, nothing leaves. Within it is an infinite (*anant*) number of beings (*jīvs*) who cycle and recycle from death to birth to death again. Except for the liberated, this wandering from existence to existence is eternal, for the cosmos was never created nor will it ever cease to be.

Humanity's physical surround is the terrestrial world, which is a flat disc with Mount Meru at its center[23] Here, and only here, are to be found human beings and animals. At the middle of this disc, and serving as Mount Meru's base, is a circular continent called Jambūdvīp, which is subdivided into seven regions separated by impassable mountains. The most important of these regions are Mahāvideh, Bharat, and

Airāvat. Mahāvideh is a broad belt running east and west across the continent and is divided into thirty-two rectangular subdivisions. At the extreme south and north of the continent are, respectively, the much smaller regions of Bharat and Airāvat. Bharat is the South Asian world, and the sole region physically accessible to us.

Surrounding Jambūdvīp is a series of concentric oceans and atoll-like circular islands continuing outward to the edge of the disc. These are said to be "innumerable" (*asankhyāt*), which means that although there is an actual limit beyond which there is simply empty space, the number of islands and oceans cannot be counted. The first two islands are divided into regions representing radial extensions of the seven regions of Jambūdvīp: Here, too, we find Mahāvidehs, Airāvats, Bharats, and so forth. Humans dwell in all of the regions of the first island, but it is possible for humans to live only in the inward-facing zone of the second island, which is separated from the outward-facing zone by a range of mountains.[24]

The most important feature of the terrestrial world is not its rather complicated physical geography (of which my brief account gives little true idea) but its moral geography. A portion of the habitable lands of Jambūdvīp and of the first two concentric islands is known as *bhogbhūmi,* "the land of enjoyment." Humans living in these regions exist in a state of continuous enjoyment without effort or struggle; subsistence is provided by trees that magically fulfill wishes, and premature death is unknown. Because asceticism cannot flourish in such an environment, Tīrthankars do not appear in these regions and liberation is not possible. Contrasting with *bhogbhūmi* are the areas known collectively as *karmbhūmi,* "the land of endeavor," in which our region is included. In these regions it is necessary for humans to earn their livelihoods through work, and premature death is possible. Because such an environment is conducive to reflection and asceticism, liberation is possible in this zone, and Tīrthankars are born here.

The terrestrial world is dwarfed by the regions above and below. Towering above is the "world of gods" (*devlok*), which is the destination of those who have lived virtuous lives.[25] The areas actually inhabited by deities are contained within the shaft-like *tras nāḍī.* There are twenty-six separate paradises in all, organized in a series of levels extending up to the top of the cosmos just below the abode of the liberated. Between the lowest heaven and the terrestrial world is a gap; here planetary and stellar bodies (the abodes of the *jyotiṣk* deities) move in stately circles around the summit of Mt. Meru. Below the terrestrial world, and extending downward as far as the heavens rise above, is the region known as hell (*narak*).[26] This is where those who have committed sins must suffer the consequences. There are seven levels of hell, and the lower the hell the more severe the punishment.

Among the more striking features of this cosmos is its sheer size. By comparison with the upper and lower worlds, the terrestrial world is tiny. The entire cosmos is often represented as a standing human figure with the terrestrial world as its pinched waist. And yet even if the terrestrial disc is viewed within a reduced frame of reference, it too turns out to be vast. The diameter of the central area of the terrestrial world—that is, the world within the circle of mountains dividing the second circular island into habitable and nonhabitable zones—is 4,500,000 *yojan*s, which (if the precise calculation is relevant) is roughly 36 million miles. The diameter of Jambūdvīp is 100,000 *yojans* (800,000 miles) and the north-south dimension of Bharat is roughly 525 *yojan*s (about 4,200 miles).

Taken together, these figures and calculations provide a basis for a certain conception of one's situation in the world. By comparison with one's immediate surroundings, Bharat is vast. But Bharat is but a tiny bite off the edge of the world-island to which it belongs. Inconceivably vaster than this world-island is the world-disc. But the world-disc itself is but a thin wafer in a cosmos that is a towering hierarchy of unimaginable dimensions. And everywhere (as we shall see) this cosmos teems with beings. Very small then—inconceivably small by comparison—is an individual's own niche in the cosmos.

## TIME

According to the Jain vision of things, in the *karmbhūmi* regions of Bharat (our region) and Airāvat, time moves through repetitive and very gradual cycles of moral and physical rise and decline. During the ascending half-cycle the human life span lengthens, body size increases, and the general level of happiness increases; these trends are reversed in the half-cycle of decline. The cycles are immensely long. According to one version,[27] a complete cycle lasts for a period of time equal to twenty *koṛākoṛī sāgar*s. *Koṛākoṛī* is a numerical expression equaling ten million multiplied by ten million, so by this reckoning an entire cycle takes $2 \times 10^{15}$ *sāgar*s. A *sāgar* (or *sāgaropam*) is a unit of time measurement. The same source (see also J. L. Jaini 1918: 90) asserts that one *sāgar* equals one *koṛākoṛī,* multiplied by ten, of units called *addhāpalyas*, and an *addhāpalya* equals "innumerable" *uddhārapalyas*, each of which in turn contains "innumerable" *vyavahārapalyas*. A *vyavahārapalya* equals the time it would take to empty a circular pit with a diameter and depth of one *yojan* (8 miles) of fine lamb's hairs if one hair were removed every 100 years.[28] The point of these abstruse and fantastic calculations is, of course, to emphasize the nearly inconceivable vastness of the periods of time portrayed.

Each half-cycle is subdivided into six eras and each era is named according to how "happy" (*sukhamā*) or "unhappy" (*dukhamā*) it is (ibid.: 89). An ascending half-cycle thus evolves from *dukhamā-dukhamā* (severely unhappy) through *dukhamā* (unhappy), *dukhamā-sukhamā* (more unhappy than happy), *sukhamā-dukhamā* (more happy than unhappy), *sukhamā* (happy), to *sukhamā-sukhamā* (extremely happy) (renderings partly from P. S. Jaini 1979: 31). The declining cycle is the reverse of this. We (in Bharat) are currently in the fifth age (often called the *pañcam kāl*) of a declining half-cycle. When a descending half-cycle begins, all human wants are effortlessly satisfied by wish-fulfilling trees, and human beings attain an age of three *palyas* (presumably *addhāpalyas*) and a height of 6 miles. By contrast, the last age is a time of extreme discomforts and lawlessness; miserable, dwarfish, with a height of one and one-half feet, humans live a mere twenty years. In a declining cycle such as ours, Tīrthankars exist only during the fourth age (the first Tīrthankar appearing at the very end of the third), and it is only during this period that liberation is possible. During the first three ages the general happiness discourages ascetic exertion, and during the last two ages the misery is too great. Our current fifth age began just after Lord Mahāvīr (the last Tīrthankar of our half-cycle) left the world; it will last only 21,000 years.

These cycles, however, do not occur in all regions of the terrestrial world. The most significant exception is Mahāvideh, half of which is *karmbhūmi*. This means that there are Tīrthankars active at the present time in that region.

The social and cultural world we know was the creation of Ṛṣabh, the first of the twenty-four Tīrthankars of our declining half-cycle.[29] As P. S. Jaini (1979: 288) points out, Ṛṣabh occupies the functional niche of a creator deity in a tradition that denies creation. Prior to his advent, the world was a precultural paradise.[30] Because of the magical wish-fulfilling trees, toil was nonexistent. Old age and disease were unknown. Religious creeds did not exist. There was no family, no king or subjects, no social organization. As just noted, humans were 6 miles tall and their lives were eons long. Born six months before their parents' death, these extraordinary beings (called *yugliyās*) came into the world as mated sibling pairs. Each pair lived as a couple after puberty, and in time produced two similar offspring. In uncanny parallel with the theories of Lévi-Strauss and other anthropologists, the Jains see presocial humanity as humanity without the incest taboo.

With the passage of the first three eras conditions deteriorated. The magical trees began to disappear and this resulted in shortages of food and other necessities. This led to the development of anger, greed, and conflict. Because of the crime and disorder, the frightened people met together and formed small family groups (*kul*s), and set persons of special ability in positions of authority. Here is Hobbes in a Jain guise. These individuals were called *kulkar*s, and by establishing property rights and a system of punishments, they were able to maintain order as paradise dwindled away. The last of the *kulkar*s was named Nābhi,[31] and he was the father of Ṛṣabh.

Ṛṣabh was the inventor of society, polity, and culture in our half-cycle of cosmic time. He was the first king, made so by the twins because of the troubles then occurring. He introduced the state (*rāṣṭra*), the enforcement of justice by punishment (*daṇḍ nīti*), and society (*samāj*) itself (these terms are from Lalvānī 1985:31).[32] He established the system of *varṇa*s, the ancient division of Indian society into functional classes.[33] He also taught such necessary arts as farming, fire-making, the fashioning of utensils, the cooking of food, and so on. His was also the first nonincestuous marriage, which established the current system of marriage. In the end he abandoned the world and became the first Tīrthankar of our half-cycle of cosmic history. He was also the first to receive the *dān* (merit-generating gift) of food from a layperson, which in this case was sugar cane juice. So important was this event that Jains commemorate it in a calendrical festival (*akṣay tṛtīyā*).

With Ṛṣabh's advent, our corner of the world became redemptively active. He was the only Tīrthankar of the third age; after him, in the fourth age, came the remaining twenty-three Tīrthankars of our current declining half-cycle. Each promulgated the same teachings and left behind the same fourfold social order of monks and nuns, laymen and laywomen. The penultimate was Pārśvanāth, with whose rite of worship this chapter began, and the last was Lord Mahāvīr. Soon after Mahāvīr's departure the window of opportunity for liberation closed.

The history of the twenty-four Tīrthankars invests what would otherwise be a featureless timescape with moral and soteriological meaning. There is no beginning or end to the cosmic pulsations of the Jain universe, and in this perspective the face of time is blank. But within the cycles the passage of time can be converted into a significant narrative, one that has a direct bearing on the nature of the world experienced by men and women at the present time. The era of the Tīrthankars thus seems to mediate between timeless eternity and the world that men and women know: The totally repetitive periodicity of the five *kalyāṇaks* belongs to eternity; the individuation of the specific careers of the twenty-four Tīrthankars belongs to the particular history of our world and era.

Mahāvīr's departure inaugurated the history of the Jain tradition itself, established by Mahāvīr's followers. The ultimate locus of the sacred for the Jains, the Tīrthankar as a generic figure, is no longer present in the world.[34] In the aftermath of their era, therefore, the task is to maintain some kind of contact with their presence as it once was. They are gone—as we have seen—utterly. But although the beneficence (*kalyāṇ*) intrinsic to their nature exists no longer in embodied form, it can be transmitted from generation to generation by means of the lines of disciplic succession that link lineages of living ascetics with Lord Mahāvīr. Their teachings also remain, although we possess only an incomplete version. Although their *kalyāṇak*s no longer occur in our world, these events can be (as we have seen) evoked through ritual. And of course the social order they established—the fourfold order of Jain society—endures still.

## BIOLOGY

The Jains have created a complex system of biological knowledge. It is a system that includes concepts of physiology, morphology, and modes of reproduction, but its main focus is taxonomy. It should not be thought of as a system of scientific analysis. Its basic motivation is soteriological, and the system may be seen as a conceptual scaffolding for the Jain vision of creaturely bondage and the path to liberation.

The beings of the world (*jīv*s) are divided into two great classes, liberated (*mukt*) and unliberated (*saṃsārī*). Liberated beings are those who have shed all forms of karmic matter, and unliberated beings are those who are in the bondage of *karma*.[35] In turn, unliberated beings are divided into two great classes: beings that cannot move at their own volition (*sthāvar*) and beings that, in order to avoid discomfort, can move about (*tras*).[36] The beings of the *sthāvar* class possess only one sense, the sense of touch, and are of five types: 1) "earth bodies" (*prithvīkāy*) that inhabit the earth, stones, and so on; 2) "water bodies" (*apkāy*) that inhabit water; 3) "fire bodies" (*teukāy* or *tejkāy*) that live in fire (and electricity); 4) "air bodies" (*vāyukāy*) that inhabit the air; and 5) plants (*vanaspatikāy*).

Plants come in two general types: *pratyek*, in which there is one soul per body, and *sādhāraṇ*, in which there are infinite (*anant*) souls in a given material body. The *sādhāraṇ* or multiple-souled forms of plant life are, in turn, of two types: "gross" (*bādar*) and "subtle" (*sukṣam*). The gross varieties include such common root vegetables as potatoes, carrots, onions, garlic, and yams, and this taxon, therefore, is extremely important from the standpoint of dietary rules. Because potatoes and similar vegetables harbor tiny forms of life in infinite numbers, they are—in theory—forbidden to Jains.[37] The ban on the eating of root vegetables is one of the principal markers distinguishing Jain vegetarianism from that of other vegetarian groups in India. The plant category also includes tiny beings, infinite in number, called *nigods*.[38] They are the lowest form of life and exist in little bubble-like clusters that fill the entirety of the space of the cosmos. They live a short time, perish, and then take rebirth as *nigod*s again (with some exceptions, as we shall see). They are a teeming sea of invisible life everywhere around us, even within our bodies.

*Tras* beings are classified on the basis of the number of sense organs they have. The *viklendriy* class, consisting of beings of two to four senses, opposes the *pañcendriy* class, consisting of beings with five senses. Two-sensed animals have taste and touch; three-sensed animals add smell; four-sensed animals add vision; and five-sensed animals add hearing. A somewhat different principle of animal classification is based on the manner of giving birth. Those born from the womb (and this includes eggs) are called *garbhaj*. Beings called *sammūrchim* are born by means of the spontaneous accretion of matter into a body. All beings of fewer than five senses are born this way, as are some five-sensed animals and human beings.

Coexisting with (and consistent with) the above scheme is yet another system of classification, and in many ways this is the most important of all. This is the system of the four *gati*s, the four "conditions of existence." These four categories are: hell-dwellers (*nāraki*), animals and plants (*tiryañc*),[39] humans (*manuṣya*), and deities (*dev*). They are ranked on the basis of the relative happiness (*sukh*) or sorrow (*dukh*) experienced by the beings within them.

The most miserable of all beings are the hell-dwellers. They exist in perpetual darkness and suffer from unrelenting hunger, thirst, and extremes of heat and cold. They are tortured in various ingenious ways by demon-like beings who perform this function. The punishment is often of the punishment-fits-the-crime variety. Picture books exist in which the punishments for various sins are depicted in vivid and rather disgusting detail, a sort of pornography of punition.[40] Hell-dwellers take birth (as do the gods) by means of instantaneous creation, and their terms of punishment are eons long. An Ahmedabad informant once told me that hell-beings remember their torments after they are reborn as humans, which—he said—is why babies cry. He then went on to say that the parents give the child a doll to stop the crying, and the child clings to it and says, "mine! mine! mine!" Then, he continued, at the age of twenty-one or so "they give you a bigger doll, and the same thing happens." The result is attachment to family and other worldly things, and so the cycle goes on.

The animals and plants (*tiryañc*) experience somewhat less misery than hell beings do, or at least this seems to be true of five-sensed animals. However, birth anywhere in the *tiryañc* category is extremely undesirable. Their natural place of habitation is the world-disc, but they can live in many areas barred to human beings.

Human beings experience more happiness and less sorrow than those in the *tiryañc* category. As noted already, humans occupy only the restricted central area of the world-disc; they are distributed, of course, between the two moral zones of *karmbhūmi* and *bhogbhūmi*. The humans in *bhogbhūmi* are born as twins of the same sort that exist in our world during the paradisaical age; their lives are spent in sensuous enjoyment, and liberation is impossible for them. Humans can be either womb-born (*garbhaj*) or born by spontaneous generation (*sammūrchim*). The latter are generated from various impurities (such as excrement, urine, phlegm, or semen) produced by the bodies of womb-born humans. They are without intelligence and cannot be detected with the senses; their bodies measure an "uncountably" small part of a finger's breadth. They die within one *antarmuhūrt* (forty-eight minutes) without being able to develop the full characteristics of a human body.[41] Certain rules of ascetic discipline are based on the injunction to avoid harming these beings. For example, after eating, some ascetics and extraorthoprax laymen drink the liquid residue from washing their hands and plates or bowls. This is to prevent the spontaneous generation of millions of little replicas of themselves, for whose deaths they would then be responsible, in the meal's remains. Just as the category of multiple-souled plants invests Jain vegetarianism with a distinctive character, this category provides the basis for certain distinctive features of Jain asceticism.

The truly crucial fact about human existence, however, is that liberation is possible only in a human body. As we know, liberation is not possible for *all* humans, but it is possible *only* for humans. This is a fact with momentous consequences, as we shall see in the next chapter.

The gods and goddesses are, in some ways, mirror images of the hell-beings. Hell-beings are being punished for their sins; the gods and goddesses are being rewarded for their virtuous acts in previous existences. The question of the cosmic functional niche of the gods and goddesses will be addressed in the next chapter. For now it is sufficient to note that, as are the hell-dwellers, the gods and goddesses are stratified. The lowest are the *bhavanvāsī*s, "those who dwell in buildings," who live in the uppermost of the seven hells but are not subjected to hellish torments. Residing in an intermediate level between the uppermost level of hell and the earth are deities known as *vyantar*s who inhabit jungles and caves. They can help human beings, but can be malicious, too. The *jyotiṣk* deities (planetary deities) dwell in the region between the earth and the heavens above. They belong to two basic categories, moving and stationary.

The most important deities are the *vaimānik*s, so named because they inhabit heavenly palaces (*vimān*s) of various kinds. They are divided into two basic types. Lowest are the *kalpopapan*s, those who are born in paradises (*kalpa*s). Residing in palaces above the *kalpopapan* deities are the *kalpātīt* deities (without *kalpa*s), who are of two kinds: the *graiveyak*s, who dwell in nine palaces above the topmost of the heavens of the *kalpopapan* deities, and the *anuttar*s, who live in five palaces higher still. The *kalpopapan* deities perform the celebrations of the Tīrthankars' *kalyāṇak*s. They also live in organized societies in which there are kings, ministers, bodyguards, villagers, townsmen, servants, and so on. The *kalpātīt* deities do not participate in rituals and are not socially organized. Goddesses are found dwelling only in the first and second heavens of the *kalpopapan* deities and below, although they may visit higher heavens. In these lower regions the gods have sexual relations; at higher levels, sexual relations become progressively etherealized: from mere touch, to sight, to hearing, to thought, and finally to no sexual activity at all.[42]

The Indras are the kings of the gods. There are sixty-four of them in total: twenty who rule the *bhavanvāsīs*, thirty-two for the *vyantars* (and a subcategory known as *van vyantars*), two for the *jyotiṣks*, and ten for the twelve paradisaical regions. As we shall see in the next chapter, the Indras (and Indrāṇīs, their consorts) are symbolically central to ritual action among Jains.

## RULES

The Jain universe might be likened to a three-dimensional board game. The board is *saṃsār,* the world of endless passage from existence to existence.[43] The playing pieces are infinite in number and are, subject to the rules of the game, free to move anywhere on the board. The object of the game is to leave the board. The game has no beginning or end; it has been going on from beginningless time (*anādi kāl se,* as Jains always say) and will continue for an infinite time to come (*anant kāl tak*). Nor does it reflect the purposes of some divine creator; there is no rhyme or reason to it—the game simply is. Most player/pieces are not even aware of the game, to say nothing of the possibility of winning; they merely wander "without a goal" (*lakṣyahīn*) from existence to existence, leaving pain and havoc in their wake.

The various taxa of living things are the stopping places of player/pieces between moves; moves occur at the moment of death. There are rules of play (often called *śāśvat niyam,* "eternal rules," in the materials I have seen) determining which moves are possible and which are not. The human and *tiryañc* classes share one critical feature: After death, humans and subhumans can be reborn in any class at all. They can return to their previous classes, or they can switch from *tiryañc* to human, or vice-versa. Or, on the basis of sin or merit, they can ascend to heaven or descend to hell, and it should be noted that this is true of animals as well as of humans.[44] By contrast, the divine and hellish classes are one-stop existences. Gods and hell-beings must be reborn either in the human or *tiryañc* class.

These various rules of play result in a game with certain general features. Victory, which is moving off the board of play, is extremely difficult to achieve. Even to have a chance at winning, one must first take birth in the human class, and this in itself is hard to do. Forward and upward progress is hard; falling backwards from the goal is easy. There is no opting out of the game. The game goes on eternally, and, short of victory, there is no way at all to discontinue play.

## COSMOS AS PILGRIMAGE

The soul's career in the cosmos is sometimes likened to a pilgrimage. A good example of the use of this metaphor is to be found in a book (Aruṇvijay, n.d.), put into my hands by a Jaipur friend, consisting of a collection of rainy season discourses given by a Tapā Gacch monk named Aruṇvijay.[45]

The soul, he says, is on a pilgrimage through the cosmos (a *saṃsār yātrā*), with the final destination being liberation. His account begins with the *nigod*s, beings who have not yet begun the pilgrimage. Infinite in number and packed into every cranny of the cosmos, these tiny beings mostly just wink from one identical existence to the next. The *nigod*s, he says, are a kind of "mine" (*khān*) or reservoir of souls, infinite in extent and inexhaustible. To begin the pilgrimage, a soul must leave this condition; only then does a soul enter the "dealings" (*vyavahār*) of *saṃsār.* Can a *nigod* leave this condition by means of its own effort? No, says Aruṇvijay. It is a law of the cosmos that in order for one *nigod* to leave that condition, one soul in the universe must attain liberation. Given the vast number of *nigod*s and the relative infrequency of liberations, it follows that this is an extremely rare event, and that we—those of us now in a higher condition—are fantastically fortunate even to have left the condition of *nigod.*

Having left the status of *nigod,* he says, the soul enters various existences as *bādar sādhāraṇ vanaspati* (coarse vegetable bodies that live together in infinite numbers in a single plant or portion thereof) and finds itself packed within masses of similar souls in the form of moss on a wall, a potato, or the like. It then takes birth as various kinds of earth and water bodies before graduating upward to the status of *pratyek vanaspati* (that is, the vegetable bodies that live one to a plant or portion thereof). It then goes on to inhabit air bodies and fire bodies. In this way the soul takes "uncountable" (*asankhya*) births among the one-sensed beings.

Aruṇvijay says that the soul progresses because of the accumulated effect of merit resulting from virtuous actions performed in various births. Exactly how merit is generated by the activities of such humble beings he does not explain, and his overall characterization of the soul's destiny does not emphasize ethical retribution. Rather, the image he stresses repeatedly is the "wandering" (*paribhramaṇ*) of the soul. His favorite metaphor is that of the ox tied to an oil press. The wretched beast goes round and round in a circle (the four *gati*s); he is blindfolded, and has not the faintest idea of where he has been or what his destination will be.

The pilgrimage continues. The soul takes "uncountable" births as it advances from two to four-sensed bodies. But it can also regress and even fall back into the one-sensed category again. In the end the soul may at last enter the category of five-sensed beings. It now spends countless years in this class. It must take birth as every form of water beast, then every kind of land animal, then all the varieties of birds. It takes "violent births" (*hiṃsak janams*) in the form of such animals as lions or tigers. As a carnivore it commits the sin of killing five-sensed creatures, and now it descends into hell.[46] The soul spends eons (*sāgaropanms* of years) in hell, and moves back and forth between hell and the *tiryañc* class many times. It even falls back into the four-, three-, two-, and one-sensed classes yet again. Eons more pass. And then progress resumes.

At long last, after infinite existences from beginningless time, the soul/pilgrim enters a human body. Alas, it sins and falls into hell, and from there takes birth all over again in the sub-five-sensed classes. As a result of truly fearsome (*bhayankar*) sins commited as a human, the soul can even fall back into the condition of *nigod*. How often, our author exclaims, has the soul gone downward and how far it has fallen! Our soul/pilgrim may also become a deity on the basis of merit earned by deeds. From this condition, however, it must return, and Aruṇvijay says that it may well fall all the way down to the lowest classes of life again. These transformations will occur again and again. The soul/pilgrim goes through the four *gati*s, the five *jāti*s (classes of beings with from one to five senses), and the entire 8,400,000 kinds of births that exist. This is the nature of the cycle (*cakra*) of the soul's great pilgrimage through the cosmos. And there is more. Aruṇvijay reminds us that not only have we all been through this cycle, but we have been through it an infinite number of times.

What is Aruṇvijay's main point?[47] Almost everything he says converges on one fundamental assertion, namely that one's birth in a human body should not be wasted.[48] This reflects the ascetics' view of things, a view that exists as a perpetual rebuke to the more comfortable lay view that routine piety is enough. It is possible, he says, for human births to be repeated; in theory it is possible to have seven or eight in a row. But this is very difficult and requires an immense amount of merit. Human birth is "rare" (*durlabh*) and in this vast cosmos very difficult to obtain. Sin is so easy, and the sins of one life can pursue you through many births. Not only will sins send you to hell, but they will result in many births in the classes of two- to four-sensed creatures after you have emerged from below. Aruṇvijay reflects at length on the sin of abortion, and it is significant that, in his eyes, part of the horror of abortion is that it cuts the newly incarnated soul off from the possibility of a human existence.

His conclusion is that one must set a "goal" (*lakṣya*) of release from the cycle of rebirth in the classes of living things. The contrast is between one who has such a goal and those who are "without a goal" (*lakṣyahīn*). Those who are without a goal wander blindly and aimlessly. You have sinned an infinity of times, but now you have gotten the Jain *dharm* (Jainism). If you set the goal of release, he says, then it is easy to get rid of sins. What is needed is a full effort in spiritual endeavor. This is the real point of everything he has said. He is not much interested in the whys and wherefores of the wandering soul's entry into one kind of body or another. More important is the sheer *scale* of things. The soul takes many, many births—infinite births—in its endless wanderings through this vast cosmos. At long last has come the opportunity for deliverance, and this opportunity must not be allowed to slip away.

Aruṇvijay uses this vision of the soul's pilgrimage to reinforce the plausibility of central Jain values. Large numbers abound: uncountablities and infinities. The universe is inconceivably vast in size. The timescape is infinite in extent. The taxonomic system is enormous and labyrinthine. The potential for doing harm to other beings is boundless. Liberation is possible only in a human body, and human bodies are hard to get. The zone of human habitation is tiny by comparison with the cosmos as a whole, as is the human taxon by comparison with the teeming multitudes of other forms of life with which the cosmos is filled. Indeed, even a human body is not in itself enough, because liberation is actually available during the merest sliver of time in comparison with all of time. And even in eras and places where Jain doctrine can be heard, not everyone hears it. Here, then, is the pilgrim at last in human form and in contact with Jain teachings. Lucky is such a pilgrim, and so valuable an opportunity must not be wasted.

Aruṇvijay's main concern is not with proselytizing asceticism. His primary goal is to raise the general level of piety of his lay audience. But the vision he projects is one that places a context around the core values that inform the text of Pārśvanāth's five-*kalyāṇak pūjā*. Ascetic withdrawal is the central meaning of Pārśvanāth's last life. The only truly rational and morally defensible response to this cosmos is the most radical withdrawal from it. This is not the way most Jains live, but it is a constant undertow in Jain religious life, and one that creates strains and ambivalences. It cannot be ignored. How could it be, when it is dramatized on a daily basis by living ascetics?

## LIVING ASCETICS

Perhaps the first thing that should be said about Jain *sādhu*s and *sādhvī*s, monks and nuns respectively, is that they are not hermits. Indeed, in some ways the very opposite is true. Jain ascetics—particularly ascetics of consequence with lay followings—are public persons, and to be in their presence is to be in the center of a more or less constant hubbub. In the midst of the coming and going it is sometimes hard for the inquiring field researcher to get a word in edgewise. This life is not reclusive, and in fact it cannot be. Jain ascetics are totally dependent on the laity for every physical need; they cannot even prepare their own food. Among many other things, this means that ascetics and laity must come into constant contact among the Jains. Nor does the tradition define the ascetic's role as socially exterior. Readers will recall that every Tīrthankar reestablishes the fourfold order of Jain society—the *caturvidh sangh*—which consists of monks and nuns, laymen and laywomen. Ascetics are obviously not householders, but they are nonetheless included in a wider social order.[49]

Although the primary focus of my research was the religious life of lay Jains, I was constantly being urged to consult ascetics. The reason for this is that ascetics are regarded by the laity as the sole true experts on Jain matters, a confidence not always well placed. While I was in Ahmedabad it was easy to meet both monks and nuns. It was the *cāturmās* season, which meant that ascetics were in permanent residence, and the Tapā Gacch, the ascetic lineage dominant in Ahmedabad, is large. It was more difficult to meet monks in Jaipur, even during *cāturmās,* for the simple reason that there are very few monks belonging to the Khartar Gacch, the image-worshiping ascetic lineage dominant in that city. As a result, monks were usually not present at all, although I encountered them from time to time. I did have the privilege of meeting many Khartar Gacch nuns in Jaipur, who were almost always present in the city. During the course of the year in Jaipur I had also had numerous conversations with monks belonging to the flourishing, nonimage-worshiping Terāpanthī sect. Most of my image-worshiping friends held the Terāpanthī ascetics in high esteem and saw nothing untoward about my contact with them. A well-known Digambar *muni* was also kind enough to allow me to spend a lot of time in his presence. This was a valuable source of comparative data on lay-ascetic interactions, especially in the crucial area of food.

The cultural personae presented by Jain ascetics is an amalgam. At one level they are personal exemplars. Here, their very existence suggests, is the kind of life one *ought* to want to lead. At another level they are the tradition's teachers. They give discourses, sometimes learnedly and sometimes not. Many lay Jains develop intensified relationships with a particular ascetic whom they regard as their *guru* (religious preceptor).[50] Jain ascetics frequently admonish and scold lay Jains for laxity in their behavior. I have been told that some lay Jains avoid contact with ascetics for fear of being asked awkward questions about their diet. They also instigate fasting and other religious/ritual behavior. Indeed, a layperson must make a vow before an ascetic (or in front of a Tīrthankar-image if no ascetic is available) before undertaking ascetic practices such as fasts; without such a vow the exercise will be without results.

Ascetics are also, in their persons, objects of worship. This cannot surprise us, for Jains, as we know, worship ascetics. Although the *namaskār mantra,* the all-important formula with which this chapter began, singles out the Tīrthankars as foremost among the worship-worthy, it also includes living ascetics, *sādhu*s (and by extension *sādhvī*s). When Jain friends urged me to take my questions to ascetics, the content of what they might say was, perhaps, less important than the fact that *they* were the ones who would be saying it. After all, living ascetics participate in the sacredness of the Tīrthankar, though at a great remove, and any interaction with them necessarily falls in the paradigm of worship.

## ORGANIZATION

According to a survey of rainy season retreat locations for the year of my research in Jaipur (B. Jain 1990: 62), in 1990 there were 6,162 ascetics (1,373 monks and 4,789 nuns) among image-worshiping Śvetāmbar Jains. The Sthānakvāsīs had a total of 2,738 (532 monks, 2,206 nuns), and the Terāpanthīs had 719 (157 monks, 562 nuns) (ibid.). Digambar ascetics are very few by comparison with the Śvetāmbars. According to the same source, in 1990 there were only 225 *muni*s and

130 *āryikās* (nuns who, unlike Śvetāmbar nuns, do not take full vows), giving a total of 355 Digambar ascetics (ibid.: 63).

The temple-going Śvetāmbar ascetics are distributed among several currently existing ascetic lineages. An ascetic lineage, called a *gacch,* is an order of male and female ascetics tracing ritual and spiritual "descent" through links between preceptors and disciples. As far as I am aware, all currently active ascetic lineages trace their descent to Sudharmā, who was one of Lord Mahavir's eleven chief disciples.[51] As John Cort points out (1991b: 554), the formation of a *gacch* is typically conceptualized in relation to spiritual lapses and reform. A charismatic ascetic arises in response to laxity in ascetic discipline; having reestablished the proper ascetic rigor, he becomes the apical spiritual ancestor of a new *gacch.* The survey of rainy season retreats lists the following currently functioning *gacch*s in order of numerical strength: Tapā Gacch, Acal Gacch, Khartar Gacch, Tristuti Gacch, Pārśvacandra Gacch, and Vimal Gacch (B. Jain 1990: 61–62). These differ greatly in size and influence. The Tapā Gacch, especially influential in Gujarat, is the largest and most flourishing today: In 1990 it had a total of 5,472 ascetics (1,246 male, 4,226 female) divided into sixteen subgroups (*samudāy*s). No other *gacch* comes near it in size; the next largest, the Acal Gacch, has a total of only 231 ascetics listed, and the smallest, the Vimal Gacch, lists only six ascetics.

A *gacch* is further subdivided into *samudāy*s, which in turn are further subdivided into *parivār*s (on these points, see Cort 1991b: 559–63). The model is that of the descent group. A *samudāy* consists of those who are, by disciplic succession, the spiritual descendants of a particular *sādhu,* the apical spiritual ancestor. He is typically a charismatic *ācārya* whose career seems to his followers to have represented a "new beginning" of some kind or another (ibid.: 559). Cort suggests that, from a social point of view, the *gacch* is the equivalent of *jāti* (a term usually rendered as "caste" or "subcaste" in English), with the *samudāy* then emerging as an ascetic analogue of the lineage and the *parivār* as the ascetic version of the family (which is in fact the meaning of the word) or small lineage segment (ibid.: 560). As Cort also points out, these ascetic institutions reflect the agnatic values prevailing in the wider social world: monks constitute the core of these entities, and nuns are attached to monks' lineages, just as women become attached to the families and lineages of their husbands by marriage.

As noted already, Ahmedabad and Jaipur are dominated by two different *gacch*s. The predominant influence in Ahmedabad is the currently flourishing Tapā Gacch. The organization of the Tapā Gacch has been well described by Cort (1989: Ch. 3). More relevant to the concerns of Chapters Three and Four of this book, however, is the Khartar Gacch, to which most of the temple-going Śvetāmbar Jains of Jaipur are linked. With a total of only 214 ascetics, 22 monks and 192 nuns (B. Jain 1990: 62), the Khartar Gacch is obviously small. Only two *samudāys* are now extant: Sukhsāgarjī's and Mohanlāljī's (so named for their founders). A third, Kṛpācandrajī's, became extinct around midcentury, and the remaining nuns (there were no monks) were absorbed by Mohanlāljī's *samudāy*. The principal Śvetāmbar temples of Jaipur are affiliated with the Khartar Gacch, although there is one large Tapā Gacch temple in the old city. Moreover, the cult of the Dādāgurus (see Chapter Three), a Khartar Gacch phenomenon, is a dominant feature of the religious lives of the Śvetāmbar Jains of the city. The Khartar Gacch also has significant numbers of followers in Gujarat, Madhya Pradesh, Maharashtra, and other areas of Rajasthan.

In addition to monks and nuns, there remain today a very few *yatis* in the Khartar Gacch. The *yatis* are ascetics who own property, maintain residence in one place, and are in some instances noncelibate. This institution is today in a state of nearly total desuetude, and has apparently completely disappeared in the Tapā Gacch (Cort 1989: 97–102; Laidlaw 1995: Ch. 3). There are still a few Khartar Gacch *yatis*—especially, I am told, in Bikaner—but I met only one in Jaipur, an elderly gentleman and a rather sad figure, a vestige of a bygone era. In the past, however, they were very important figures in the Khartar Gacch. The standard *pūjā* of the Dādāgurus (to be discussed later) was authored some ninety years ago by a *yati* whose name was Ṛddhisār.

An apparent effect of the shortage of monks in the Khartar Gacch (currently only 22) is the relatively high status of nuns. In the Tapā Gacch, for example, it is not customary for nuns to preach publicly (Cort 1991b: 557), but this is quite common in the Khartar Gacch. In fact, because of the relative scarcity of monks in the Khartar Gacch community, the preaching function of ascetics seems to have gone largely by default to nuns (see Reynell 1991: 60–61). In Jaipur the two most respected and beloved ascetic figures of recent times were both nuns. One was Vicakṣaṇśrī, who died in 1980. Her image is now enshrined in an imposing memorial at Mohan Bāṛī (the site of our five-*kalyāṇak pūjā* of Pārśvanāth). The community's major *upāśray* (community hall for religious functions) is named Vicakṣaṇ Bhavan after her. The other beloved nun, Sajjanśrī, died in 1989. A memorial structure for her, also at Mohan Bāṛī, was under construction at the time of my stay. As far as I am aware, no monks have attracted such strong veneration among Jaipur's Khartar Gacch Jains in recent times.[52]

## MENDICANCY

The ascetic life is based on five "great vows" (*mahāvrats*) to which initiates commit themselves as part of the initiation (*dīkṣā*) process.[53] The vows are the same for male and female ascetics. The vows are mostly negative—that is, they are vows not to do a given thing—and apply to three modes and at three levels of action. The actions in question must not be done with mind (*man*), speech (*vacan*), or body (*śarīr*). Moreover, monks must vow not to do them (*karnā*), not to cause them to be done (*karvānā*), nor to admire their being done (*anumodan karnā*).

The first vow, and in many ways the most important, is that of *ahiṃsā,* which is the vow to harm no living thing. Jain laity are also required to avoid harming life forms, but the ascetic's vow is more inclusive, extending even to one-sensed beings. Many of the most conspicuous features of ascetic life are shaped by this requirement. Ascetics drink only boiled water so as to avoid harming small forms of life that would otherwise be present. Their food must be carefully inspected to be sure that it is free of small creatures. They must avoid walking on ground where there might be growing things, and they do not bathe so as not to harm minute forms of water-borne life. An ascetic carries a small broom (*oghā*) with which to brush aside small forms of life before sitting or lying. He or she also carries (and in the case of Sthānakvāsīs and Terāpanthīs permanently wears) a mouth-cloth (*muhpattī*) with which to protect small forms of life in the air from one's hot breath.[54] They may not use fire. They may not fan themselves lest harm come to airborne life. Although they are permitted to sing (and do so during rituals), they are not permitted to clap or count rhythm on their knees because of the potential lethality of the percussions. They may not use any artificial means of conveyance. This list of prohibitions could be greatly extended.

The vow of *ahiṃsā* is the basis of the four-month rainy season retreat called the *cāturmās* (or *comāsu*), which begins at the very end of the lunar month of Śrāvan (July–August). One of the most important requirements of the ascetic life is movement; ideally, ascetics, traveling in groups of at least two, should never spend more than a few days at a given place. During the four rainy season months, however, ascetics must establish semipermanent residence in one place, the basic idea being that travel would endanger the many growing things that flourish on the ground during the rains. The practice plays an important role in reinforcing the ties between laity and ascetics. Because resident ascetics give daily sermons and exercise a more than ordinary influence on the community, the rainy season retreat is a season of enhanced piety among lay Jains. Local communities are eager to invite particularly distinguished or charismatic ascetics to spend their rainy season retreats among them, and arrangements are often made years in advance.

The period of the rainy season retreat is the most important of the Jain ceremonial year. During this period there are two ascetically-oriented annual observances. One is the eight-day period of Paryuṣaṇ, the most solemn occasion of the Jain year.[55] Lasting for eight days, it is an occasion for extensive sermonizing by ascetics, and for fasting and the performance of the confessional rite of *pratikramaṇ* by laypersons. The high point of Paryuṣaṇ is the public recitation of the *Kalpasūtra* (see Vinaya Sagar 1984) by ascetics, and the high point of the recitation is a dramatization of the fourteen dreams seen by Mahāvīr's mother at the time of his conception (as described in this text).[56] Also occurring during the retreat period is a fast, not observed by many, known as *navpad olī*. It centers on nine days of fasting coordinated with the worship of the nine positions of the *siddhcakra* figure.

The second vow is *satya,* to tell the truth. The third is *asteya,* not to take what is not freely given. The fourth, *brahmacarya,* is a vow of complete celibacy. An important implication of the vow of celibacy is that there should be no physical contact between an ascetic and a member of the opposite sex. This requirement extends even to animals of the opposite sex. Indirect contact is also barred; an ascetic should not touch an object that is being touched by a member of the opposite sex. Thus, if a man wishes to give, say, a book to a nun, he must first place it on a neutral surface, after which she will pick it up.

The fifth and final vow, *aparigraha,* is that of propertylessness. The importance of this vow in regulating ascetic behavior is exceeded only by the vow of *ahiṃsā*. This vow is the basis of the peripatetic ascetic life; constant movement ensures that there can be no attachment to a particular place. Ascetics may own nothing. They do, however, carry some items. Śvetāmbar ascetics wear clothing, and they also carry certain paraphernalia, such as their staffs, brooms, mouth-cloths, the special ritual devices used while preaching (*sthāpanācārya*), the receptacles they use for collecting food, and personally needed items like eyeglasses. They may not, under any circumstances, handle money. Some ascetics, however, in effect control quite large sums because of their influence on wealthy laity. Ascetics can even be involved in property transactions while nonetheless adhering to the letter of nonpossession. On one occasion in Jaipur I saw an ascetic "purchase" some carved religious objects intended for display in a museum this ascetic was promoting. Money actually changed hands, but it was not touched by either of the ascetics who were present. Instead it was counted out and given to the seller by a "servant" who accompanies these monks on their travels carrying money and other items.

The vow of nonpossession has extremely important implications for the ritual culture of the Śvetāmbar Jains. Ascetics cannot perform worship that involves physical offerings, although they can engage in mental forms of worship. This is because, having taken the vow of nonpossession, they have nothing to offer. In major rites of worship such as Pārśvanāth's five-*kalyāṇak-pūjā,* when ascetics are present they frequently sing the Sanskrit verse coming before the offering formula, but they cannot repeat the offering formula itself, which is sung by a lay worshiper. Their singing of the verse is a concession to their supposed knowledge of Sanskrit, but the offering formula is off limits because of their inability to make offerings.[57]

## EATING

Ascetics are completely dependent on the laity for the most basic necessities of life, including nourishment. The transaction in which ascetics are fed is probably the most important lay-ascetic interaction. Eating itself is highly problematical to Jains. All eating is dangerous; it is at the root of the fatal attachment of the soul to the body and it is also a form of sense enjoyment (see Dundas 1985 on food and the Tīrthankars). Moreover, producing and preparing food inevitably result in the sin of violence. For these reasons, fasting is central to the religious praxis of both ascetics and lay Jains (especially women). Nonetheless, ascetics must consume food in order to live. They are forbidden to prepare food (and indeed cannot even ignite the fire to cook it), and therefore ascetics must go on daily (or more) rounds to seek nourishment from lay households. The food they are given must of course conform to the strictures of nonviolence that apply to the diet of ascetics. Obviously there can be no tubers or the like, even if members of the family do consume such items on other occasions, and the food must be prepared under conditions of scrupulous cleanliness. The ideal is that food be taken only from lay households and persons of the highest piety and orthopraxy. There is, however, some latitude in these matters, for I myself was once honored with the privilege of donating a small amount of food to a Terāpanthī monk.

Fundamental to this transaction is the idea that the food taken by an ascetic can never be prepared on his or her behalf.[58] This has the effect of insulating the ascetic from the violence that went into the food's production and preparation; these things were not done at his or her instigation. The sin is that of the preparer of the food, but presumably it is offset by the merit (*puṇya*) generated by feeding the ascetic. As Laidlaw stresses, the issue is probably not so much that of the ascetic being contaminated by the sin of food preparation, but that he or she should not be the cause of the householder's sin, which would be in complete contradiction to the ascetic's role of teacher and exemplar (1995: Ch. 14). The ideal of ascetic subsistence is that the ascetic wanders totally at random from household to household, taking just a little bit of sustenance from those households worthy to give. The food-seeking rounds are likened to a cow's grazing; the idea is that the ascetic should take a little here, a little there. As a nun once put it to me, it is the opposite of the grazing of a donkey, "who gobbles up everything in one place." In theory, at least, the food is then consumed without enjoyment and in the spirit of complete detachment.[59] Some ascetics simply mix all of their food with water into a uniform gruel and gulp it down.

Food-seeking by ascetics is neither called nor considered a form of "begging."[60] The usual term, in fact, is *gocarī*, a term meaning roughly "a cow's grazing." The ascetic himself has something of great value to offer the householder whose dwelling he approaches, namely, the opportunity to gain merit and/or spiritual advancement by feeding ascetics. "I say to myself," as an Ahmedabad informant put it, "I'm really lucky that a *sādhu* has come to my house." The gift of food to an ascetic belongs in the general South Asian category of merit-generating gifts called *dān*, and in Jainism a gift to an ascetic is among the most efficacious forms of *dān*.[61] The giver therefore wants to give, but at least in theory the ascetic receiver is disinclined to take because taking compromises his or her asceticism.[62] Indeed, because the asceticism of the ascetic receiver is vital for the efficacy of the gift, the odd circumstance arises that the giver wishes most to give to the ascetic least likely to take. As we shall see, this fact has much to do with the inner logic of Jain worship.

The ascetic on food-seeking rounds says to the householder, "*dharm lābh!*" Whether uttered as an invitation to be given food or as a final blessing, it expresses the idea that the "profit" or "benefit" (*lābh*) of "religion" (*dharm*) will accrue to the giver. The reference is clearly in part to the "merit" (*puṇya*) and its fruits that will result from gifting food to an ascetic. As Laidlaw has shown, however, the acceptance of one's gifts by ascetics can signify more than mere merit; it can also be seen as emblematic of the spiritual progress of the donor. "For a renouncer to accept food from a household," Laidlaw points out, "is to recognize that it follows a comprehensive regime, at least with regard to food, which is comparable to that of the renouncers themselves" (1995: 322). Thus, the expression *dharm lābh* allows two potential meanings: good fortune in both the worldly and spiritual senses (ibid.: 322–23, 325; also Cort 1989: 457). We have not seen the last of this type of ambiguous doubleness.

As with all religious acts, the crux of the matter is the spirit (*bhāv*) in which it is done. As an Ahmedabad informant once put it to me, a person might well go to the *upāśray* in the morning and say to an ascetic, "*lābh dījiye*" ("Please give me the benefit/profit of religion," meaning "Please come to my house for food today."). Such a layperson might feel that because it is the first of the month he will get good business if the monk or nun accepts. But only if there is a real feeling of "I should give" will merit result. And—my friend went on to say—if gifting to an ascetic is done truly in the right spirit, it will even result in the removal of *karma* (*nirjarā*).

Consistent with the Jain view of the moral suspectness of eating, death by self-starvation is one of the highest spiritual ideals among the Jains. Among Digambars, with whom the practice is known as *sallekhanā,* such a death is apparently expected of ascetics (Carrithers 1989: 224). Among Śvetāmbars the practice is called *santhārā* and seems to be less common than among Digambars (Cort 1991b: 152–53). In Jaipur, however, I heard of instances of laypersons who made deathbed vows of *santhārā.* During the year of my research in Jaipur a very distinguished Sthānakvāsī *ācārya* named Hastīmaljī Mahārāj (author of a history of Jainism cited in this book) took *santhārā.* This occurred in April 1991 and was regarded as an event of sufficient importance to be widely reported in the Rajasthan press.

## OBJECTS OF WORSHIP

Living ascetics are objects of worship to lay Śvetāmbar Jains. Lay Jains greet ascetics formally with a rite of obeisance known as *guru vandan;* it consists of bowing in coordination with the recitation of a prescribed formula (see Cort 1989: 328). This is a form of worship. Ascetics are also overtly worshiped in a small rite known as *guru pūjā.* In the Tapā Gacch this is based on a transaction involving a yellow powder called *vāskṣep,* a mixture of sandalwood powder and saffron (ibid.: 331–33). The layperson puts a small amount of it on the ascetic's big toe; the ascetic then sprinkles the same type of powder on the back of the bowing worshiper's head (Figure 4). The *vāskṣep*-exchanging pattern appeared to me to be less strong among Khartar Gacch Jains in Jaipur. As I have seen it in Jaipur, the worshiper touches the ascetic's feet (if they are of the same sex) while the powder is bestowed as a blessing on the worshiper's head or shoulders. I have never seen the powder being used among the Sthānakvāsīs and Terāpanthīs.

*Vāskṣep* powder is an important substance among Śvetāmbar Jains. This yellow powder, in effect a material vehicle for a nonmaterial power, is said to have been sprinkled by Lord Mahāvīr himself on the heads of the eleven *gaṇdhar*s to signify their successful assimilation of his teachings. Indra supposedly held the platter from which it came. The powder is also associated with miraculous occurrences. I have heard various stories about miraculous rains of *vāskṣep* in temples; in one case (in Ahmedabad) it was interpreted as a message from a recently deceased nun who had achieved rebirth in the first heaven. It is also used in the empowerment of images by officiating ascetics. In other South Asian traditions, liquids are frequently used in similar contexts. Jains use powder, I believe, because of its dryness; it can be handled by ascetics without fear of harming the microbes that swarm in liquids.

There is nothing distinctively Jain about the worship of ascetics. It is, in fact, a widespread South Asian pattern. There is, however, one very significant difference between the veneration of living ascetics among Śvetāmbar Jains and the worship of holy persons in most Hindu traditions. Relations between worshipers and holy persons in non-Jain traditions are typically rich in two-way transactions.[63] The guru is given food, but then the remnants of his or her meal are consumed by devotees as a kind of blessing. Such returned food is known as *prasād,* which is seen as divine grace in a substantial, consumable form. The same basic pattern is fundamental to image worship in many (though as we shall

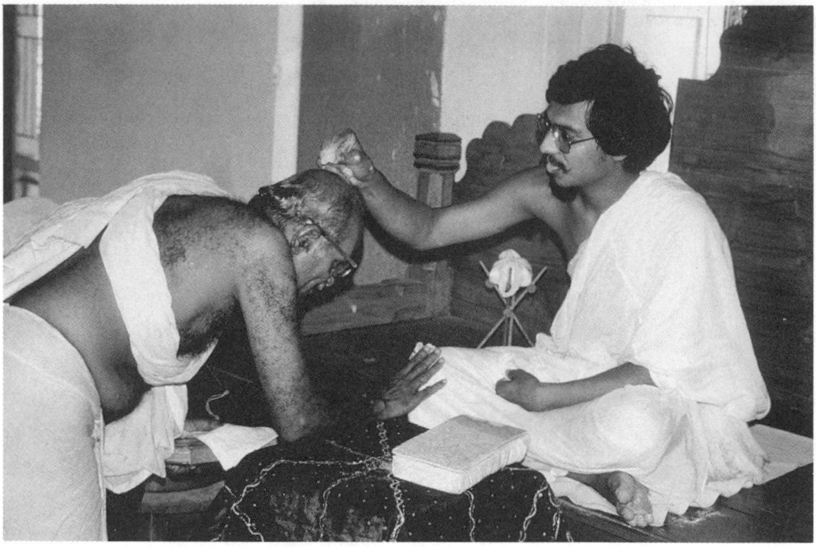

Figure 4. Receiving a blessing from a monk. A Tapā Gacch monk places *vāskṣep* on the head of a layman in Ahmedabad.

see, not all) Hindu traditions. However, the remnants of ascetics' meals are never returned to donors as blessings among Śvetāmbar Jains.[64] This is part of a wider pattern. We have already learned that offerings are not returned to donors in the five-*kalyāṇak pūjā* with which this chapter began. In the next chapter we shall see that the nonreturn of offerings is a general characteristic of Śvetāmbar image-worship. This is a matter of great importance having centrally to do with Jain conceptions of relations between human beings and the sacred.

## WORSHIP-WORTHINESS

The cosmos as visualized by the Jains is one to which radical asceticism is the only rational and moral response. Whether radical world rejection is an emotional or practical possibility for most people is another matter. In their persons, ascetics exemplify the path to liberation; in their interactions with nonascetics they draw others—less advanced than they—along in the right direction. Given these roles, ascetics emerge as the only beings truly worthy of worship. The Tīrthankars, as the ultimate ascetics, epitomize worship-worthiness, and Pārśvanāth's five-*kalyāṇak pūjā* has taught us what the ingredients of this kind of worship-worthiness are. Living ascetics partake of the same qualities, though in far lesser degree. They too are worthy of worship, though not to the same extent.

The Tīrthankars and living ascetics may therefore be said to represent the two poles of a continuum of worship-worthiness. As will be seen in Chapters Three and Four, the middle region of this continuum is, in fact, populated. Here we find distinguished deceased ascetics, the Dādāgurus, who are not Tīrthankars but whose veneration is nonetheless of great importance for the Śvetāmbar Jains of Rajasthan. These figures turn out to be vital elements in the integration of the Śvetāmbar Jain tradition as manifested in Jaipur.

This chapter has examined the role of objects of worship among temple-going Śvetāmbar Jains. Jains, we see, worship ascetics—of various degrees and kinds. It is now time to turn the matter around. Who, we must now ask, *are* these Jains who worship ascetics? How is their identity constructed in ritual? Of what significance for the worshiper is the fact that the object of his worship is an ascetic? These are questions to be addressed in the next chapter.

CHAPTER TWO

# Kings of the Gods

Rites generate fruits. The nature of the fruits produced by Jain rites of worship, however, is an ambiguous matter. As we shall learn, many Jains, especially ascetics, stress the soteriological benefits of rites; from this perspective they are seen as mere aids along the way to the sole legitimate goal, which is liberation from worldly bondage. But rites of worship also bear worldly fruits. Thus, there is potentially more than one way in which a Jain worshiper can interpret his or her acts of worship. The coconuts deposited for each of Pārśvanāth's five *kalyāṇak*s in the rite with which we began the preceding chapter clearly stand for good results, but *what* good results? As this chapter will show, this doubleness of potential interpretation—worldly versus spiritual benefits—is a deep feature of the Jain worldview.

In the actual theatrics of ritual performances, the emphasis often seems to be on the worldly side of the equation. Suggestions of prosperity, increase, and worldly benefit abound. Many major rites, for example, end on a note of true sumptuousness. An elaborated *svastik* (of the design called *nandyāvart*) is often executed on a large table standing in front of the image being worshiped. Here a huge pile of sweets and fruit is deposited by multiple participants just prior to the final lamp offering. Although the sweets and fruit are construed quite differently in normative interpretations of worship (as we shall see later in this chapter), in this context they strongly suggest overflow and abundance. Rites I saw in Ahmedabad often ended in a ceremony of benediction (called *śānti kalaś*) in which liquids used in the preceding *pūjā* are poured into a pot until it overflows. The pouring is done in a continuous stream until the accompanying verbal formulas have been completed. At the moment of overflow, participants throw rice and reach for the liquid, which they apply to their heads and foreheads; a female participant then circumambulates the ritual site with the pot on her head and takes it as a moveable blessing to another location. The liquid carries a kind of beneficial power which, among other things, can aid those seeking children.[1]

In rites of this sort the juxtapositions of worldliness and otherworldliness are startling, even jarring. The appearance of overflow and abundance is mobilized in a celebration; and, indeed, people believe that the celebration itself can bring into existence the very overflow and abundance—even fertility—that outward appearance suggests. But the celebration is *of* a state of being that is the very negation of overflow and abundance. Devotees belt out songs in jubilation, but the songs are about the cessation of all jubilation—indeed, the cessation of all affect. What, then, is the devotee doing? What does it mean for the devotee's identity that the object of his or her devotion is an ascetic who pushes asceticism to its practical and even logical limit? *Who* is such a devotee? This chapter deals with these questions by examining two rites of worship. One, the *snātra pūjā,* dramatizes with particular vividness the ritually constructed persona of the Jain worshiper. The second rite, the *aṣṭprakārī pūjā* or "eightfold worship," illustrates the peculiar consequences of the asceticism of the object of worship for the relationship between the Jain worshiper and the object or his or her worship. We shall see that this relationship is—in Śvetāmbar ritual culture—ambiguous, tense, and finally unstable.

## THE LORD'S BATH

### TEMPLES

Jain temples abound in both Jaipur and Ahmedabad, but in a different mix of sectarian affiliations. Ahmedabad is a Śvetāmbar world, and the city's temples reflect that fact. A well-connected Jain of Ahmedabad told me that there are about 280 temples in that city. In Jaipur, most Jain temples belong to the Digambars, who substantially outnumber the Śvetāmbars. A recent directory of Digambar Jain temples in Jaipur and environs (Nyāyatīrth 1990) lists a total of 127, large and small. Śvetāmbar temples are many fewer; in the old city there are only four large ones. Still, I found no shortage of Śvetāmbar temples to visit in Jaipur. In both cities the oldest temples are in the older sections of the city; newer structures, usually architecturally far less distinguished, have arisen in outlying areas as Jains have begun to move to suburbs.

A Jain temple (*mandir;* in Gujarat often called *derāsar*) is a place where consecrated images of the Tīrthankars (Figure 5) are worshiped. Images of ancillary deities and revered ascetics of the past are usually present in Jain temples, but the Tīrthankars are central. Some of the images in a temple are fixed; others are smaller and moveable. In essence, a temple is a physical replica of the *samvasaraṇ,* the universal assembly of those who come to hear a Tīrthankar's preaching (P. S. Jaini 1979: 196). It is also a place of ritual isolation. Prior to consecration, Tīrthankar images are simply inert objects of stone or metal; afterwards, they are sacred things that must be treated in accord with exacting rules. A temple is a protected zone in which such images can be shielded from the physical and spiritual impurities of the outside world.

Those who enter the temple should do so in a condition of ritual purity. The stringency of this requirement, however, depends on the worshiper's intentions. A Jain temple is divided into two zones of sacred space: the main hall and the inner shrine in which the Tīrthankars' images are stationed. Some types of worship can be performed in the main hall, while other require entering the inner shrine. Persons in deep pollution (such as menstruating women or those in whose families there has been childbirth or a recent death) are barred from the main hall. One's mouth should be rinsed out before entering the temple. The worshiper should also avoid wearing items of clothing made of leather. My experience has been that Digambars enforce this rule more strictly than do Śvetāmbars.[2] More demanding rules govern access to the inner shrine. Although Jains tend to be rather unfussy about the categories of persons who can enter this inner space (even non-Jain foreigners are not barred), those who enter must be freshly bathed and wearing special garments used only for this purpose. Men's clothing should be unstitched; for women, some stitching is allowed. While in the inner shrine, worshipers should also cover their mouths with a cloth, which has the purpose—as we have already noted—of preventing impurities from being breathed on the images.

The movement of worshipers across the boundaries of a temple's zones of relative purity is marked by a simple vocal rite of transition

Figure 5. An image of Mahāvīr. The main image in the Mahāvīr temple at Osiyā.

representing stages of separation from the outer world. When entering a temple from the outside, one should say *nisīhi* three times (although many temple-goers omit this step). This signifies one's intention to give up, while within, all speaking or thinking about worldly affairs; speaking or thinking about temple-related matters is permitted. Upon entering the inner shrine one should utter this formula again. This time it signifies an intention to give up all speaking or thinking even about temple affairs. At the conclusion of one's attentions to the image, the formula should be repeated yet a third time; this time it marks a further stage of removal from the world, namely, the transition from material worship (*dravya pūjā*) to a form of mental worship (*bhāv pūjā*), which occurs after the material worship is completed.

A temple's main image, called the *mūl nāyak* (literally, "root lord"), sits at the center of the altar platform with other Tīrthankar images to either side. Many of the images in a temple are portable; these can be taken off the altar for worship elsewhere. A temple visitor should perform obeisance to the main image first, then to other images. Every consecrated Tīrthankar image is supposed to be worshiped once per day. If no ordinary worshiper is available to do this, then it is the responsibility of the temple's *pujārī* (temple servant).

It should be stressed that the role of "temple priest," in the strict sense, is absent among Śvetāmbar Jains. In both Hindu and Jain temples are found functionaries known as *pujārīs*. The term *pujārī* means "one who does *pūjā*"—that is, one who worships—and in Hindu temples they function as actual ritual mediators between human devotees and deities. This whole idea, however, is fundamentally alien to the Śvetāmbar Jain conception of a worshiper's relation to sacred beings. For them there is no mediation; the worshiper himself or herself does the worshiping, which is consistent with the more encompassing Jain conviction that the beings of the world must, in the final analysis, pursue their spiritual interests on their own. The *pujārīs* in Jain temples are, accordingly, regarded as menial temple servants; they are ritual assistants, not priests. They prepare the materials used in worship and assist worshipers in various other ways, but they worship images only as stand-ins for absent Jains. For reasons that will be addressed later in this chapter, in Jain temples these ritual assistants are almost always non-Jain.[3] In Ahmedabad I never met a Jain *pujārī;* in Jaipur I heard of an Osvāl *pujārī* at one temple who was said to have taken up the work because of poverty.

Observant Jains normally visit temples as part of their usual morning activities. Unless it is a special occasion there is generally not much happening in a Jain temple during the evening hours; an evening lamp-offering ceremony (*āratī*) is part of the normal daily schedule, but it tends to be sparsely attended. A temple's routines may be seen as an assortment of loosely coordinated opportunities for individuals to choose from a variety of standardized modes of encounter with the divine images. People do whatever their own inclinations and inspirations lead them to do. Some merely stop by to take the images' *darśan* (auspicious vision). In the full rite the *darśan*-taker should greet the Tīrthankar images with folded hands, saying "*namo jiṇāṇam,*" and should then circumambulate the images, ideally three times, moving around the images (through a special hallway found in most temples) in a clockwise direction. Many, however, abbreviate this procedure. After taking *darśan* a worshiper might also perform a *caitya vandan.* This is a rite consisting of oral recitations of praise-verses coordinated with a series of physical obeisances.[4] Or the worshiper might perform what is called the *aṣṭprakārī pūjā,* the "eightfold worship," or some portion of this rite. The eightfold worship will be described later in the chapter. Another possibility is to perform a rite known as the *snātra pūjā,* the "bathing rite." This is one of the most important rites in the Śvetāmbar repertoire and is the point of departure for this chapter.

During my stays in both Ahmedabad and Jaipur I was a frequent morning visitor to temples. In Ahmedabad there was a flourishing temple not far from the Gandhi Ashram where I was living, and this was my destination most mornings. In Jaipur I attempted to branch out as much as possible, but many of my morning visitations were to a small temple and *dādābāṛī,* not yet fully built, in one of the newer suburbs quite close to my flat. In both these temples the *snātra pūjā* was performed on a regular basis. In the temple in Ahmedabad it was performed every day by a permanent group of four or five devotees. In my neighborhood temple in Jaipur it was performed, again by a small group of regulars, on the eighths and fourteenths of every lunar fortnight. Because it is also performed as a preliminary to all major rites of worship (an example being Pārśvanāth's five-*kalyāṇak pūjā*) I had many other opportunities to observe it.

## DEVCANDRAJĪ

As is the case with Pārśvanāth's five-*kalyāṇak pūjā,* the performance of the *snātra pūjā* centers on the singing of a text. This rite, too, is seen as an expression of *bhakti,* devotion, and the spirit of the singing should, at least ideally, reflect that fact. The version of the *snātra pūjā* performed in Khartar Gacch temples, the variant to be described here, was written by an illustrious Khartar Gacch ascetic named Devcandrajī. He is an interesting figure, one of considerably greater renown than Kavīndrasāgar, the author of Pārśvanāth's five-*kalyāṇak pūjā.*

Devcandrajī was born in 1689 C.E. in an Osvāl family belonging to the Lūṇiyā *gotra* living near Bikaner, and it is said that prior to his birth his mother had a dream in which she saw sixty-four Indras and other deities performing the *janmotsav* (birth celebration) of a Tīrthankar's image on the summit of Mount Meru.[5] It is said that she also saw—while half asleep and half awake—the moon enter her mouth. An ascetic was later to tell her that these visions meant that she would bear a son who would either be a king and rule the earth, or would become a great spiritual teacher and rule the "hearts of worthy (*bhavya*) people." As we shall see, these reported auguries resonate powerfully with the dominant theme in the *snātra pūjā,* the rite of worship he most famously authored.

Initiated at the age of ten, he went on to a career of great distinction as an author, scholar, and spiritual leader. He was also a magically powerful ascetic who performed many miracles. As we shall see in the next chapter, this trait is a feature common to the careers of some of the most revered ascetics in the Khartar Gacch tradition. He died in 1755. Many Śvetāmbar Jains believe that currently he is living in the continent of Mahāvideh in "*kevalin* form," by which is meant that he will attain liberation after his present existence ends. A knowledgeable Jaipur friend told me that Devcandrajī's current existence in Mahāvideh is known because it was announced to a Jain gathering somewhere in Gujarat by a mysterious stranger who then miraculously vanished.

## MERU'S PEAK

As does the text of Pārśvanāth's five-*kalyāṇak pūjā,* the text of Devcandrajī's *snātra pūjā* tells a story. The story, which we encountered briefly in the last chapter, is the tale of how the Tīrthankar comes into the world and how he is given his first bath (*janamābhiṣek*) by the gods on the summit of Mount Meru. The bath, as Laidlaw points out (1995: 44), superimposes two images: it is a baby's bath but also an *abhiṣek,* an anointing associated with the consecration of a king. Unlike the text of Pārśvanāth's five-*kalyāṇak pūjā,* however, this text is generic: It is not about the birth and first bath of any Tīrthankar in particular, but of all Tīrthankars, past, present, and future. All five *kalyāṇak*s are regarded as axial events in the Jain tradition, but the story of the Tīrthankar's birth and first bath has a special significance. It is the narrative most often told in Jainism, and has an importance roughly equivalent to that of the nativity story for Christians.

Devcandrajī's text is a description of these events. In contrast to

Pārśvanāth's five-*kalyāṇak pūjā,* performers of the *snātra pūjā* not only sing the text but act it out as well. The text is therefore unambiguously the "script" for a dramatic performance.[6] The language is difficult for most participants to follow. According to the editor of the *sārth* version I consulted (Jargaḍ 1959b, pp. *kha* and *ga*), the language of Devcandrajī's *snātra pūjā* is a mixture of Prākrit, Rājasthānī, Gujarātī, and Hindī, with Rājasthānī predominating. The Prākrit, in particular, is a hurdle for many. My impression, however, is that most performers of the rite can follow its gist on the basis of word recognition and familiarity with the main story line, which is certainly quite well known by most Jains. Some know the text by heart.

Those who perform a *snātra pūjā* should be bathed and dressed appropriately for worship. They should have at hand the various materials and utensils used in the rite. The focus of worship is a small metal image of one of the Tirthankars and a *siddhcakra,* which are placed on a "lion throne" atop a three-tiered stand.[7] In other rites the stand represents the *samvasaraṇ,* the assembly of listeners to the Tīrthankar, but here it doubles as Mount Meru. The many necessary paraphernalia are kept on a low platform in front of the stand. During the rite itself, performers should have their mouths and nostrils covered by the usual cloth to prevent breathing impurities on the image. They should stand with men to the image's right and women to the left.

A brief sequence called *sthāpnā* precedes the rite. In other South Asian traditions the purpose of *sthāpnā* is to invoke a deity's presence. But as we know, the Tīrthankar's presence cannot be invoked because he is a liberated being, and therefore this is obviously a problematical ritual gesture for Jains. It is probably for this reason that no *sthāpnā mantra* (a verbal formula to accompany *sthāpnā*) is included in Devcandrajī's text, but the procedure is nevertheless considered essential.[8] A coconut (always associated with auspiciousness) with currency tied to it is placed on a *svastik*-mark below the image on one of the supporting tables or the floor. Most worshipers merely repeat the *namaskār mantra* while doing so. An experienced ritualist told me that while doing *sthāpnā* one should cultivate the inner feeling that "this is Mt. Meru and we are about to give the Lord his *janamābhiṣek* (postpartum bath)."

What follows is a description of the *snātra pūjā* comparable to the description of Pārśvanāth's five-*kalyāṇak pūjā* given in the last chapter. I have abstracted the performative aspects somewhat and have given special emphasis to the text. It should be borne in mind that performances of the rite can vary tremendously in elaboration and enthusiasm, depending on the context.

## THE SNĀTRA PŪJĀ

The rite begins with a succession of welcoming flower offerings (*kusamāñjalī*) made to each of five Tīrthankars (Ṛṣabh, Śāntināth, Nemināth, Pārśvanāth, and Mahāvīr). The "flowers" consist of saffron-colored rice which may be mixed with cloves or real flowers. Worshipers stand, holding the "flowers," while singing lines of praise from the text. Then comes a formula of offering, at which point the "flowers" are deposited at the image's feet. After each of these offerings, worshipers apply spots of sandalwood paste to the image's body: after the first offering, to the feet, next to the legs, and then to the hands, shoulders, and head. At the conclusion of the five offerings, celebrants sing the Tīrthankars' praises, and some wave or dance with whisks known as *cāmar*s.

Now begins the rite's narrative, which is the story of the holy birth and first bath. As the story unfolds, the participants take on the personae of gods and goddesses who assist in, and celebrate, the events depicted. I now describe the actions of participants and summarize the text.

Worshipers stand with flower offerings in their hands. The story opens. The text begins by telling of how a Tīrthankar-to-be earns the *tīrthankar nām karm* in the third birth before his incarnation as a Tīrthankar, and how he takes human birth in a kingly family in the continents Bharat, Airāvat, or Mahāvideh. At the time of his descent into a human womb his mother is visited by the fourteen auspicious dreams (listed in the text).[9] She informs her husband. He declares that she will give birth to an "honor-mark of the three worlds" who will establish the path to liberation. Then the throne of the Indra of the first heaven shakes; he sees the descent by means of the clairvoyant knowledge he possesses as a god and knows that a great savior has come into existence. He rises from his lion-throne and closes his hands in salutation. He steps forward, bows, and then announces the descent to the gods. He sings a hymn of praise. There is rejoicing in heaven and in the mother and father's house, and all the beings of the three worlds (including the denizens of hell) experience an instant of happiness. Cries of felicitation ring out everywhere.

Figure 6. Participants in a *snātra pūjā* performing *caitya vandan* in Jaipur. Note the special posture, prescribed for *caitya vandan,* with the left knee raised.

At this point participants make a congratulatory offering of the flowers to the image, and then circumambulate the image three times. Then, while seated in a special posture, they recite (or one among them recites) a *caitya vandan* or a portion of it (Figure 6). Commonly, participants recite the *Namutthuṇam Sūtra* (also known as the *Śakra-stava*), which is believed to be sung by Indra at the time of a Tīrthankar's conception.[10] They then wash and dry their hands. They mark their right hands with *svastik*s, tie ceremonial strings on their right wrists, and stand ready for the next phase of the rite.

The tale resumes. The fifty-six Dikkumārīs (a category of goddesses) learn of the birth by means of their clairvoyant knowledge. Singing praises, they go to the mother and clean impurities from the site of the birth. At this point human worshipers make a gesture of cleaning the floor before the image. The Dikkumārīs light a lamp. Worshipers likewise show a lamp. The Dikkumārīs display a mirror. Worshipers do the same. The Dikkumārīs fan the mother and child. Worshipers wave a fan. The Dikkumārīs fashion a house from banana trees and bathe the mother and child within. Then they tie a protective thread on the child's wrist. At this point worshipers place a ceremonial string on the image's lap.

On the night of the Lord's birth, says the text, there is brilliance everywhere,[11] and at the auspicious moment of birth Indra's throne trembles. Wondering what "opportunity" (*avsar*) has arisen, Indra learns of the birth by means of his clairvoyant knowledge and is filled with the highest bliss. To announce the birth he causes a bell to be rung. At this point worshipers ring a bell. Indra then goes to the summit of Mt. Meru and orders the other gods to do the same; by washing the Lord's feet, he says, they will wash their sins away. Tens of millions of gods assemble there. Now Indra goes to the Lord's mother and does obeisance. The worshipers now make a flower offering. He explains that he will convey the infant to Mt. Meru. Taking the child in his hands, he multiplies himself into five Indras who bear the child to the mountain. There the waiting gods and goddesses sing, dance, and praise the infant as the teacher and Lord of the world and as their shelter and support. At this point worshipers dance.

Indra takes the infant to the Pāṇḍuk Grove,[12] where he seats himself on a lion-throne with the infant on his lap. The other sixty-three Indras arrive. Acyutendra, the lord of the eleventh and twelfth heavens, orders tens of millions of gods and goddesses to bring water for the Lord's bath. With hands joined in salutation, they obey. The human worshipers now stand ready with water pots.

The gods go to the milky ocean and all the great pilgrimage places on watercourses in order to obtain pure water and other things needed for the Lord's bath. One thousand and eight pots of eight different kinds are prepared. The gods return, and when they see the Lord in Indra's lap their hearts are filled with ecstasy. Acyutendra exhorts all gods to take the Lord's *darśan.* Then, at his command, they stand ready with pots in hand. The gods ask the Indra of the first heaven, "Who is that wondrous form in your lap?" Indra answers that it is the world's savior and tells them to perform *abhiṣek*—that is, to pour liquid on the infant. They do so. At this point the human worshipers, following the divine model described in the verses, pour water on the image's feet.

The Indra of Īśān Devlok (the second heaven) now asks the Indra of the first heaven if he might hold the infant for a while. Permission granted, he does. Worshipers again pour water on the image's feet, and, as the story continues, the worshipers pour water and milky water over the entire image (Figure 7). On special occasions they anoint the image

Figure 7. Bathing the image in *snātra pūjā*. Note the seated image of the Tīrthankar with the flat *siddhcakra* below.

with what is called *pañcāmṛt,* a mixture of five substances: milk, curds, sugar, saffron, and clarified butter. Participants take turns in the pouring, and sometimes several participants at once touch the pot as the water is being released. The basic idea is that everyone should take part in the bathing. The image's final bath is with plain water.

The text continues. The Indra of the first heaven takes the form of four bulls and pours water over the Lord from the eight horns. Worshipers often imitate this act by pouring water on the image from a bull-shaped pot. Afterwards Indra garlands and ornaments the infant. The assembled gods cry "victory" and dance: The "chief of the convoy" on the road to liberation has come. They then give a gift of 320 million golden coins. At this point a worshiper circles a coin in the air before the image (a gesture known as *nyauchāvar*) and deposits it in the bowl into which the run-off liquids from the image's bath have been collecting. Indra returns the infant to his mother's lap, and then goes to Nandīśvar to worship the eternal Tīrthankar images there. The gods return to their normal abodes while saying how much they look forward to the *kalyāṇak*s of the Lord's initiation and attainment of omniscience.

At the end of the text Devcandrajī identifies his disciplic lineage and names himself as the composer of the rite. Those worthy (*bhavya*) beings, he says, who perform this birth-rite will plant the seeds of the tree of enlightenment in their hearts and will fill the *sangh* (the Jain community) with bliss. The final lines are an exhortation to perform the Lord's *pūjā;* it benefits one's soul and carries one across the ocean of existence. Afterwards the image is carefully wiped dry and replaced in its former position. The *snātra pūjā* proper is followed by a version of the eightfold worship, the *aṣṭprakārī pūjā* (to be described later in this chapter). Sometimes, especially when the *snātra pūjā* is being performed in conjunction with a major congregational ceremony, the offerings given in the eightfold worship are quite festive and elaborate. The entire series normally concludes with lamp offerings (*āratī* and *mangal dīp*).

## DEITIES

What does the *snātra pūjā* teach us? The story it tells, in word and deed, is obviously the key. It is, first and foremost, a celebration of the birth and first bath of the Tīrthankar, and it tells us something about this event. But it can also be seen as a statement about the nature of ritual itself. It tells us, that is, something about what it *means* to worship a Tīrthankar, and this is what I want to stress.

This story, the most reiterated narrative in Jainism, deals with the basis of the redemptive economy of the cosmos as seen by the Jains. The basic elements are two, and both are established in the narrative and in the rite based on the narrative. The first element is the *advent* of one who establishes the path of liberation, namely, the Tīrthankar. Here the focus is on the descent of the Tīrthankar-to-be into a human womb, the dreams, the birth. The second element, indispensable to any concept of Jainism as an actual tradition, is the establishment of a *relationship* between such a being and other beings. This is, in fact, the axial relationship in the Jain tradition, and in the birth narrative and the *snātra pūjā* it is represented by the worshipful attentions of the gods and goddesses. Everything comes together in the *janamābhiṣek*, the postpartum bath. Here is the infant, and here are the deities. The infant represents the promise of redemption. The deities, for their part, worship the infant. This ritual thus symbolically establishes what must exist if a Jain tradition is to exist, namely, a modality of relationship between the Tīrthankars and those who worship Tīrthankars. And those who worship the Tīrthankars are, paradigmatically, the deities.

Accounts of Jainism sometimes treat the tradition's deities as marginal figures. This is because they are not the primary focus of worship in Jainism; indeed, it can even be said that they are not true objects of worship at all. This is because to be truly worthy of worship is (as we know) to be a Tīrthankar or one who is like a Tīrthankar, and the deities are not Tīrthankars, nor are they remotely like Tīrthankars. But to conclude from this that they are unimportant is to miss the point, for they represent the other side of the equation. They are Jainism's model worshipers. To understand the meaning of the worshiper's role, therefore, we must know more about the deities.

As we saw in Chapter One, Jainism's deities and hell-beings are inversions of each other.[13] The hell-beings live in the lower regions of the cosmos, the deities in the upper regions (though not at the very top). The hell-beings must suffer eons of torment because of sins committed in previous births. The deities, by contrast, are beings who exist in a state of continuous enjoyment as a consequence of merit (*puṇya*) earned in previous births. The hell-beings exist to suffer; the deities exist to enjoy.

In comparison with humans, deities have special powers and knowledge. They are vastly wealthy. They have the ability and sometimes the willingness to use their powers to assist human beings, although some deities, apparently only those belonging to the marginal *vyantar* category, can also act maliciously. Their bodies—which contain no blood, meat, or bone—are beautiful, luminous, and free from illness. They are not subject to birth or death pollution (*sūtak*). Their breath is perfectly sweet (as a nun once told me). They do not eat as humans do; when they feel the desire for food, nourishment automatically enters their bodies in the form of pure atoms (*pudgal*s). When they are born they simply appear on divine beds in the form of youths of sixteen. They are perpetually young, and their lives are immensely long. They learn of their deaths six months in advance; at this point their flower garlands wilt and their faces lose luster. When they die the atoms of their bodies are dispersed like camphor, and there is no odor.

The deities' lives may be said to represent every kind of worldly happiness in a perfected state, and if the Tīrthankars are apotheosized ascetics, the gods and goddesses are the apotheoses of worldly felicity. They exist for the sole purpose of the very enjoyment the ascetic rejects. This contrast may represent a Jain version of what T. N. Madan characterizes as a general opposition between the good life and its renunciation in the Hindu tradition, between *yogī* (ascetic) and *bhogī* (enjoyer) (Madan 1987: 10, 98).

There is, however, a very serious flaw in this happy picture. Despite their special powers, the gods cannot achieve liberation, for this is possible only in a human body. They serve and worship the Tīrthankars, listen to their discourses, and also worship Tīrthankar images. They are capable of spiritual progress. But the gods are "enjoyers" by definition; as such, they cannot be ascetics, and asceticism is the key to liberation. As a nun once explained it to me in Jaipur, "the gods have plenty of *sukh* (happiness); but because they don't eat they can't fast, which means they can't achieve *mokṣ* (liberation)."[14]

The relevant distinction was brought home to me with special force when I asked an Ahmedabad respondent whether the gods are *śuddh* (pure). This seemed a perfectly reasonable question, for in Hindu traditions the gods are certainly seen as pure. My friend, however, rather vehemently responded that the deities have nothing whatsoever to do with purity in this sense. The word *śuddh,* he said, has only to do with the removal of *karma* (*nirjarā*). He then went on to say that the terms *śubh* and *aśubh,* meaning "auspicious" and "inauspicious" respectively, both belong to the category of things that are "impure" (*aśuddh*). The auspicious, having to do with *puṇya* (merit), and the inauspicious, having to do with *pāp* (sin), are *both* discarded in the end. In this sense, the gods cannot be said to be truly pure.

The Jain tradition does not completely condemn the deities' happiness, for it affirms that it can be gained by means of meritorious action, including the performance of acts of worship. Indeed, one of the highest worldly rewards of asceticism itself is rebirth in heaven as a deity. Moreover, in their felicity the deities clearly represent what John Cort (1989, esp. Ch. 8) has shown to be an entire "realm of value" in the Jain world, that of auspiciousness and worldly well-being. But the message the deities send is mixed. Their happiness is great but transient, for although their lives are eons long, they must perish and fall from heaven in the end. And, as deities, they cannot attain the supreme goal.

## DEITIES AS MODELS

The *snātra pūjā* illustrates with particular clarity and explicitness a principle vital to understanding Jainism as a ritual culture and as a lived tradition: When human beings engage in acts of worship, they take on the roles of gods and goddesses. Moreover, Indras and Indrāṇīs, the kings and queens of the gods, are the principal figures emulated by human worshipers. In many important *pūjās* worshipers wear tinsel crowns to symbolize this identity (Figure 8).[15]

We see, therefore, that in the redemptive economy of the Jain cosmos the deities' role is not to serve as *objects* of worship, but to serve as the tradition's archetypal *worshipers*. They are not ascetics, and (as we know) ascetics alone are true objects of worship to the Jains. Instead, they are *lay* Jains who project an ideal image of what lay Jains must do as ones who worship ascetics. As an Ahmedabad friend once put it to me, the deities are really "like our brothers and sisters" in the sense that they, too, worship the Tīrthankars. This role is reiterated whenever the five *kalyāṇak*s occur. On infinite occasions through infinite time the gods and goddesses have come forward to be the prime admirers and supporters of those who are truly worthy of worship, the Tīrthankars. This is the paradigm for the worshiper's role in Jainism.

It is true that certain Jain deities are offered a type of worship, but this illustrates the more general principle that only ascetics are truly worthy of worship. Jains believe that some gods and goddesses will respond to prayers, as Tīrthankars do not and cannot, with worldly boons. The ancillary deities (*adhiṣṭhāyak dev*s) of the Tīrthankars serve this function, and some (such as Padmāvatī and Cakreśvarī) have cults of their own. The guardian deities of temples (called *kṣetrapāl*s) are also believed to come to the aid of worshipers, and some of these have likewise become important deities in their own right. But they are never truly independent objects of worship, and their worship is seen as a kind of postscript to the worship of the Tīrthankars. Jains say that all such deities come to the aid of human beings because of their approval of piety directed, not toward them, but toward the Tīrthankars.

A good example of such a deity is Nākoṛā Bhairav, who is the guard-

Figure 8. A crowned worshiper in Ahmedabad

ian deity of Pārśvanāth's image at a famous temple complex at Nākoṛā (near Bālotrā in western Rajasthan). This god is reputed to be extremely powerful, and has a very large following in Jaipur where his image is commonly installed in temples and household shrines. Many businessmen consider him to be a business partner and pledge a certain percentage of their profits to him.[16] Most pilgrims who go to Nākoṛā do so to worship Bhairav in order to seek his aid in worldly matters. When I was present, the sums paid[17] for the privilege of performing rites for Bhairav were considerably higher than for the Tīrthankar. Nonetheless, it is Pārśvanāth, not Bhairav, who is—in theory—the principal object of worship at this temple, and Bhairav is seen as his worshiper and protector. It is significant that the promotional brochures distributed by the temple's Trust give only passing mention to Nākoṛā's main claim to fame, which is Nākoṛā Bhairav, stressing instead the images of the Tīrthankars, the quality of the artwork, and so on.[18] This illustrates the more general principle that from the standpoint of the tradition's dominant values—values which the authors of the brochure are willing to articulate in print—the seeking of worldly boons is an awkward feature of the situation that needs to be minimized, and that, in any case, it is the Tīrthankars, not deities like Bhairav, who are the real objects of worship. Bhairav is really a lay Jain who, out of fellow feeling, will come to the aid of other pious lay Jains.

The theme of identification between worshipers and deities is familiar to students of the ancient Vedic sacrifice; in these rites the sacrificer is divinized. From Brian K. Smith (1989: 104–12; see also F. M. Smith 1987: 20) we learn that during the course of the sacrifice the sacrificer attains a divine self (*daiva ātman*), a "godlike status within the ritual," and goes on a "journey" to heaven (*svarga loka*). This is, however, only a temporary condition, for the worshiper must return to his mortal existence with the conclusion of the rite. For the sacrificer a permanent sojourn in heaven comes only after the present life; in the ritual he is in heaven "just long enough to mark out and reserve a space for the next life" (ibid.: 109). The Jain rite of worship (*pūjā*) is seen as a form of sacrifice, the one form of sacrifice acceptable to Jains, and is often referred to as *ijyā* or *yajña* (Williams: 216). The identity between worshipers and the denizens of heaven in Jain ritual may thus have an ancient pedigree. However, in Jainism the ideological and symbolic surround is very different. For the Vedic sacrificer the heavenly realm, attained completely only after death, was a fully legitimate goal. For the Jains it is not. The worshiper may indeed become a deity after death, but such felicity is finally declared to be a kind of spiritual fool's gold. The wise ritualist aims not at heaven but at liberation beyond heaven.

It is significant, therefore, that the *snātra pūjā* does not glorify the roles of the gods and goddesses. It is the Tīrthankar, and not even mighty Indra, who is the actual object of worship. The Tīrthankar stands for ascetic values, not for the felicity that the deities embody. The true goal of asceticism is not the world's delights but a state of being beyond all delights and sorrows. A subtext of this and similar rites is that worshipers prosper in the same way the deities do (and can indeed someday *become* deities) as a consequence of worship. But as we shall see later, so decisively is asceticism asserted as the transcendent value that there is a strong tendency in the tradition to interpret human acts of worship as ascetic acts.

Deities and ascetics are therefore opposed, and their opposition reflects a basic contrast between two unequally valued modes of religious practice. This choice, in turn, is embedded in Jainism's conception of how Jain teachings enter history. This brings us to the crucial matter of kingship.

## KINGSHIP AND THE TWO PATHS

It is difficult to exaggerate the importance of the fourteen dreams that visit the mother of a Tīrthankar-to-be. In accounts of the Tīrthankar's conception and birth they are almost always enumerated. They are ritually dramatized during Paryuṣaṇ, the most sacred occasion of the year. They are also reiterated in the *snātra pūjā* and in many other rites. Why are these dreams described and enacted so often? I suggest that it is because they reach to the values and choices that lie at the very heart of the Jain tradition's vision of the soul's opportunities and destiny.

As we saw in the last chapter, the dreams have a double meaning: They are the dreams that announce the birth of a universal emperor, but they also announce the birth of a Tīrthankar. In other words, a Tīrthankar is one who *might have been* an earthly king but became an ascetic instead.[19] In this connection it is important to note that a Tīrthankar-to-be is *always* born into a family belonging to the Kṣatriya *varṇa,* the social class of warriors and kings (P. S. Jaini 1985: 84–85). Put otherwise, the Tīrthankar renounces earthly kingship to become a spiritual king. Kingly martial valor is transposed to a transcendental plane; instead of victory over earthly sovereigns, the Tīrthankar becomes a "victor" (*jina*) over attachments and aversions. Asceticism thus turns out to be a spiritualized martial virtue.

The Tīrthankar's spiritual kingship is the highest manifestation of the ascetic path. Others, however, prosper in the world and use their worldly wealth and power to *serve* ascetics—and by implication, those who serve ascetics prosper in the world. Earthly kingship, rejected by the Tīrthankar, is the highest manifestation of this path, which is dramatized by the heavenly projections of earthly kingship, the Indras and Indrāṇīs who are the kings and queens of the gods. It is, as well, the path of nonascetic Jains, who, as worshipers, identify with the kings and queens of heaven. Having renounced earthly kingship, the Tīrthankar becomes a king of the spirit who is worshiped *by* kings, both heavenly and earthly.

Those who inhabit human bodies find themselves at the crossing point of these two paths. Unlike the gods, humans can be ascetics.

However, as we noted in the last chapter, those who take ascetic vows cannot (as do the gods) worship with material things; being possessionless, they have nothing to offer.[20] Indeed, we now see that there is an even more basic impediment to ascetics worshiping with material things. There is a fundamental resonance between the role of the worshiper and heavenly/earthly enjoyment as embodied by the gods and goddesses. To worship with material things is to step into this paradigm, which is seemingly inconsistent with the ascetic ideal. Lay Jains, on the other hand, are in a perpetual condition of being able to choose. They can worship with material things, but they can also engage in various forms of asceticism, especially fasting, for which lay Jain life is justly famed. It might be said that for pious lay Jains life is, in effect, a constant oscillation between these two modes of praxis.

The ascetic practices of lay Śvetāmbar Jains have been well described by Cort for Gujarat (1989: Ch. 5) and Laidlaw for Rajasthan and Jaipur (1995: Part III). As both authors show, asceticism does not radically divide ascetics under permanent vows from the laity. Although lay ascetic practice is formally conducted under the aegis of ascetics (who administer the vow that is required for an ascetic practice to be efficacious), asceticism is a central feature of lay Jain life. In both regions the principal lay ascetic practices are the same. There is, first, the practice known as *sāmāyik,* which is a forty-eight-minute period of meditation.[21] Lay Jains who perform *sāmāyik* typically do so after visiting the temple in the morning. An extended version of *sāmāyik* is *poṣadh* in which a layperson in effect becomes a mendicant for a period of twelve or twenty-four hours. Another important ascetic practice is *pratikramaṇ,* an arduous and complex rite of confession and expiation of the performer's sins.[22] It is required of mendicants in the morning and evening. Only the most serious lay Jains perform it frequently, but virtually all Jains perform it once per year during the holy period of Paryuṣaṇ.

Undoubtedly, however, fasting (*upvās*) is the mode of austerity that Jains have most brought to a high art. Food is an essential part of the body's karmic imprisonment, and obviously, therefore, the attenuation of eating—tending toward cessation—is necessarily among the tradition's most valued modes of praxis. The Jains have elaborate taxonomies of fasting based on length of time and types of consumption allowed or forbidden. The tradition's admiration for fasting is indicated by the fact that successful fasters are often felicitated in public ceremonies. It is certainly not the case that most lay Jains are serious fasters. Most of my male friends in Jaipur did little of this sort of thing apart from the bare minimum at the time of Paryuṣaṇ. As is the case in the surrounding Hindu world, among Jains lay austerities are practiced mainly by women, especially older women, and by men in retirement. It is, however, the case that the ideal of asceticism—as expressed in fasting and other types of ascetic performances—casts a kind of cool light over Jain life in general. Austerity and renunciation are the tradition's highest values, and even those whose styles of life are far from austere know that they *should* be pursuing these values.

While the centrality of asceticism stems from the fact that ascetic practice directly causes the eradication of *karma,* asceticism also brings about good worldly results; that is, it brings prosperity in the here and now and favorable rebirth.[23] Put somewhat differently, it is associated with merit (*puṇya*) as well as karmic removal (*nirjarā*). And, as always, the key issue is the *bhāv*—the "spirit"—in which austerity is conducted. It should be conducted in the spirit of true nonattachment. If it is, as Laidlaw points out, then good fortune can enter the situation by the back door; the faster's undesire for good results is somehow essential to bringing them about (1995: Ch. 10). Here, as in so many areas of Jain life, we find ourselves in the presence of an ambiguous doubleness.

## REFLEXIVITY

Jains worship ascetics. But Jains also live in the world. What then is to be the relationship between one who lives in the world and the ascetic? All ascetic traditions must grapple with this problem. In Jainism, however, the problem is particularly acute. This is so because the asceticism of the tradition's most idealized ascetics, the Tīrthankars, is so complete that they cannot engage in transactions of any kind with those who worship them. This dilemma is dramatized by the ordinary daily rite of temple worship to which we now turn.

### THE EIGHTFOLD WORSHIP

The eightfold worship (*aṣṭprakārī pūjā*) is performed in the morning, usually in a temple. It is the daily rite of worship for orthoprax Jains; as such, it is the most important institutionalized form of worship for Jains. It differs from what we have seen thus far. The other rites we have looked at have been congregational; that is, they are designed to be performed by groups of worshipers—in the case of Pārśvanāth's five-*kalyāṇak pūjā* (and rites like it), by a group of potentially very large size. The eightfold worship, however, is strictly individual. Although many people may perform it at the same time in a temple, each worshiper is engaged in what amounts to a solo operation. One may say, perhaps, that as a performance it represents the ultimate conflation of performer and audience: in effect they are one and the same person. Moreover, there is no text for the rite as such. Some perform the rite in silence; others recite or sing verses that are provided by various layman's manuals. The verses can also be meditated upon while the rite is being performed. One of my Jaipur friends used only Sanskrit verses, which he knew by heart. As in everything connected with Jainism, there is great variation in individual practice.

A worshiper intending to perform the eightfold worship must come to the temple in a state of purity sufficient to allow him or her to touch the images.[24] Having uttered *nisīhi* and entered the temple, and having greeted and circumambulated the temple's main image, the worshiper should apply a sandalwood paste mark to his or her forehead. He or she then utters *nisīhi* a second time and enters the inner shrine to begin worship.

As the name of the rite implies, it has eight separate components. The first of these components is called *jal pūjā* ("worship with water"; also known as *prakṣāl pūjā* or *abhiṣek*). If necessary, the image is first carefully and gently cleaned of all adhering remains of the previous day's worship. The worshiper (or each worshiper if more than one is participating) then pours liquid over the image, usually a mixture of milk and water first, and then pure water. The verses supplied by layman's manuals for meditation upon or recitation during this act (Muktiprabhvijay n.d.: 50; Hemprabhāśrījī 1977: 35) express the worshiper's desire that his or her *karma*s be washed away. After the bathing, participants often touch the wet base of the image and then bring the moisture to their forehead and eyes. In temples in Ahmedabad the liquid run-off drains into receptacles below the altar. In Jaipur the liquid is commonly mopped up with a cloth, which can then be wrung into a receptacle. In either case, a small amount of this liquid is made available to other temple visitors who do not perform the eightfold worship. Worshipers anoint their eyes and foreheads with it and occasionally take small quantities to their homes in bottles. The remainder is disposed of in a river or at some out-of-the-way place where it is unlikely to come under anyone's feet.[25] At the conclusion of *jal pūjā* the image and its base are carefully and completely dried with three separate cloths.

*Jal pūjā* enacts the infant Tīrthankar's first bath on Mount Meru, and is precisely the same ritual gesture that we have seen in considerably more elaborated form in the *snātra pūjā*. This interpretation is in no way arcane or obscure. One acquaintance (in Ahmedabad) compared the sensation of drying the image after *jal pūjā* to the pleasure of drying an infant after his or her bath. The reclaiming of residual liquids, moreover, is not unique to this rite. Bathing an image is central to most rites of image worship, and the liquids used are normally available to worshipers afterwards.

Part two of the eightfold worship is called *candan pūjā* or sometimes *kesar-barās pūjā*. Camphor (*barās*) is sometimes applied to the entire image as part of this rite, but the main ritual act is the application of sandalwood paste (*candan*), sometimes mixed with saffron (*kesar*), to nine points on the image's body. With the ring finger of his or her right hand the worshiper applies the sandalwood paste to the right and left large toes, knees, wrists, shoulders, top of head, forehead, neck, heart, and navel. In Ahmedabad worshipers usually apply single dots to the body parts in question; in Jaipur extra dots are commonly added.

In his layman's manual, the ascetic author Muktiprabhvijay (n.d.: 50) renders the sentiment of the couplet he provides for this portion of the rite as follows, "O Lord, just as *candan* is cool, I wish that by means of this *candan pūjā* my mind (*cit*) will also be removed from the heat of lust, anger, etc., and become cool and peaceful."[26] In South Asian cultures there exists a concept of metaphysical temperature. Certain things and substances, especially edibles, are classified as inherently "hot" or "cool," irrespective of physical temperature. Sandalwood paste is seen as "cool" in this sense, and this provides a metaphorical bridge to the notion of the spiritual equanimity that the rite is supposed to produce. Muktiprabhvijay also provides separate couplets for each of the nine annointings (ibid.: 51–53); the emphasis is on the soteriological significance of the anointing of each separate body part.[27]

Adorning the image with flowers (*puṣpā pūjā* or *phul pūjā*) is the third part of the eightfold worship. The flowers should be fresh, flawless, and fully bloomed. Muktiprabhvijay renders the sentiment of the verse he provides for the rite as: "Oh Lord, by means of worshiping you with flowers, may my life also become fragrant with the five-colored flowers of *pañcācār* and *jñān-darśan-cāritra*" (ibid.: 54).[28]

Worshiping with flowers is in fact problematical for Jains because of the violence inflicted on the flowers and the plants from which they were picked. This leads Muktiprabhvijay to some fairly desperate casuistry (ibid.: 55–57). He says that the flowers in question are picked by the Mālī (gardener) for his livelihood, and therefore when a layman pays a price for the flowers there can be no question of sin (*pāp*) or fault (*doṣ*). He adds that when the layman purchases such flowers he should think that, if he does *not* buy them, they will go to some wrong believer (*mithyātvī*) who will burn them in a (Hindu-style) sacrifice. It could also be that these flowers might go to some debauched person who will make them into a necklace or bouquet to give to his mistress or concubine. The flowers might then become a bed to be wallowed upon in lust; or they might end up on some woman's neck, and in this way cause someone to become infatuated and thus pushed in the direction of sin. "Therefore," the buyer should think, "it is good that I buy these flowers and use them in the holy activity of the Lord's worship." The author concludes by saying that we sin when see a goat fall into the hands of a butcher because we have made no effort to save it. We commit the same kind of sin by not buying the flowers; in fact, we obtain great merit (*puṇya*) from buying flowers and using them in the Lord's worship.

The first three parts of the eightfold worship, as just described, occur within the inner shrine. As a group they are called *ang pūjā,* limb worship, because they focus on the image's body and its parts (*ang*). The remaining five rites are known collectively as *agra pūjā,* worship performed "in front of" (*agra*) the image.[29] *Ang pūjā* and *agra puja* together form the category of *dravya pūjā,* "worship with material things," as opposed to *bhāv pūjā,* "mental worship." *Ang pūjā* involves intimate physical contact with the image. *Agra pūjā* occurs at a distance; as suggested by its name, this type of worship is performed before the image in the temple's main hall. The focus of *ang pūjā* is honorific bodily attentions: bathing, anointing, adorning. The various gestures comprising *agra pūjā* are in some ways very heterogeneous, but an important aspect of this sequence is the offering of edibles. *Agra pūjā* is specifically associated with food (*āhāra*) in some texts (Williams 1963: 218).

A worshiper who has completed *ang pūjā* leaves the inner shrine, washes his or her hands, and then commences *agra pūjā.* Because these rites take place in the temple's main hall and do not involve contact with the divine image, their performance does not require the special personal purification and dress necessary for *ang pūjā*. Many temple visitors, therefore, perform only *agra pūjā*.

The fourth rite of the eightfold worship, and the first of the *agra pūjā* series, is *dhūp pūjā*, worship with incense (*dhūp*). The worshiper circles incense before the image while standing at the door to the inner shrine. Muktiprabhvijay renders the associated verse as, "O Lord, just as the incense [offered] before you causes inauspicious atoms (*aśubh pudgal*) to go away and fragrance to spread, so by means of worshiping you with incense, may my inauspicious inner thoughts vanish and my life become perfumed" (Muktiprabhviyay n.d.: 57).

Then follows the fifth rite, called *dīpak pūjā*, worship with a lamp (*dīpak*). Still standing at the inner shrine's door, the worshiper circles a lamp before the image. The accompanying couplet expresses the feeling that, "O Lord, by means of worshiping you with a lamp, may the darkness of my heart's ignorance be dispelled and may the lamp of the knowledge that lights up the universe burn" (ibid.: 58).

The sixth, seventh, and eighth parts of the eightfold worship form an integrated group of rites. These consist of a series of offerings, or offering-like gestures, that are made on an elevated surface. In Ahmedabad this is usually done on a low table positioned directly in front of the worshiper as he or she sits, facing the image, on the floor of the temple's main hall. In Jaipur it is usually done on the upper surface of the *bhaṇḍār* box (a box with a slotted top for temple donations), which is typically situated directly in front of the entrance into the inner shrine, or on a special low offering table located in front of the main shrine's entrance. I think this difference merely reflects the larger number of worshipers that typically attend Ahmedabad temples in the morning hours. In any case, this is the most visible part of Jain worship, and it is what most non-Jain visitors notice when they visit a Śvetāmbar temple.

The first rite of this group, and thus part number six of the eightfold worship, is called *akṣat pūjā*, meaning worship with unbroken rice grains (*akṣat*). The worshiper forms a diagram on the surface of the platform using perfect and nonviable grains of rice: first a *svastik*, above it three small heaps of rice, and above these a crescent surmounted by a dot (see Figure 9). The significance of the nonviability of the rice is that this is consonant with the worshiper's hope not to be reborn. Muktiprabhvijay renders the associated couplet as, "O Lord, by means of worshiping you with *akṣat* may I rapidly attain the imperishable (*akṣay*) stage" (ibid.: 58).[30] The *svastik*'s four arms represent the four classes of unliberated beings: deities, humans, hell-dwellers, and animals and

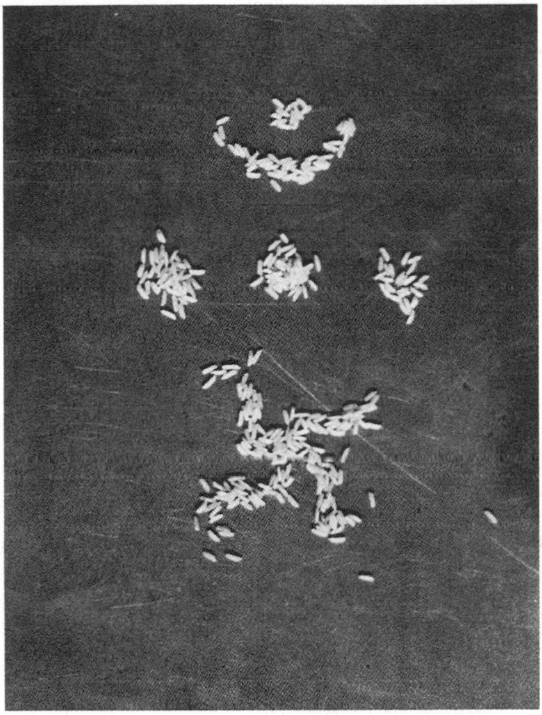

Figure 9. The diagram of rice formed in *akṣat pūjā*. Offerings will be placed on the diagram in the following phases of the eightfold worship.

plants. The three small heaps are the "three jewels" of the Jain tradition (knowledge, insight, and right conduct), and the crescent and dot signify liberated souls in their abode at the apex of the universe. The whole figure is thus a representation of the rudiments of the Jain belief system, depicting the situation of unliberated beings, the means of liberation, and liberation itself.

The seventh part of the eightfold worship is *naivedya pūjā*, the offering of food. Usually sweets of some kind (often rock sugar) are offered. The offered items are placed directly atop the *svastik* at its vertex. Many worshipers also offer a coin, usually by placing it on the middle heap of rice above the *svastik*. Although the food offering is certainly associated with notions of food and nourishment, it is not conceived as a "feeding" of the Tīrthankar. It is linked instead with the notion of the renunciation of food in imitation of the Tīrthankar. This we see clearly from the sense of the verse associated with the rite, which Muktiprabhvijay renders as "O Lord, I have eaten and am weary of eating, and you remain non-eating (*aṇahārī*) and obtain the highest happiness. You are non-eating and I am one who eats (*āhārī*). By doing your *pūjā* with this *naivedya* (food to be offered to a deity) I want to obtain from you the non-eating stage (*aṇāhārī pad*)" (ibid.: 60). In the symbolism of the rite, the offering of food is actually a rejection of eating and the bondage that eating represents.

*Phal pūjā,* worship with fruit (*phal*), is the eighth and final part of the eightfold worship. A fruit is placed on the dot and crescent at the top of the diagram that represent final release. It should be noted that in *naivedya pūjā* the food, the eating of which is inherent to our unliberated state, is put at the vertex of the *svastik,* which symbolizes the round of birth and death through the four classes of unliberated beings; in effect, the worshiper leaves food precisely where it belongs (Cort 1989: 375–76; Humphrey and Laidlaw 1994: 128). The depositing of the fruit at the top of the diagram (representing the summit of the universe) then elevates the worshiper to the highest goal. Any of various fruits can be used. The fruit offering is associated with the ultimate "fruit" of spiritual effort, which is liberation; the sentiment of the associated verse is, "O Lord, by means of worshiping you with fruit, may I obtain the libertion which is the fruit of the highest spiritual endeavors" (Muktiprabhvijay n.d.: 61).

The offerings made in the *agra pūjā* phase of the rite can be seen as a kind of symbolic paragraph in which the worshiper's situation in the world is represented and his or her hoped-for liberation through renunciation is enacted. The *svastik* stands for *saṃsār,* the "from what" of liberation. Above it are represented the means of liberation, and above these, the ultimate goal of liberation, which is marked by the offering of fruit. Of special interest in this context is the offering of food. As we have seen, giving food in worship is giving up food in emulation of the Tīrthankar. And indeed it is symbolically giving up the body itself, bodily existence being dependent upon eating and the very condition of worldly bondage. In the eightfold worship, therefore, adoration grades into *tyāg,* relinquishment, and culminates with the symbolic shedding of all residues of worldly existence. With these offerings made, the eightfold worship is completed.

If the offerings have been made on the surface of the *bhaṇḍār* box they are simply left there. Periodically these materials are swept into the slot, where they fall into the box below. If the rite has been performed on a different surface, then the offerings can be removed later by the temple's *pujārī* or *pujārīs*. But whatever is done, the materials used in worship are not returned to the worshipers. As will be seen, this is a very important fact about Jain ritual culture.

After finishing the eightfold worship, and having said *nisīhi* once more, one should perform *bhāv pūjā,* which is mental or internal worship as opposed to the now-completed physical worship (*dravya pūjā*). The object of *bhāv pūjā* is inward contemplation of the Jina and the qualities he represents. The essence of *bhāv pūjā* is praise, and ideally it should take the form of the rite known as *caitya vandan.* Afterwards the worshiper leaves the temple; in doing so the worshiper should not turn his or her back on the Tīrthankar.

## REFLEXIVITY

While there exists no "authoritative theory of the *puja*" within the tradition (Humphrey and Laidlaw 1994: 42), there is nonetheless a strong tendency among ascetic commentators and laypersons influenced by the views of ascetics to interpret *pūjā,* and the eightfold worship in particular, as an expression of soteriological ideas. This is not a coherent "theory" but a general point of view, one that happens to be extremely influential. It is expressed with greatest clarity in the interpretations of the eightfold worship provided in various layman's manuals (such as Muktiprabhvijay: n.d. and Hemprabhāśrījī: 1977) as cited above. Although many people perform worship in order to gain worldly benefits (a point to be addressed later in this chapter), these interpretations nonetheless emphasize the theme of liberation. As we have seen, the act of bathing the image is said to express the worshiper's hope of washing away the impurities that have accumulated on his or her soul from beginningless time, and the application of sandal paste (a cooling substance) is held to express the worshiper's desire for coolness of soul (that is, the eradication of passion). The remaining acts are interpreted in similar ways. The last offering, the fruit, stands for the "fruit" of the rite, liberation, which is why it is placed on the part of the diagram that represents the liberated state.

It will be noted that in none of this is there any suggestion of aid from the Tīrthankar. It is a fact of the highest importance about Jain ritual culture that worshipers do not engage in any transactions whatsoever with the Tīrthankars. The reason of course is the fifth *kalyāṇak,* the Tīrthankar's liberation. This *kalyāṇak* is not the focus of very much Jain ritual,[31] but it has a great deal to do with the definition of the ritual situation because it establishes the Tīrthankar as a liberated being. Liberation is a complete withdrawal into a nontransactional state. Ascetics who are on the road to liberation attenuate their transactions with the rest of the world; liberation is the complete cessation of such transactions. Many Jains obviously feel strong emotions while engaged in acts of worship, and there seems little doubt that, in the context of these emotions, the Tīrthankar is in some sense "present." "Of course he hears prayers," an Ahmedabad respondent once said to me; "he's omniscient." But from the standpoint of transactional logic the Tīrthankar is absent. He responds to no prayers or petitions, and dispenses no saving grace; he exists as an "other" in the relationship constructed by the rite, but transactionally he is nonexistent.[32]

The efficacy of worship, therefore, has to be *reflexive;* that is, whatever ritual does is done by the human ritual actor to himself. This is among the most important themes in Jain ritual culture, and a good illustration of it is provided by the following passages taken from a layman's manual authored by a Khartar Gacch nun named Hemprabhāsrījī: Worship (*pūjā*), she says, results in "purity of soul" (*ātmaviśuddhi*) (1977: 27). Elsewhere she says, "Just as the *darśan* of the supreme soul (*paramātmā,* meaning the Tīrthankar) makes the mind pure and becomes the means of the removal of *karma* (*karm nirjarā*), so the *pūjā* of the Lord encourages the arising of [the proper] feelings (*bhāv*), and the spark of these feelings will burn *karma*s and reduce them to ashes. Worship (*ārādhnā*) is done in order to destroy sensual vices and eradicate *karma.* Just as austerity and self-denial eradicate *karma,* in the same way the Lord's *pūjā,* done with devotion, also destroys *karma*s and provides many worldly benefits (*lābh*) besides. Auspicious feelings (*śubh bhāv*) will result in the adhesion of merit (*puṇya*), and, from merit, material (*paudgalik*) happiness is automatically acquired" (ibid.: 25).

As we see, from her standpoint, worship is really a kind of substitute form of world renunciation, which in Jainism is the principal means of shedding the *karma*s that impede the soul's liberation. In this sense the act of worshiping an ascetic becomes—itself—an ascetic act. She also says that these ritual acts result in worldly benefits by means of that (relatively) positive form of *karma* called "merit" (*puṇya*). It is important to note, however, that she nowhere says that any benefit of the rite—material or spiritual—will actually come from the object of worship, the Tīrthankar. This is not an obscure point among Jains; it is widely understood.

It should be noted also that she places great emphasis on the "feelings" or "sentiment" (*bhāv*) of the worshiper, which in her mind is clearly connected with the efficacy of the rite. This idea was echoed in the statements about the nature of worship made to me on many occasions by lay Jains. One should worship in the spirit of "devotion" (*bhakti*). This means that one should worship in the spirit of love for the Lord and with a sincerity of heart that Humphrey and Laidlaw have aptly characterized as "meaning to mean it" (1994: Ch. 9). But it needs to be stressed that in the ascetic commentaries on *pūjā* (such as Hemprabhāsrījī's) the portrayal of *bhāv* is pushed in the direction of *asceticism*. The worshiper is supposed to feel like an ascetic. This view is often articulated by lay Jains as well. An Ahmedabad informant put it this way: The meaning of worshiping with offerings (that is, *dravya pūjā*), he said, is that "Oh Lord, I have these things, but I really don't want them—I want to leave them."

## THE UNRETURNED OFFERING

All items offered in the Tirthankar's worship instantly acquire a negative ritual status in relation to the givers. This is true of all such rites (including, as we have seen, Pārśvanāth's five-*kalyāṇak pūjā*), not just the eightfold worship. These items become what Śvetāmbar Jains call *devdravya* (the Lord's goods), which means that they enter a category of things inviolably earmarked for the Tīrthankar (or, by extension, the temple).[33] This does not mean that they are actually possessed by the Tīrthankar. My Jain friends stressed, and Jain doctrine unambiguously affirms, that the Tīrthankars possess nothing. The most important meaning of the concept of *devdravya*, rather, is the absolute and unalterable separation between the thing given and the giver or givers. It is a major act of ritual "disrespect" (*āśātnā*) for even a single grain of rice offered in *pūjā* to pass a Jain's lips. Even if you accidentally have a piece of candy in your pocket during a temple visit, you cannot eat it afterwards. One mendicant author goes so far as to say that, if you take medicine into a temple, it cannot be used afterwards by you (Bhadrabāhu Vijay 1989: 56).

Offerings in temple worship are normally deposited in the offering box at the front of the main hall or are otherwise gathered up by the temple's *pujāris*. The items are generally given to the temple's *pujārī* or *pujārīs* and other servants, and are regarded as payment for services rendered. This practice is probably one of the reasons that *pujārīs* in

Śvetāmbar temples are almost always non-Jains.[34] The small sums of money given in *agra pūjā* go directly into temple funds. Grains and other materials used in major occasional rites are sometimes given in charity. When this is done, care should be taken to ensure that the recipients are not Jains. It does not matter who in particular receives such materials; the critical thing is that Jains do not.

The nonreciprocity between worshiper and object of worship in Jainism is one of the single most important differences between Jain ritual culture and the ritual cultures of some varieties of Hinduism. The crucial issue is the treatment of food offerings. Among Hindus there is considerable variation in the nature of deity-devotee transactions, a matter to be explored in detail in the final chapter. For the present it will suffice to say that in most Hindu traditions the offering of food to a deity is reciprocated. The food returns from the altar to the donor, and brings with it something of the virtue and power of the deity to whom it was offered. The returned offering is called *prasād,* a word that has the double meaning of a deity's blessing or grace as well as a reciprocated food offering. From this standpoint, the most salient fact about Jain ritual culture is that there is no *prasād.*

Why is this so? The answer lies in the inherent nature of an ascetic as an object of worship. As the ultimate ascetic (that is, a fully liberated being), the Tīrthankar can neither accept from nor give to a worshiper. He is an object of worship, but he cannot be a transactional alter. When a Hindu recovers offerings from the object of his devotion, the basic idea is that they have been transformed by their divine receiver. But, in the case of the Tīrthankar, there *is* no divine receiver, and therefore the offerings cannot be transformed.

Moreover, the offerings carry an onus of a very special sort. Because the Tīrthankar engages in no transactions, the worshiper cannot connect with him. Instead, the only relationship possible is one of emulation. Therefore the food offering is seen through the lens of ascetic values; one cannot *become* the Tīrthankar, but one can become *like* him. He represents an ideal, fixed in the form of an image before the worshiper's eyes, of a state of existence the worshiper hopes—or is supposed to hope—to attain at some future time. And if worship is emulatory, then the offering is necessarily spiritually insalubrious. To emulate the Tīrthankar is, above all, to renounce the world, to get rid of the harmful accretions that weigh down the soul and prevent its liberation. This is precisely how the food offering is interpreted in the eightfold worship. The food offering is not—as we have seen—in any sense "given to" the Tīrthankar; it is "given up" in emulation of his giving up of food. To take back what is given up is clearly to undo the good that has been done. Thus, the impossibility of the very idea of *prasād.*

Spiritually insalubrious to start with, and accepted by no divine receiver, the offering remains in that betwixt-and-between state that Arnold Van Gennep (1960) called "liminal." Given but not taken, in ritual logic the offering hangs suspended, trapped between a giver who cannot take it back and a receiver who is not there. It must therefore be pushed off the edge of the Jain world by being passed to a non-Jain.

## APPARENT EXCEPTIONS

There are certain ostensible exceptions to the generalization that Jains do not take *prasād,* but they all turn out to be special—and instructive—cases. For example, favors (often cash or sweets) are handed out to departing guests at the conclusion of various Jain ceremonies. These gifts, however, are not *prasād.* Known as *prabhāvnā,* they are distributed as an expression of the good wishes of the ceremony's sponsor. What is critical is that they are not redistributed offerings.[35]

Certain Jain pilgrimage centers are famed for the distribution of *prasād.* One example is the celebrated temple complex at Mahuḍī, just north of Ahmedabad in Gujarat. Sweets are indeed distributed to worshipers here, and they are in fact *prasād.* They are not, however, a Tīrthankar's *prasād,* for they have been offered not to the Tīrthankar but to a deity named Ghaṇṭā Karṇ Mahāvīr, who is much celebrated for his miraculous interventions (*camatkār*s) in his worshipers' worldly affairs.[36] In an interesting twist, his *prasād* may not be consumed outside the Mahuḍī temple's premises. The prohibition is said to have been instituted by the god himself at the time of the temple's founding, and tales abound concerning the misfortunes of those who have broken the rule.

In Rajasthan a similar pattern obtains at the pilgrimage center at Nākoṛā. As at Mahuḍī, *prasād* is distributed at this temple complex, but it is not the Tīrthankar's *prasād;* it is that of Nākoṛā Bhairav. A pilgrim purchases sweets outside the temple compound. He or she then takes a portion into the temple building, and the rule is that anything going into the temple building cannot be eaten and cannot be taken outside. Presumably it goes to the temple staff. The portion remaining outside the temple building becomes Nākoṛā Bhairav's *prasād,* and it must be consumed within the temple compound and cannot be taken outside. One friend told me of how, when he was on a family visit, one of his grandchildren accidentally put some *prasād* in his pocket. While driving away from Nākoṛā they had engine trouble and an engine fire. They finally discovered the hidden *prasād,* which of course was the reason for the trouble. The boy ate the *prasād,* they prayed for forgiveness, and were able to continue their journey.

The reason *prasād* can be taken from the altars of these deities is that they, unlike the Tīrthankars, are unliberated. This means that they are able, as the Tīrthankars are not, to engage in transactions with worshipers. Therefore, offerings made to them can indeed be transformed by them and then returned as blessings to devotees. This is true of all Jain deities. Why the *prasād* in these cases cannot be consumed outside these temple complexes is unclear. It may be that the relationship between deity and worshiper (as opposed to Tīrthankar and worshiper) is being quarantined. If worldly give-and-take is normally kept outside the Tīrthankars' temples, at Mahuḍī and Nākoṛā it is subordinated to higher values by keeping it within. It is also possible that the restriction has been instituted because it has the effect of maintaining high attendance at the shrines by ensuring that the benefits of a visit are not portable. But whatever the case, the *prasād* in question is not the Tīrthankar's.

Another apparent exception to the no-*prasād* rule, this in the Khartar Gacch tradition, involves the worship of the deceased ascetics known as Dādāgurus. Here too *prasād* is recovered from worship and consumed by devotees. But here, too, this is possible because the Dādāgurus are not, as are the Tīrthankars, in a liberated condition. This is a matter to be discussed in detail in the next chapter.

## THE POWER OF RITUAL

Although worshipers of the Tīrthankars do not recover food offerings as *prasād,* they do utilize the residual water left from the bathing of the Tīrthankar's image. This presents us with a puzzle. When worshipers recover small amounts of this liquid and apply it to their bodies, this seems to express a reciprocal relationship in which sacred power is being transmitted from the image to the worshiper. That power is involved is shown clearly by the belief that the image's bathwater has healing properties. In illness or injury it can be applied directly to the afflicted parts of the body with beneficial results. Similar power can be carried by the detritus that is cleaned from the images in the morning. This raises two general questions. The first is that of how the water can be power-charged if there is no transaction with the Tīrthankar. The second is the more basic question of how ritual can be materially efficacious at all.

Jains believe that worship can indeed produce good worldly results, but the mechanism by means of which this is done is always a cloudy matter. Various kinds of explanation, each plausible in its own way, free-float around the issue.[37] Most Jains agree that good results cannot come from the Tīrthankar himself. One friend in Ahmedabad, however, opined that the power does indeed come from the Tīrthankars; it descends from above, he said, as a gentle rain of compassion with the temple's flag acting as an antenna.[38] Many say that good results come from the positive nature of the act of worship itself. It produces merit (*puṇya*), which will inevitably yield positive fruit. Another common explanation is that the act of worship pleases the Tīrthankar's ancillary deities, who are the specific guardian deities particularly associated with him. He, of course, cannot be pleased or displeased, but his associated deities are glad to see the act of worship and will reward the worshiper. Many Jains believe that the most powerful temples are those of Ṛṣabh and Pārśvanāth precisely because of the extraordinary power of Cakreśvarī and Padmāvatī, goddesses who are associated with these two Tīrthankars respectively.

It is also clear that the images themselves, quite apart from the beings they represent, can be repositories of power. This is shown by the fact that some images are regarded as more powerful than others.[39] A particular image's power may be related to its history—how it was created, or how it was discovered, for many images are believed to have been miraculously recovered from burial. An image's power is also associated with the *mantra* (power-charged utterance) pronounced by the officiating ascetic at the time of the image's consecration. Jains sometimes say that an image's power is proportional to the spiritual attainments of the ascetic who performed the consecration. Much like the charge of a battery, the *mantra*-induced power can dissipate over time and can be replenished by ritual means. Such power does indeed have links to the Tīrthankar, but only indirectly through the line of disciplic succession that connects the officiating ascetic to him over the gulf of intervening ages.

In any case, the water recovered from a Tīrthankar's worship can indeed transmit sacred power to the recipient. But it is highly significant that even though it transmits sacred power, the liquid taken from a Tīrthankar's altar should not be drunk.[40] This restriction contrasts with the corresponding Hindu practice in which devotees do indeed consume the bathwater and bodily detritus of deities, and it goes directly to the heart of a basic tension in Jain ritual culture.

Applying such substances to one's body is an expression of respectful and loving intimacy with the Tīrthankar's image. In the eightfold worship the context of this act is *ang pūjā,* a phase of the rite that emphasizes humble bodily service. Taking materials used in such services on one's own body intensifies and extends the intimacy and is a further expression of homage. Because of their close contact with the images, such materials can also transmit beneficial power from image to worshiper. But there is a limit to the intimacy, for there can be no consubstantiation between worshiper and Tīrthankar in Jain ritual culture. The prohibition of eating or drinking anything taken from the Tīrthankar's worship seems to obviate the notion that one could express or achieve any sort of "union" with a Tīrthankar by internalizing his emanations. The Tīrthankar is not present in the image, and in any case union with such a being is neither possible nor sought. What then remains as a ritual possibility is emulation, not connection—at most an intimacy of surfaces (as opposed to alimentary intimacy) with an empowered Tīrthankar image (as opposed to the Tīrthankar himself).

## AMBIVALENCE

The eightfold worship is the most important of all Jain rites of worship. In a sense, all other physical forms of worship (as opposed to *bhāv pūjā*) may be seen as variations or elaborations of this core rite. The *snātra pūjā,* for example, can be seen simply as a highly embroidered version of the *ang pūjā* portion of the eightfold worship. The entire eightfold worship is then reiterated at the end. Rites such as Pārśvanāth's five-*kalyāṇak pūjā* elaborate the *agra pūjā* portion of the eightfold worship (the emphasis being on the table offerings), but all elements of the eightfold worship are present. Not only is *ang pūjā* reiterated at the beginning of each of the five offerings, but if the five-*kalyāṇak pūjā* is analogous to *agra pūjā,* then the *snātra pūjā,* which always precedes the main rite, becomes the functional equivalent of *ang pūjā* in the sequence as a whole.

To a significant degree, therefore, the question of what is really taking place in rites of worship is the question of what is taking place in the eightfold worship. And the answer to this question is never quite clear. On the one hand, Jains certainly believe that worshiping the Tīrthankars can generate worldly prosperity and happiness in this life or another. Many Jains—some Jains would say most—engage in ritual activities precisely for this reason. Indeed, we have seen that even the ascetic commentator Hemprabhāśrījī gives implicit sanction to this idea by explaining how worldly benefits result from the merit generated by worship. The desire for worldly benefits, however, is inconsistent with the ascetic values expressed by normative interpretations of the rite. How could things be otherwise? Given the very nature of the object of worship—an ascetic—the rite is a celebration of asceticism. In consistency with this, one often hears *dravya pūjā* devalued in comparison with the more ascetic *bhāv pūjā*. "*Dravya pūjā,*" an Ahmedabad friend said to me, "takes you to the twelfth *devlok,* but *bhāv pūjā* takes you to *mokṣ* (liberation)."[41] Moreover, we have seen that normative interpretations characterize the eightfold worship as *itself* a kind of substitute form of world renunciation. All this meshes poorly with the idea of worship as a source of worldly well-being. Both ascetic and worldly values exist in Jain ritual culture, but we see that the relationship between them is necessarily ambiguous.

As Laidlaw has shown (1995), there is in fact a deep ambivalence on this issue that is present in many different contexts in the Śvetāmbar tradition. At its most abstract it is manifested in the idea that good *karma* (the name for which is *puṇya,* "merit") is there to be gained by the virtuous, but that the highest goal is the removal of *karma* (*nirjarā*). I encountered many lay Jains who were quite articulate about this distinction. A very common image for this idea as enunciated by ordinary Jains, one already alluded to, is that of *puṇya* as a chain of gold—gold indeed, but for all that a chain. But while the conceptual distinction between good *karma* and the removal of *karma* is clear, Laidlaw perceptively and rightly says,

> there is no correspondingly clear distinction between the practices that might cause these internal processes. The workings of *karmik* cause and effect are unknowable, except to those with supernatural insight. Thus what appears from the outside to be two instances of the same act will have different effects, depending on the *karma* already present in those who perform them and the mental attitude (*bhav*) with which they are performed. To make a donation is more likely to bring merit, and so luck and good fortune, but insofar as it is motivated by non-attachment to material possessions . . . or mercy . . . and so non-violence . . . , it might also effect the purification of the soul. Conversely, ascetic practices such as fasting or con-

> fession are most naturally thought of as removing *karma*. . . . But even in the case of the most pious monk, only distant future events will reveal whether he has succeeded in destroying his *karms* or only in gaining more merit. (ibid.: 28)

We find, in fact, a similar ambiguity right at the heart of Hemprabhāśrījī's interpretation of the eightfold worship. Readers will recall that she says that the rite removes and "burns" *karma*s. But at the same time she asserts that it generates merit and material happiness. We know which interpretation she prefers; she gives clear emphasis to the removal of *karma*. But she never quite chooses between them in the sense of telling us, once and for all, what *pūjā* actually "is." The Tīrthankar makes a great choice between the path of worldly felicity and the path to liberation. We see that this same choice is presented to the worshiper by every act of worship. Only one who knows his or her heart perfectly can know for sure what choice has been made, and who truly knows his or her own heart?

In the symbolism of worship this ambivalence is manifested in an instability in the metaphor of the worshiper as Indra or Indrāṇī. The worshiper takes the role of wealthy and powerful Indra (or Indrāṇī). The ritually adopted persona of Indra carries with it the image of worldly well-being, and this fits well with the worshiper's expectation that worship will result in earthly versions of heavenly felicity (or even in heavenly rebirth). But the problem is that, although the worshiper's well-being is given due recognition, the ascetic's path alone possesses unquestioned legitimacy. As a result, normative interpretations of the ritual act emphasize mimesis. Metaphor gets tightened into actual analogy; the worshiper's identity as a regal deity gives way to the idea that he is a renouncer who imitates his spiritual king: the Tīrthankar. At this point, kingly largess becomes the ascetic's giving up. But the worshiper's role is finally ambiguous. Who is the worshiper? The matter is never quite settled. At one level the worshiper is powerful and prosperous, but this image is always challenged by omnipresent ascetic values.

Given the tradition's bias in favor of ascetic values, the values most attuned to the tradition's highest aspiration of karmic eradication, and given also the inevitable pull of worldly necessity for most people, this ambiguity must take the form of a tension. There is not the slightest doubt, moreover, that this tension is felt as quite real by many lay Jains. This was revealed to me especially in the constant hedgings and evasions that characterized the many discussions I had with Jain friends about the fruits of worship.[42] I was told repeatedly that although many

Jains (some said most Jains—indeed some included themselves) seek good worldly results from their temple-going and other religious activities, they *should not* be seeking such things. Such persons, I was told, are "ignorant" about what Jainism really is; Jainism is about *tyāg,* giving things up, not about getting things. As an Ahmedabad respondent vividly expressed it, "Jainism is '*choṛo, choṛo, choṛo*'! ('relinquish, relinquish, relinquish!')." The entire matter of the worldly results of worship is awkward, even embarrassing, precisely because many Jains do indeed seek worldly benefits from worship while knowing that there is something deeply questionable about doing so.

The tradition thus allows worldly values a sphere of legitimacy. Indeed, worldly felicity is a potential result of every ritual act. But the sphere of worldly values is subordinate; their legitimacy is, at the tradition's highest levels, defensive. Among Jaipur's Śvetāmbar Jains, however, there is another domain of religious practice in which the worshiper's role is recast in a much more stable form. Here worship is focused not on the Tīrthankars but on certain ascetics of the more recent past. This pattern will be the subject of the next chapter.

CHAPTER THREE

# Magical Monks

## *A Ritual Subculture*

It is time to return to the temple complex at Mohan Bāṛī in Jaipur where we observed Pārśvanāth's five-*kalyāṇak pūjā*. This is not the community's most important temple, but it is of great interest to us because it exhibits a range of diverse ritual subtraditions in close physical juxtaposition.[1] As we know, the main shrine is dedicated to Ṛṣabh; here he is represented (unusually for a Tīrthankar) by a pair of feet (*caran*s) carved in stone. The other structures in the complex do not contain representations of the Tīrthankars at all; rather, they are shrines dedicated to various monks and nuns of the past. One shrine contains an image of Śānti Vijay, a monk famous for his miracles, who died in 1943. There is also a large structure at the spot where the last rites were performed for a much beloved Khartar Gacch nun named Vicakṣaṇśrī, who died in 1980. Within is her very lifelike image, protected by a glass case. In 1991 a similar shrine was under construction nearby for a nun named Sajjanśrī, who died in 1989. Yet another shrine houses the footprint images of four very distinguished Khartar Gacch monks, known as Dādāgurus or Dādāgurudevs, who lived centuries ago. There are foot images of other deceased monks and nuns as well. The representations of all these ascetics of the past are objects of worship.[2]

The temple complex at Mohan Bāṛī encourages us mentally to rotate the cult of the Tīrthankars slightly so that we see it at an unaccustomed angle. At first glance the worship of the Tīrthankars seems discontinuous with any wider ritual context at all. Such a view is encouraged by the tradition's own habitual emphasis on the idea that the worship of the Tīrthankars is a kind of physical enactment of soteriological ideas and values. Mohan Bāṛī teaches us that this impression is in some ways quite misleading, at least for the image-worshiping Śvetāmbar Jains of Jaipur. We see that to the sensibilities of those who constructed and use this temple, the worship of Tīrthankars has a natural home among mortuary cults—indeed that it *is* a particular kind of mortuary cult, albeit one with exceptional characteristics.[3]

This chapter deals with the worship of deceased ascetics who are not Tīrthankars, and in particular with the cult of the Dādāgurus. This means that our regional focus now shifts decisively to Rajasthan and Jaipur, and to the Khartar Gacch.[4] The chapter will show that, as sacred personae, the Dādāgurus are in some ways quite Tīrthankar-like. If we focus specifically on transactions, however, we see that their relationship with worshipers is very different from that of the Tīrthankars. This difference supports, and is supported by, a symbolic surround that shares some similarities with the cult of the Tīrthankars but is strikingly different in its orientation toward worldly values. The cult of the Dādāgurus is, I therefore suggest, a ritual subculture with a regional (Rajasthan) and ascetic-lineage (the Khartar Gacch) focus. It utilizes many of the ritual idioms and usages described in the preceding two chapters, but it does so in a very different context, a context in which overt recognition is given to the worldly ambitions and desires of devotees. If ascetic and worldly values are in tension at the tradition's highest levels, in this ritual subculture they are brought into a far more stable relationship.

Our point of departure will be an exploration of how an ideal ascetic career is conceptualized. We shall see that this conceptualization is a bridge between ascetic values and a certain kind of ritual response *to* such values. We then examine the Dādāgurus and the ritual subculture of which they are the focus.

## ASCETIC CAREER AS RITUAL CHARTER

We normally think of hagiography as the portrayal of exemplary lives, and this is certainly true of the abundant Jain hagiography. These materials typically concern ascetics' lives that embody the tradition's central values and highest aspirations. But in some of the hagiography of the Khartar Gacch there is also a subtheme of great interest. The main dish is the ascetic's life, but also important is his death and its aftermath. As were the Tīrthankars, these figures were ascetics—but of course they were in no sense at the same spiritual level. As did the Tīrthankars, they departed this world—but of course in no sense was their departure as complete. And just as the Tīrthankar left something behind, so did they. They left a continuing pattern of helpful response to the supplications of devotees.

To illustrate this principle I now present a highly abstracted version of a posthumously written biography (Jinharisāgarsūri 1948) of a distinguished Khartar Gacch monk named Chagansāgar. The biography was written by one of his disciples, Jinharisāgarsūri,[5] and it shows us how in this tradition hagiography can become a charter for ritual.

## AN ASCETIC'S LIFE

Chogmal (his original name) was born on Mahāvīr Jayantī[6] in 1839 C.E. in the town of Phalodī in what was then Jodhpur State (Marwar). His father belonged to the Golechā clan (*gotra*) of the Osvāl caste. Our biographer reports that Chogmal's birth was preceded by an augury. One night his mother was awakened by a remarkable dream of the sun. In the morning his father asked his guru to interpret the dream. The guru said that a son as lustrous as the sun would be born in his house, one whose brightness would light up *saṃsār.*

Our author tells us little of Chogmal's childhood, and his narrative hits its real stride only with his young adulthood. We learn that Chogmal married the daughter of a wealthy merchant, and that after his father's death he entered business with his two brothers and began the life of a householder. Unfortunately, business went badly and the brothers fell out and separated. Chogmal then decided to depart Phalodī and seek his fortune elsewhere. He left his wife behind, and, after many difficulties on the road, he found his way to a village named Bārsī. For three years he worked there in the shop of a man named Rangājī. He then returned to Phalodī, where he stayed for a year and begot a son. After this he made his way back to Bārsī, and later—how much later is not clear—he again returned to Phalodī. After his wife bore him a second son, he took to the road once again, this time to Hyderabad. I suspect that these comings and goings were typical of men of his class and background.

It was in Hyderabad, our biographer tells us, that his life began to change. Here he began to associate with pious individuals with whom he engaged in a variety of ascetic exercises and ritual activities. His biographer tells us that during this period his spiritual life flourished along with his financial affairs, and that his life became a "model" of religion (*dharm*) and prosperity (*dhan*). Later, he again returned to Phalodī, and during this stay he came under the influence of a leading Khartar Gacch ascetic named Sukhsāgar, who held the rank of *gaṇādhīśvar* (group leader).[7] This is, of course, the selfsame Sukhsāgar who founded the *samudāy* that bears his name (Chapter One). Chogmal asked him for initiation. Sukhsāgar was encouraging but counseled delay because, as he put it, Chogmal still had some "enjoyment (*bhog*) *karmas*" remaining. Chogmal then had another son. After the birth of this son he and his wife took a vow of celibacy. He also arranged the marriages of his two older sons and his daughter.

His initiation was finally precipitated by hearing a sermon delivered by a well-known Khartar Gacch nun of those days. Inspired by what he heard, he asked his wife for permission to leave the householder's state and begged her pardon for any hardships he might have caused her. In response she expressed the wish to become a nun. On the tenth day of the bright fortnight of the lunar month of Vaiśākh (April/May) in the year 1885 C.E., Chogmal received initiation from Sukhsāgar.[8] As a monk, his name became Chagansāgar, and he became a member of Sukhsāgar's *samudāy*. At the same time his wife became a nun with the name Cāndśrījī.

At the direction of Sukhsāgar, Chagansāgar became the companion of a senior monk named Bhagvānsāgar. Their first journey together was to the village of Khīcand near Phalodī where Chagansāgar began his period of studies prior to final initiation (*baṛī dīkṣā*). Although Chagansāgar's officially designated guru was an ascetic named Sthānsāgar, this individual is hardly mentioned in our account; Bhagvānsāgar seems to have played the actual role of his teacher and senior mentor. Many laymen begged to have the final initiation performed in their own villages; to sponsor an initiation is, of course, highly meritorious. In the end, it was performed by Sukhsāgar in the village of Lohāvaṭ (about 16 miles from Phalodī) on the eighth day of the bright fortnight of the lunar month of Jeṭh (May/June) in the year 1885. Bhagvānsāgar and Chagansāgar then set out together on their ascetic wanderings; they would continue to travel as a pair until Bhagvānsāgar's death in 1900.

The biography now becomes an account of their travels. This record need not be summarized in detail; it is enough to say that they visited villages, towns, temples, and pilgrimage centers, and they took the *darśan* of many important images. They also participated in important pilgrimage parties organized by laymen, and they undertook notable fasts. Chagansāgar achieved particular fame for his ascetic practices, and as a result became generally known as Mahātapasvījī (practitioner of great austerities). As the author puts it, they "obtained *lābh* (benefit)" by means of these activities, and they "gave *lābh*" to the people as well. Their travels were punctuated by their rainy season sojourns, which our biographer clearly sees as defining episodes in their careers. He puts great stress on the role of laymen's entreaties in bringing them to a given locale for the rainy season retreat and on the benefits their presence bestowed on the communities in which they stayed.

Lying below the particular details in this account are certain recurrent themes. Perhaps the most important of these is the biographer's constant emphasis on the role played by the two ascetics as instigators of lay piety. As the author puts it, the two constantly engage in the *pracār* (promulgation) of religion. This they accomplish by means of their discourses and also by the powerful example of their learning and asceticism. We are told how they inspire laymen and laywomen to take the twelve vows of the *śrāvak dharm* (or *gr̥hasth dharm*).[9] They inspire people to give up cannabis and tobacco. They induce some to take vows of celibacy. They inspire laymen and laywomen to undertake ascetic practices (such as fasts) and also to take initiation as ascetics. Indeed, our biographer himself was initiated by Chagansāgar.[10] There were many others, some of whom became quite well known as ascetics. For example, a Maheśvarī of Pireu (in Marwar) took initiation from him in 1906; his ascetic name was Navnidhisāgarjī, and he became quite famous, with many disciples of his own. Many nuns were also drawn to initiation because of Chagansāgar.[11] He had, our author asserts, much "influence" (*prabhāv*, an important word, as we shall see in the next chapter) over Jains and non-Jains alike.

Another strong theme in this account is that of the powerful ascetic as the protector of Jainism. Examples are abundant in the text. In the town of Meḍtā, Chagansāgar successfully debated an erudite Brāhmaṇ who claimed that Jains were atheists (*nāstik*). In Kolāyatjī, a Vaiṣṇava pilgrimage center, he debated another distinguished Brāhmaṇ scholar, and did so in Sanskrit; the Brāhmaṇ was "influenced" (*prabhāvit*), and declared, or so our biographer says, that in future he would hold Jain teachings in honor and that he regretted his past opinion that Jains were atheists. In Bikaner, Chagansāgar debated a famous Terāpanthī ascetic named Pholmaljī, and defended the practices of charitable giving and *dravya pūjā* (the worship of images with material things). He also defended *dravya pūjā* in a debate in Deśnok. On this occasion he stated that the materials and items used in worship are produced by householders for their "enjoyment" (*bhog*), and that enjoyment is what makes the world go round (*bhog se saṃsār baṛhtā hai*). Thus, by using these things in devotion to the Lord instead of enjoying them, the householder is in fact engaged in world renunciation. His point, of course, was that worship is properly seen as a form of asceticism, a view that we encountered in the last chapter.

Another theme is that of the miraculous. Chagansāgar possessed great supernatural power and performed a large number of miracles. Our author is careful to state that he performed miracles only for the *prabhāvnā* of *dharm*—that is, for the glorification of Jainism. Early in his career he and Bhagvānsāgar had gone to Mt. Abu, and there he practiced special kinds of meditation and obtained certain *siddhi*s (accomplishments; in this context, magical powers). After this, he saw a lion on the pathway. "Influenced" (*prabhāvit*) by Chagansāgar's new power, the lion bowed humbly and departed. In Pālī, where he and Bhagvānsāgar spent the 1890 rainy season, the people were being tormented by *ḍākiṇī*s (malign female supernaturals). Once, while Chagansāgar was delivering a discourse there, a woman lost consciousness as a result of possession (*praveś*, literally "entry") by a *ḍākiṇī*, and began to dance. He quelled the disturbance by putting *vāskṣep* powder on her, and she was never troubled again. Indeed, on numerous other occasions he benefited individuals by means of what our author calls his "miraculous (*camatkārik*) *vāskṣep*." He relieved many victims of ghost-possession (*bhūtāveś*). For example, he once encountered a Rājpūt and his wife on the road from Nāgaur to Khīvsar. She had become possessed by a ghost, and the Rājpūt begged for his assistance. Chagansāgar said that if the Rājpūt would give up meat and liquor, all would be well. The Rājpūt did so, and his wife recovered completely. In Pīpaḍ he quelled a cholera epidemic. He even relieved Nāgaur of a drought.[12]

Because of Bhagvānsāgar's increasing age and frailty, Chagansāgar and he spent the rainy season of 1893 in Lohāvaṭ, and in nearby Phalodī in 1894. From this point on they spent the rains in one or the other of these places. In 1900, Bhagvānsāgar died, and Chagansāgar thereupon became his successor. Bhagvānsāgar had succeeded Sukhsāgar upon the latter's death in 1885, and so Chagansāgar became the third leader of this *samudāy*.

Chagansāgar continued his travels and work as before. Eventually, however, his own advancing age and the entreaties of local Jains persuaded him to spend the rains only in the vicinity of Phalodī and Lohāvaṭ. In 1908 and 1909 he spent the rainy season in Lohāvaṭ, and, at the beginning of the 1909 retreat, while doing *caturmāsik pratikramaṇ*[13] with members of the community, he sneezed—highly inauspicious during *pratikramaṇ,* and an ill omen. That evening in a special vision he became aware of his impending death. When his death came it was directly related to his propensity for austerities. After rigorous fasting during that year's Paryuṣaṇ, and despite the entreaties of the community, he extended his *saṃvatsarī* fast (the fast on the final day of Paryuṣaṇ) for an extra day. Normally this fast occurs on the lunar fourth of the fortnight; he extended it to the fifth, saying that it was only because of Kālkācāryajī that *saṃvatsarī* is observed on the fourth and that the time-honored date is the fifth.[14] He died on the day after this; after blessing the community he passed away while meditating on the five *parameṣṭhins*.[15] The actual date of his death was the sixth day of the bright fortnight of the "second" lunar month of Śrāvan (July/August). Normally, Paryuṣaṇ ends on the fourth day of the bright fortnight of the lunar month of Bhādrapad (August/September), which is the month coming after Śrāvan. As occasionally happens, however, an extra (intercalary) Śrāvan was added that year in order to bring the lunar and solar years into coordination. Because of this, that year's Paryuṣaṇ was observed during the second of the two Śrāvans, and his death thus occurred in that month.[16]

The community, our author says, felt the pains of separation deeply. Chagansāgar's obsequies took place near a local *dādābāṛī,* and a certain Ray Badrīdāsjī Bahādur of Calcutta built a *chatrī* on this spot. The term *chatrī* refers to the umbrella-like memorial cenotaphs with which deceased individuals of distinction are commemorated. The custom of marking the cremation sites of the dead with these structures is associated especially with the Rājpūt aristocracy, but religious figures of note are also memorialized in this fashion.[17] In the latter case the deceased individual is symbolized by an image of his or her feet. Chagansāgar's feet were duly installed in his cenotaph, and here they are still being worshiped.

Our author ends his narrative with a series of crucial assertions. Local Jains, he says, sponsor an annual ceremony at the *chatrī* on the anniversary of Chagansāgar's death. In Jaipur, Jodhpur, Bikaner, Phalodī,

Lohāvaṭ, and elsewhere, devotees perform *pūjā* (worship), *tapasyā* (austerities), and *jāgraṇ* (all-night singing of devotional songs) on bright sixths (that is, the day of the month on which he died) and on the bright sixth after Paryūṣaṇ.[18] Every year, he adds, devotees come to Lohāvaṭ to this memorial, which is located just in front of the Campāvāḍī railway bridge. Chagansāgar was peripatetic in life—we note—but now his devotees come to him. This great monk, says our biographer, had miraculous powers in life (that is, he was "*camatkārī*"), but *now too* his miracles occur for the faithful. In times of trouble (*sankaṭ*), meditation on Chagansāgar can help. Happiness, good fortune, health, progeny, and an increase in wealth can be gotten by invoking his name.

Our biographer reiterates the basic facts of Chagansāgar's life in his final chapter in accord with a standard formula for texts of this kind. He opens this recapitulation by tracing Chagansagar's lineage of disciplic succession. He begins with Mahāvīr and his disciple, Sudharmā, who is the source of all Śvetāmbar disciplic lineages. He ends with Chagansāgar's nominal guru, Sthānsāgar. Sthānsāgar was in the seventy-third disciplic generation from Mahāvīr. "Thus," says our author, "Mahātapasvījī Śrīmān Chagansāgarjī Mahārāj was in the seventy-fourth."

## VIRTUE AND POWER

Jinharisāgarsūri's biography of Chagansāgar teaches us an important lesson about Jain ascetics. A distinguished ascetic is certainly an exemplar of virtues. But he may also be a wielder of great magical power.[19] Indeed, in Chagansāgar's career these two things seem to blend nearly seamlessly.

We note first that his career, as portrayed in our biography, echoes themes found in the lives of the Tīrthankars. This important idea is signaled early in the account when we learn that before his birth his mother had a dream of the sun, a dream that was interpreted—or so we are told—as an augury of his future greatness. The parallel with the fourteen dreams of the mother of the Tīrthankar-to-be is obvious.[20] We know, too, that just as the Tīrthankar develops equanimity toward the pleasures of the world—indeed toward the pleasures of heaven—prior to his renunciation, Chagansāgar likewise became detached from the world. His biographer is eager to show us that, for Chagansāgar, world renunciation was never a virtue made of necessity. He had everything that truly matters to the worldly—progeny and wealth. His life as a layman was a perfect blend of wealth and piety (*dhan* and *dharm*), but in the end he gave up everything. His career as an ascetic was likewise a model career. He was scholarly, influential, a protector of Jainism, a teacher, and an able custodian of the virtue and piety of the lay community. He was also a great master of ascetic practices.

All this provides an important context for the fact that Chagansāgar also possessed and exercised great magical power. In his biography this power has been completely embedded in Jain values and aspirations, and in this way has been legitimized in Jain terms. To begin with, the power is clearly associated with his virtuosity in Jain ascetic praxis. Furthermore, his use of the power is connected always with two linked goals: to protect Jainism and Jains, and also to increase the glorification (*prabhāvnā*) of Jainism. Finally, our biographer reminds us at the very end of his account that Chagansāgar was connected, by disciplic succession, to the ultimate source of all legitimacy in the Jain world, namely, the Tīrthankar himself. Chagansāgar's power was a Jain power, legitimately employed to help Jains and Jainism.

When Chagansāgar dies, this power crystallizes into a *ritual effect.* The legitimacy of the power is guaranteed by the original paradigm of its application: to help Jains and Jainism, to glorify the Jain creed. Its efficacy is guaranteed by its association with a recurrent time (the lunar day of Chagansāgar's death) and permanent place (the site of his death rites). In fact, to this day the anniversary of his death continues to be noted in Khartar Gacch almanacs. In this way, hagiography is refocused into a charter for a mortuary cult. The relationship between Chagansāgar and his followers is *preserved* in the form of a pair of permanently available ritual roles: powerful monk and lay follower in need of assistance. The Tīrthankars are, of course, departed ascetics too. But a crucial difference in the case of the Tīrthankars is the fact that, because of the fifth *kalyāṇak* (liberation), this relationship cannot truly be preserved; thus, as we have seen, the core of worship must be emulation, not connection. With Chagansāgar, however, connection remains a postmortem possibility.

Jinharisāgarsūri's biography thus discloses an alternative possibility for ritual action in Śvetāmbar Jainism—the veneration of ascetics who wield power on behalf of devotees in need of assistance, and whose power becomes posthumously available in the form of an institutionalized pattern of worship. This is the general principle underlying the ritual subculture of the Dādāgurus.

## DĀDĀGURUDEVS

The worship of deceased ascetics of note is a central feature of the religious life of Śvetāmbar Jains associated with the Khartar Gacch. Of these the most important by far are the figures known as Dādāgurus or Dādāgurudevs.[21] The Dādāgurus are past Khartar Gacch *ācārya*s who are singled out from others because of their roles as defenders and reformers of Jainism, and as miracle workers and creators of new Jains. The four are: Jindattsūri (1075–1154 C.E.), Jincandrasūri "Maṇidhārī" (1140–1166), Jinkuśalsūri (1280–1332), and Jincandrasūri II (1541–1613). These figures are the focus of a widespread cult.[22]

Most temples affiliated with the Khartar Gacch contain images of the Dādāgurus. There are also many shrines—called *dādābāṛī*s, "gardens of the Dādā"—dedicated specifically to them. The temple complex at Mohan Bāṛī is, in fact, a large *dādābāṛī*. Even in *dādābāṛī*s, however, images of the Tīrthankars are present—as we see in the case of Mohan Bāṛī—and, in theory, are the primary objects of worship. *Dādābāṛī*s are basically mortuary structures. Although many of them have been enveloped by urban growth, the ideal is for *dādābāṛī*s to be away from population centers, as would be appropriate for a place where funerary rites take place. The complex at Mohan Bāṛī functions in this way today.

There are several *dādābāṛī*s in Jaipur, the most important being a temple located on Motidungri Road to the south of the old city. This temple is owned by the Śrīmāls and is a major Jain landmark in Jaipur. The most famous *dādābāṛi*s of all, however, are located at Ajmer, Mehraulī (near Delhi), and Mālpurā (some 80 kilometers southeast of Jaipur). Those at Ajmer and Mehraulī are located on the spots where, respectively, Jindattsūri's and Jincandrasūri Maṇidhārī's obsequies took place. The *dādābāṛī* at Mālpurā was supposedly founded as a result of a vision that Jinkuśalsūri gave just fifteen days after his death (to be discussed later). A directory of *dādābāṛī*s published in 1962 lists 344 independent shrines and 210 larger temples in which the Dādāgurus are represented, mainly in Rajasthan and Madhya Pradesh (Jośī 1962). Many more exist now.

The Dādāgurus are usually worshiped in the form of foot images, but anthropomorphic images have become more common in recent times (Figures 10, 11).[23] It is clear, however, that footprints are more fundamentally in character for the Dādāgurus than anthropomorphic images, because even when there is an anthropomorphic image there are usually footprints too.[24] The structures in which the Dādāgurus' im-

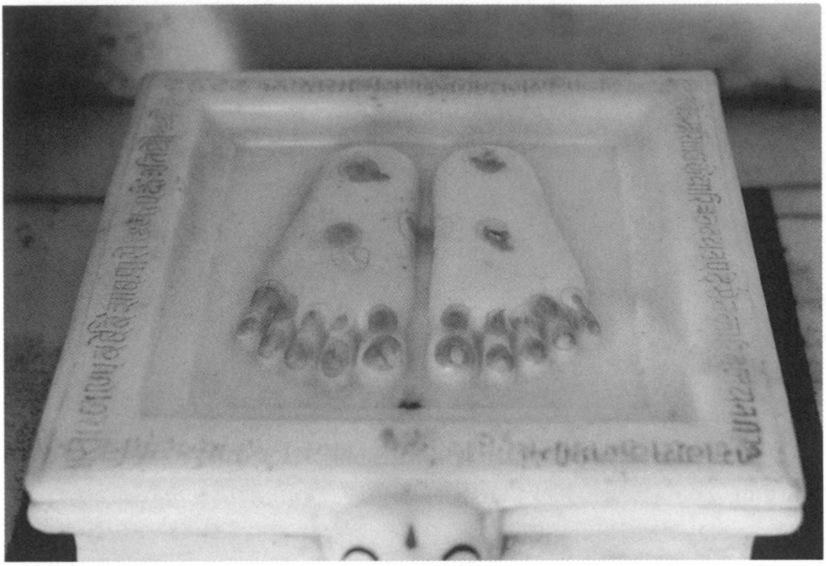

Figure 10. Footprint image of a Dādāguru at Sāngāner, near Jaipur

ages are housed are modeled on the funerary cenotaphs that are so common a feature of Rajasthan. Even where temple-like buildings have been erected for the Dādāgurus, their images—whether footprints or anthropomorphic figures—are usually housed in cenotaph-like shrines within.

We may say that deceased ascetics constitute a general class of objects of worship. The Dādāgurus are different in degree from other deceased monks, not different in kind. They are the most beloved, respected, and powerful of them all, but—as we have seen in the case of Chagansāgar—other ascetics have achieved postmortem recognition. As I have already suggested, the Tīrthankars can also be seen as members of this class, but this statement requires qualification. The distinction between the Tīrthankars and ordinary deceased ascetics is never in doubt; the Tīrthankars have achieved omniscience and liberation, whereas even ascetics as distinguished as the Dādāgurus have not. The *namaskār mantra* establishes a clear hierarchy among ascetics, with the Tīrthankars unambiguously at the top. But at the same time, Tīrthankars are deceased ascetics too. As noted before, Ṛṣabh is represented at Mohan Bāṛī by feet, not by an anthropomorphic image.[25] Moreover, these footprints are stationed under a *chatrī*-like structure. This is an unusual arrangement, but the fact that it is a plausible arrangement suggests that

Figure 11. Image of Jincandrasūri "Maṇidhārī" at a neighborhood temple in Jaipur

in some respects the Tīrthankars are thought of as belonging to the same category as other deceased ascetics. The physical homologies seen in the arrangements at Mohan Bāṛī suggest a common conceptual substratum. Ṛṣabh is a deceased ascetic too, who has left footprints behind.

The Dādagurus are absolutely central to the beliefs and practices of Śvetāmbar Jains associated with the Khartar Gacch. They are objects of worship, and in some ways are ritually more prominent than the Tīrthankars themselves. To understand their role we must learn something about their place in history, and this in turn requires that we learn something of the history of the Khartar Gacch.

## REFORMERS

The Khartar Gacch was at first a reform movement among ascetics.[26] In medieval times, possibly as early as the eighth century C.E., ascetics known as Caityavāsīs, "temple-dwellers," had become prominent in western India. These were ascetics who, contrary to the Jain ideal of the peripatetic mendicant, lived in permanent establishments. Their leaders were learned, were held in high esteem at court, and in general exercised great influence over the Jain laity. But the Caityavāsīs had their critics as well, and the Khartar Gacch began as a protest movement against what was viewed by critics as the stagnation and backsliding of these false ascetics.

The story begins with a late tenth- to early eleventh-century ascetic named Vardhmānsūri. He was initiated originally as a Caityavāsī, but ultimately left the Caityavāsīs because of his growing disgust at their lax ways. He then became the student of a learned ascetic named Udyotansūri, who taught him "true" Jain doctrine. He later went forth to propagate teachings opposed to those of the Caityavāsīs, and died in 1031 C.E. His most important disciple was Jineśvarsūri, one of the truly great figures of Śvetāmbar history. Said to have been of Brāhmaṇ origin, Jineśvarsūri and his brother apparently met Vardhmānsūri while still boys and were quickly initiated by him. Both went on to distinguished ascetic careers.

Jineśvarsūri was an able scholar and powerful debater, and his most celebrated deed was the defeat of the Caityavāsīs in a famous debate. Vardhmānsūri had decided to confront the Caityavāsīs on their own ground and had gone to Pāṭaṇ with his disciples. This city, then the capital of Gujarat, was a great center for the Caityavāsīs. Because of the Caityavāsīs' influence in the city, Vardhmānsūri and his followers had difficulty finding a place to stay. In the end, however, the scholarly Jineśvar so impressed the king's chief (Brāhmaṇ) priest with his Sanskrit learning that the priest invited the monks to stay with him. The Caityavāsīs then put it about that they were spies dressed as mendicants. When word of this reached King Durlabhrāj, he called his priest, who defended the mendicants. The Caityavāsīs then decided that the best way to get rid of this threat would be to challenge and defeat them in a debate.

The debate was joined in the presence of King Durlabhrāj in a Pārśvanāth temple in the year 1024 C.E. Sūrācārya, the leader of the Caityavāsīs, sat with eighty-three other local Caityavāsīs. Vardhmānsūri and his followers were summoned.[27] When they arrived, the king offered them betel, which apparently the Caityavāsīs were quite accustomed to taking. In response, Vardhmānsūri produced a couplet from the *Śāstras* that said that for celibates, mendicants, and widows, taking betel is equivalent to the sin of eating beef.

As the debate then unfolded,[28] Jineśvar (who carried the burden of the debate) asked the king whether he—the king—followed new political policies or those of his ancestors. The king replied that he followed the policies of his ancestors. Jineśvar pointed out that the followers of Vardhmānsūri were simply trying to do the same thing, namely, to follow the original teachings of the Tīrthankars. Jineśvar then reminded the king that he and his fellows had come from far away and noted that they did not have the books they needed to debate properly. He asked the king to have books brought from the Caityavāsīs' *maṭh* (monastery). The bundle of books was duly produced, and when it was opened the first thing that came to hand was the *Daśavaikalikasūtra,* and from this book the first thing that met the eye was a stanza that read: "An ascetic (*sādhu*) must live in a place that is not specifically for ascetics but which is designed for any other purpose, and in which there are facilities for eating and sleeping, and in which there is a proper designated place to urinate and defecate, and from which women, animals, eunuchs, etc., are forbidden."[29] The king, who was an impartial judge, found this extremely convincing. The king then asked for thrones to be brought for Jineśvar's group to be seated upon. Jineśvar responded that it was improper for monks to sit on thrones and backed up the assertion with a couplet from the *Śāstras*. In the end, Jineśvar's victory was total, and the king took him and his companions under his protection. The Caityavāsīs left the temples and the kingdom, and were replaced with Brāhmaṇ temple priests.[30]

This dissident reforming sect, founded by Vardhmānsūri and consolidated and propagated by Jineśvarsūri, was at first known as the *vidhimārg* (the path of [proper] method).[31] However, it is said that at the time of the great debate the admiring king Durlabhrāj applied the term *khartar* ("fierce") to Jineśvar. This sobriquet later became the name of the *gacch*.

## JINDATTSŪRI

Vardhmānsūri and Jineśvarsūri had many illustrious successors. Among them, however, the ones who stand out most in the ritual life of Jains associated with the Khartar Gacch are the four Dādāgurus. And of the Dādāgurus, none is of greater importance than the first, Jindattsūri.

Jindattsūri was born in 1075 C.E. at a place called Dholkā.[32] His clan was Humbaḍ and his given name was Somcandra. When he was a small boy he once accompanied his mother to discourses being given by some Khartar Gacch nuns. They noticed auspicious marks on the boy, became convinced that he was destined for greatness, and sent news of their discovery to a senior monk named Dharmdevjī Upādhyāy. This monk then came to the village and asked the boy's mother if she would be willing to "give the boy to the *sangh*" (the conventional expression for allowing a child to be initiated). Parental permission was given, and the boy's initiation occurred in 1084 when he was only nine years old.

Somcandra demonstrated cleverness and great independence of mind from the start. His education was put in the hands of an ascetic named Sarvadevgaṇi. Dharmdevjī told Sarvadevgaṇi to educate the boy in every particular of the mendicant's life, and even to take the boy with him to the latrine.[33] Somcandra, however, was very young and ignorant of the rules of ascetic discipline. Knowing no better, he uprooted some plants in the field. In his exasperation, Sarvadev took away the boy's mouth-cloth and broom and told him to go home. The boy responded that if Sarvadev wanted him to go, he'd go, but first he'd like the hair that had been taken from his head (in his initiation ceremony) returned. Sarvadev was highly impressed by this spunky response, as was Dharmdevjī when it was reported to him.

After his studies were completed, Somcandra began his wanderings from village to village. He impressed everyone with his learning, meditation, and piety. As time passed his reputation grew to such an extent that, when Jinvallabhsūri—the leader of the Khartar Gacch at that time—passed away, Somcandra was his logical successor. He attained the status of *ācārya* at Cittauṛ in the year 1112, at which point he acquired the name Jindattsūri and assumed the leadership of the Gacch.

Wishing to know where he should go in his wanderings, the newly elevated Jindattsūri engaged in a program of meditation and fasting. According to the hagiographies, a deceased ascetic named Harisingh-ācārya came to earth from heaven in response. He told Jindattsūri that he should go to Marwar and places like it. Jindattsūri followed this advice, first going to Marwar and then to Nagpur, and later through countless villages and towns. He taught, he protected the Jain faith, and he converted many non-Jains to Jainism. His rainy season sojourns were sources of inspiration in the communities in which they occurred. He performed numerous consecrations of images and initiations of ascetics. He was also a great reformer. Under his influence, large numbers of Caityavāsī *ācāryas* abandoned their former ways and took initiation with him. He had many admirers among great kings and princes. Arṇorāj, the then-ruler of Ajmer, was one of the kings of the period who numbered among his devotees.

He seems to have been tough-minded and earthy, qualities of character that probably served him well in a pattern of life that was surely merciless in its physical and psychological demands. Once in Nagpur a certain rich man presumptuously tried to advise Jindattsūri on how to gain more followers. The monk responded with a verse that reveals a man with a short fuse who did not suffer fools gladly. This verse is translated by Phyllis Granoff (1993: 55) as follows:

> Do not think that just because he has many hangers-on a man is honored in this world
> For see how the sow, surrounded by all her young, still eats shit.

He was, above all, a great worker of miracles, as were all the Dādāgurus. It is extremely important to emphasize that the hagiographies insist that these miracles always had a higher purpose than merely solving someone's worldly problems. From the standpoint of Jainism's highest ideals, ascetics are not supposed to be magicians. As we have already seen in the case of Chagansāgar, the hagiographers must therefore legitimize this power by establishing a Jain context for it. One legitimizing strategy is to accentuate the point that the miraculous power is associated with its possessor's asceticism. Another strategy is to stress that the purpose of the miracles was always to glorify Jain teachings or to help Jainism flourish. The miracle-working ascetic protects Jain laity, defeats Jainism's enemies, and often aids non-Jains, who may become Jains as a result (the subject of the next chapter).

In Jindattsūri's case, however, the hagiographies establish yet another legitimizing frame of reference for magical power. It seems that Vajrasvāmī, a legendary ascetic from centuries earlier, had written a book of ancient knowledge (presumably magical).[34] Because he lacked any disciple who could make proper use of this knowledge, he secreted the book in a pillar in the fort at Cittauṛ. Others had tried and failed to obtain this book, but by means of his own yogic power (*yogbal*) Jindattsūri was able to acquire it and derive powers from it.[35] This tale makes the point that Jindattsūri's power derives both from sources internal to himself (his own yogic ability) and from an interrupted tradition of magically potent ascetics. Legitimacy is conferred on this connection, in turn, because it is embedded in the longer line of disciplic succession connecting Jindattsūri to Lord Mahāvīr.

Many of Jindattsūri's miracles—which cannot all be described here—involved subduing non-Jain powers.[36] An example is his victory over the five *adhiṣṭhāyak pīr*s of the five rivers of Punjab who once tried to disturb him in meditation.[37] It is said that because of his powers of concentration they found it impossible to budge him, and as a result the five *pīr*s conceded defeat by standing before him with hands joined, after which they became his servants. The fact that these non-Jain powers are depicted as *pīr*s, which refers to Muslim saints, may reflect the fact that Muslim influence was particularly strong in this region. It is also said that he subdued fifty-two *bhairav vīr*s (forms of the deity Bhairav), who also became his servants. Bhairav (or Bhairava) is a form of Śiva, and this episode may mirror Jain conflict with the Śaivas, which was ongoing at the time.

Another example was his defeat of sixty-four *yoginī*s: malicious, non-Jain, female supernaturals.[38] The incident occurred in Ujjain, where Jindattsūri had begun a public discourse. He told his listeners that the sixty-four *yoginī*s were coming in order to create a disturbance,[39] and that they should spread sixty-four mats and seat the *yoginī*s on them. The sixty-four arrived disguised as laywomen, and were duly seated on the mats. Jindattsūri cast a spell on them by means of his special power, and then resumed his discourse. When the other listeners rose at the end, the *yoginī*s were unable to leave their seats. They then were ashamed and said to Jindattsūri that although they had come to deceive him they had in fact been deceived themselves. They begged forgiveness and promised that they would assist him in propagating Jainism. This episode possibly reflects Jain opposition to cults of tantric goddesses and may also echo the theme of the taming of the lineage goddesses, which will be explored in the next chapter.

He also used his miraculous powers against Jainism's human opponents. Once at a place called Baḍnagar some Brāhmaṇs tried to disgrace Jindattsūri and the Jain community by having a dead cow placed in front of a Jain temple. In the morning the temple's *pujārī* discovered the outrage. He told the tale to the chief businessman of the city, who in turn told Jindattsūri. By means of his knowledge of how to enter other bodies Jindattsūri caused the cow to rise, walk, and expire again in front of a Śiva temple. Here the opponents are both Brāhmaṇs and Śaivas. In another version of the same story, the Brāhmaṇs put the corpse of a Brāhmaṇ in front of a Jain temple, and Jindattsūri caused the Brāhmaṇ corpse to rise and expire again in front of a "Brāhmaṇ" temple (Granoff 1993: 65).

Jindattsūri even defied the fury of nature on behalf of Jainism. Once, in Ajmer, a fearsome stroke of lightning in the evening threatened a group of laymen performing the rite of *pratikramaṇ*. Jindattsūri caught the lightning under his alms bowl and the rite was able to proceed.

Jindattsūri is said to have had the title of *yugpradhān* (spiritual leader of the age) bestowed upon him in a miraculous fashion.[40] It seems that in order to find out who was the *yugpradhān,* a layman named Nāgdev (Ambaḍ in some accounts) went up to the summit of Girnār[41] and fasted for three days. Pleased by his austerities, the goddess Ambikā Devī appeared and wrote the *yugpradhān*'s name on his hand, saying, "He who can read these letters, know him to be the *yugpradhān.*" Nāgdev traveled far and wide and showed his hand to many learned *ācārya*s, but nobody could read the letters. In the end he went to Pāṭaṇ, where he showed his hand to Jindattsūri. The monk sprinkled *vāskṣep* powder on the letters and they became clear. It was a couplet that read as follows: "He at whose lotus feet all of the gods fall in complete humility, and who is an oasis-like *kalptaru* (wish-fulfilling tree), may that *yugpradhān* who is Śrī Jindattsūri be ever-victorious."

Jindattsūri's life ended at Ajmer in 1154 C.E. When he realized that the end was near, he ceased taking nourishment and died on the eleventh day of the bright fortnight of the month of *Āṣāṛh*. At the time of his cremation, his clothing and mouth-cloth failed to ignite, and they are said to be preserved to this day in Jaisalmer. His successor, Jincandrasūri "Maṇidhārī," established a memorial on the spot on which his body was burned, and this was later made into a proper temple.

After death Jindattsūri became a god. According to one account (Vidyut Prabhā Śrī 1980: 11), Sīmandhar Svāmī (a Tīrthankar currently active and teaching in the continent of Mahāvideh) was once asked by his guardian goddess (*śāsan devī*) where Jindattsūri had been reborn. The omniscient Sīmandhar replied that at the present time he was in *devlok* (heaven), and that after a sojourn there he would take birth in Mahāvideh and there achieve liberation. Another author (Sūryamall 1941: 32 [appendix]) also states that Jindattsūri became a god in the Saudharma Devlok and will ultimately return to the region of Mahāvideh, whence he will attain liberation.

## JINCANDRASŪRI "MAṆIDHĀRĪ"

The second Dādāguru is named Jincandrasūri, but he is popularly known as "Maṇidhārī" because there is said to have been a jewel (*maṇi*) in his forehead from which some of his magical power emanated. He was Jindattsūri's successor, but the personality he projects as a Dādāguru is completely distinct from that of his illustrious predecessor.

According to one account (Nāhṭā and Nāhṭā 1971: 26)—a version strongly reminiscent of the Tīrthankars' birth narratives—Maṇidhārī's advent was known even before it occurred. It seems that a wealthy merchant named Rāmdev once asked Jindattsūri to say which among his disciples was worthy of becoming his successor. The monk replied that such a worthy one had not yet appeared. Rāmdev then asked, "If he's not yet here, then is someone coming from heaven?" "Just so," the monk replied. "How?" Rāmdev asked. Jindattsūri answered that on a particular day the soul who was qualified to be his successor would, having descended from *devlok* (*devlok se cyav kar*), take birth (*avtīraṇ hogā*) in the womb of the wife of Śreṣṭhī Rāsal of Vikrampur (a village near Jaisalmer). After a few days Rāmdev arrived at the house of Śreṣṭhī Rāsal. When asked why he had come, he told Rāsal to call his wife. When she appeared he garlanded her and paid her homage. Rāmdev then explained about Jindattsūri's prediction.

Maṇidhārī was born in 1140 in Vikrampur. His birth name was Sūryakumār and his clan was Mahatīyāṇ. He came into contact with Jindattsūri early in his childhood. Jindattsūri had spent the rainy season retreat in Vikrampur, and Sūryakumār's mother was a daily attendee at his discourses. Jindattsūri saw the boy with his mother and instantly knew (by means of his *jñānbal,* "knowledge-power") that the boy would be his successor. A slightly different version places this encounter in Ajmer where Sūryakumār had been taken by his mother and father.

Sūryakumār was initiated at the age of only six by Jindattsūri himself, and because of his brilliance in his studies he gained the status of *ācārya* (also conferred by Jindattsūri) and the name Jincandrasūri at the age of eight. At that time Jindattsūri warned him never to go to Yoginīpur-Delhi (Delhi is usually called Yoginīpur in these accounts) because he knew that Maṇidhārī would meet his death there. His subsequent career was very similar to that of other great ascetics. His wanderings took him to many towns and villages and his rainy season visitations were sources of inspiration in the communities blessed with his presence. He propagated Jainism, admonished backsliders, defended the faith, and consecrated numerous temples, including Jindattsūri's memorial in Ajmer. He seems to have done relatively little writing, but is reputed to have been quite learned, and is said to have been victorious in a religious debate (*śāstrārth*) held at Rudrapallī. He converted large numbers of new Jains, and his teachings inspired many laypersons to take initiation as mendicants.

As did Jindattsūri, Maṇidhārī possessed formidable magical powers, which—as is the case with all the Dādāgurus—he employed for the benefit of Jains and Jainism. His most famous miracle occurred when he was traveling in the direction of Delhi with a pilgrimage party. When the group halted near a village named Vorsidān, some bandits came near. The monk told his companions to calm their fears because Jindattsūri (that is, *his* guru) would protect them. With his stick he drew a line around the whole group, and the bandits could not see them even though they were able to see the bandits.

As Jindattsūri had predicted, Maṇidhārī's life ended at Delhi. When he and his party came near Delhi,[42] King Madanpāl arrived at the spot on an elephant to receive *darśan*. In the age-old pattern of kings falling under the spell of great mendicants, he became influenced (*prabhāvit*) by Maṇidhārī's teachings and invited him to enter the city. Remembering Jindattsūri's order not to enter Delhi, Maṇidhārī at first remained silent. But the king repeated his invitation, and at last the monk agreed to fulfill the king's wish.[43] As a result, he spent the rainy season of 1166 in Delhi.

One of his more notable achievements during his sojourn in Delhi was his subjugation of a non-Jain goddess.[44] On the ninth day of Navrātrī[45] while on the way to the latrine he suddenly saw two *mithyādṛṣṭi* goddesses (goddesses holding false views) fighting over some meat, and he was able to bring one of them under his influence. She became pacified (*śānt-citt*) and declared that she would give up animal sacrifice. He told her to take up residence in a pillar in a particular Pārśvanāth temple, and later he instructed his leading lay disciples to have an image made for her. They did so, and he performed the consecration rite at which time he bestowed the name Atibal on the goddess. The laymen made arrangements for a fine food offering (*bhog*) for her, and afterwards she was always ready to fulfill the wishes of her worshipers.

Maṇidhārī died in Delhi on the fourteenth day of the dark fortnight of the lunar month of Bhādrapad (August/September) in the year 1166. Before his death he had told his disciples that his funeral procession should not stop on the way to the burning grounds, and he also said that a *pātra* (an ascetic's alms bowl) of milk should be kept ready to receive the gemstone that would emerge from his forehead when the burning began. In addition, he predicted that Delhi's populated area would never grow beyond the point at which his body was burned. When he died his followers forgot the injunction not to set his bier down, and they lowered it to the ground to take rest at a place called Maṇek Cauk near Delhi. There his bier stuck to the earth, and not even the combined efforts of four elephants could move it. The king ordered the body burned on that spot, and this is where the Mehraulī *dādābāṛī* is located today. It is said that his followers had also forgotten about the bowl of milk for the gemstone, and that when it emerged it fell into the hands of some other "yogī." According to one account, it was later recovered by his successor, Jinpatisūri (Nāhṭā and Nāhṭā 1971: 17–18). The ultimate destiny of the gem is unclear.[46]

## JINKUŚALSŪRI

The third Dādāguru, Jinkuśalsūri, was born in 1280 in the Marwari village of Gaṛh Sivāṇā. His name was Karmaṇ and his clan was Chājeṛ.[47] As it happens, his paternal uncle was an *ācārya* named Jincandrasūri (not to be confused with Jincandrasūri "Maṇidhārī"), who at that time was the leader of the Khartar Gacch. The boy fell under his uncle's influence, and in the year 1290 (some sources say 1288) he took initiation in the village of his birth and acquired the name Kuśalkīrti. He excelled in his studies and got the title *vācanācārya* (one who interprets texts) in 1318. When Jincandrasūri realized that his end was near, he designated Kuśalkīrti as his successor. Kuśalkīrti achieved the status of *ācārya* and acquired the name Jinkuśalsūri in 1320 at Pāṭaṇ.

His career consisted of the usual travels, rainy season sojourns, temple consecrations, and initiations with which we have become familiar. As did the other Dādāgurus, he performed many miracles on behalf of Jains and Jainism. Most accounts of his life give special emphasis to two great pilgrimage parties (*sangh*s) of which he was the spiritual leader.[48] The first was organized by a Śrīmāl businessman of Delhi named Raypati. He had obtained a *farmān* from the emperor Ghiyasuddin Tughluq saying that all necessary assistance should be given to the pilgrimage party, which would be under the leadership of Jinkuśalsūri and would be traveling to Śatruñjaya and Girnār. Having obtained the *farmān*, and also Jinkuśalsuri's approval, Raypati brought his party from Delhi to Pāṭaṇ. There Jinkuśalsūri joined with his group of monks. It is reported that the expedition included seventeen monks, nineteen nuns, 500 carts, and 100 horses (Vinaysāgar 1959: 154). En route he performed various image consecrations, and when they arrived at Śatruñjaya he consecrated images of Jinpatisūri, Jineśvarsūri, and other gurus of the past.[49] After proceeding on to Girnār, the pilgrimage was completed. Jinkuśalsūri then returned to Pāṭaṇ, and the pilgrimage party returned to Delhi. Later a rich layman from Bhīmpallī obtained a *farmān* from the emperor for a similar pilgrimage party which he took from Bhīmpallī to Śatruñjaya under Jinkuśalsūri's leadership.

There were serious problems of backsliding among the Jains of Sindh at the time of Jinkuśalsūri's life. He was invited to go there by local Jains, and apparently succeeded in bringing about a major revival. It is said that because of his extraordinary charisma (*prabhāv*) he was able to convert 50,000 new Jains. He was also able to bring White and Black Bhairav, two somewhat sinister Hindu deities, under his control. These are often pictured with him—White Bhairav on his right hand, Black Bhairav on his left—each with his mascot dog and each with hands folded in the standard gesture of supplication and homage. This again reflects the theme of competition with Śaiva or Śākta traditions.

He died in Sindh in 1332. He had gone to Derāur (Devrājpur) to spend the rains there, and—knowing that his end was near—he stayed on. He named a fifteen-year-old disciple as his successor, and died on the fifth day of the dark fortnight of the lunar month of Phālgun (February/March).[50]

Since then he has been particularly prone to appearances in visions. The most celebrated of these occurred in Sindh when a certain Samaysundarjī and some companions tried to cross the "five rivers" in a boat. A great storm blew up and the boat was on the verge of sinking. Samaysundarjī meditated on Jinkuśalsūri and immediately the monk's *devātmā* (soul in its current deity status) appeared and saved the boat. This episode is a staple of the hagiographies and is frequently portrayed in the illustrations of the Dādāgurus' deeds that adorn temples. It reflects an abiding metaphor in South Asian religions, namely that of a devotee's "rescue" from the "ocean of existence" (*saṃsār sāgar*). Also, after his death he is said to have appeared in a vision at Mālpurā, where an important *dādābāṛī* was subsequently built, a point to which we shall return later.

## JINCANDRASŪRI II

The fourth and last Dādāguru was Jincandrasūri II. Readers will recall that Jincandrasūri was also the name of the second Dādāguru. Just as the earlier Jincandarasūri is distinguished by the appellation *maṇidhārī* ("gem-bearing"), the later Jincandrasūri is sometimes called *akbar pratibodhak* ("the influencer of Akbar") to distinguish him from his predecessor. He was born in 1541 in a village called Khetsar (or Khetāsar) in the former Jodhpur State. His birth name was Sultān Kumār, and his *gotra* was Rihaḍ.[51] In 1547 the leader of the Khartar Gacch at that time, Jinmāṇikyasūri, came to the village. The boy was influenced by his discourses, and was initiated forthwith. He then traveled with Jinmāṇikyasūri, and shortly after his guru's death in 1555 he was proclaimed Jinmāṇikyasūri's successor.

He was a great reformer who instituted strict new rules for mendicants and ably defended the Khartar Gacch against its detractors. Among his other achievements was his humbling of a distinguished Tapā Gacch mendicant by the name of Dharmsāgarjī. In 1560 the latter opined that Abhaydevsūri[52] did not belong to the Khartar Gacch. Jincandrasūri called a debate (*śāstrārth*) to settle the matter. Dharmsāgarjī failed to show up, and Jincandrasūri thus proved his point.

Word of his extraordinary qualities eventually reached the court of Akbar the Great. The emperor invited Jincandrasūri into his presence at Lahore, where he arrived in 1591. He impressed the emperor greatly and caused Jainism to grow in his esteem.[53] At one point Akbar's son, Salīm, fathered a daughter under inauspicious astrological influences, and the court astrologers urged that the infant be killed. Because of Jincandrasūri's teachings, however, Akbar instead had a special *pūjā* (something called the *aṣṭottrī snātra*) performed in a Jain temple to ameliorate the problem. Because of Jincandrasūri's influence Akbar protected Jain places of pilgrimage and gave orders that the ceremonies and observances of Jains were not to be hindered. He also forbade the slaughter of animals for a period of one week per year. According to Khartar Gacch sources, Akbar even bestowed the title *yugpradhān* on Jincandrasūri.

There were, of course, many miracles—performed, as always, for the benefit of Jainism. The most celebrated of his miracles took place at Akbar's court. We have seen that the miracles of the first three Dādāgurus were frequently designed to protect Jainism from its enemies, who, as the hagiographers portray them, were preeminently Brāhmaṇs, Śaivas, and Śāktas. Now, in a later and very different historical milieu, the opponents are Muslim clerics.[54] For example, once when Jincandrasūri was entering court he suddenly stopped. When Akbar asked him to proceed he said that he could not because there were *jīvs* (embodied souls) in an underground drain and that he could not walk over them. An envious Kājī (Muslim judge) had in fact concealed a goat there. The Kājī asked "how many *jīvs*?" and the monk said "three." The Kājī was quite surprised because he had placed only a single goat there, but when the drain was opened there were indeed three. The goat had been pregnant and had given birth. Akbar was duly impressed.

In another, similar incident, a Kājī tried to discredit the monk by using *mantra*-power to cause his own hat to fly up into the air and hover there. The monk sent his ascetic's broom flying after the hat; the broom retrieved the hat and set it back on the Kājī's head.[55] And once, when asked the date by some Maulvī (a Muslim scholar), one of Jincandrasūri's disciples had a slip of the tongue and said that it was the full moon day rather than the new moon that it actually was. The Maulvī then went around the city saying mockingly that a Jain monk had said that a full moon would appear in the sky on the new moon date. Even the emperor Akbar heard of this, and so for the sake of Jainism's reputation Jincandrasūri had to do something. That night he obtained a gold platter from a layman's house and threw it into the air where it shone like the moon. Akbar had the light tested, and it was discovered that the "moon" remained full for a distance of twenty-four miles.

The hagiographies also report that he exercised a good influence on Akbar's son and successor, Jahāngīr. Jahāngīr had once seen an ascetic in Jain dress engaged in some kind of dubious conduct, and as a result, in 1611, he ordered that all Jain monks should become householders or be expelled from the empire. Hearing of this, Jincandrasūri rushed to Agra to meet with the emperor. In order to prevent a breach of his imperial order, Jahāngīr forbade the monk to use the imperial road. Jincandrasūri thereupon spread his woolen mat on the Jumna river and floated to his imperial audience. The emperor was surprised and pleased. The monk then made the point that the entire Jain community should not be held accountable for one person's fault, and the emperor, agreeing, rescinded his earlier order.

While staying in the Marwari village of Bīlāḍā for the rainy season retreat of 1613, Jincandrasūri realized that his end was near. He called his disciples and lay followers together and informed them of his impending death. He named his successor, asked the pardon of the *caturvidh sangh* (the fourfold Jain community) and the *caurāsī lākh jīv yoni*s (the 8.4 million forms of life), fasted, and died on the second day of the dark fortnight of the lunar month of Āśvin (September/October).

## A RITUAL SUBCULTURE

Worship of the Dādāgurus is extremely popular among Jaipur's Śvetāmbar Jains. In fact, their worship is the principal religious activity of many Jains, and even members of the nontemple-going sects (the Sthānakvāsīs and Terāpanthīs) sometimes visit their shrines.[56] Although in some ways Jinkuśalsūri is the most popular of the four, they in fact blend into a single, generic Dādāgurudev.

The reason for the Dādāgurus' popularity is simple: They are powerful beings to whom one can appeal directly for assistance in one's worldly affairs. Moreover, there seems to be little effort to disguise the goal of gaining assistance in worldly matters from the Dādāgurus. Although some of my Jaipur friends claimed to worship the Dādāgurus solely for such reasons as "peace of mind,"[57] most devotees spoke with unembarrassed candor about the material benefits of worshiping the Dādāgurus. The general view of the Dādāgurus is that they will give you wealth, health, success in business, or any of your heart's desires (*manokāmnā*s). In praise verses they are often compared to the *kalptaru,* the wish-fulfilling tree, or to the fabled *cintāmaṇi,* the jewel that grants all desires. I have been told by tough, capable businessmen that everything they have they owe to the Dādāgurus.

The Dādāgurus are able to render assistance to their worshipers because, unlike the Tirthankars, they are unliberated and can therefore engage in transactions with worshipers.[58] They are, one might say, vastly magnified versions of Chagansāgar. They, too, are powerful and virtuous ascetics with whom ritual relationships can be maintained after death. When they died they ascended to the realm of the gods; after a sojourn there they will return to human bodies and achieve final release. Most Jains are not clear about exactly where the Dādāgurus currently are or what their status is, and the average devotee will simply say they are in "heaven." But the important thing is that although they are bound for liberation, they are not liberated yet; in the meantime they can and do dispense divine aid to their worshipers.

## MODES OF WORSHIP

Many devotees worship the Dādāgurus by simply dropping by a temple or *dādābāṛī* to take their *darśan*.[59] In doing so, devotees must always honor the Tīrthankars' images before approaching the Dādāgurus, a rule that acknowledges the Tīrthankars' supremacy. While taking *darśan,* devotees often sing a text such as the *Dādāguru Iktīsā* (a standard panegyric of thirty-one verses).[60] After singing, the worshiper usually enters the Dādāgurus' shrine, where a lamp is likely to be burning and incense smoldering in a holder. Worshipers typically proffer the incense in an abbreviated *dhūp pūjā*. Many worshipers also place their foreheads on the feet of the image, and frequently they rub the frame of the shrine with their hands and then bring their hands to their eyes and forehead. This latter gesture suggests the taking onto themselves of a liquid-like substance or power.

A temple visitor might also perform a complete individual rite of worship, which is typically a version of the eightfold worship. The image is bathed and then anointed with sandalwood paste. When the image is anthropomorphic, the sandalwood paste is applied as it would be to a Tīrthankar image. In the case of footprint images, the dots are put on nine positions on each foot.[61] Fruit and other offerings are made just as they might be before a Tīrthankar's image. The only difference is that there should be no crescent and dot formed at the top of the diagram during *akṣat pūjā*. A flag should be formed instead. This, of course, is because Dādāgurus have not achieved liberation.[62]

*Dādābāṛīs* tend to be quite crowded on Monday evenings because Monday is regarded as an especially appropriate day for worshiping the Dādāgurus. Young people (especially young men) are present in large numbers, suggesting that the cult of the Dādāgurus is currently in a flourishing state. There are also special occasions. For example, at a *dādābāṛī* near my residence in Jaipur an all-night *bhajan*-singing session (*jāgraṇ*) occurred every full-moon night. Many *dādābāṛīs* sponsor annual fairs (*melās*), and major rites for the Dādāgurus typically occur on the anniversaries of temple founding days. The aforementioned *dādābāṛī* near my residence in Jaipur sponsors major rites—some dedicated to the Dādāgurus and some focused on the Tīrthankars—on every anniversary of its consecration day.

In addition, individuals or individual families often sponsor special rites of worship for the Dādāgurus. This can be done for a variety reasons. One such family rite I attended, for example, was sponsored by a man in memory of his brother who had died the year before. However, special Dādāguru rites are probably most frequently undertaken by individuals or families in fulfillment of a vow made to the Dādāgurus in hopes of gaining assistance in some worldly matter. This can be illness, a business matter, the desire for progeny, or whatever. The usual format is that the supplicant promises to sponsor such a rite of worship (or perform some other pious act) if the request is granted; if the request is granted, the promise has to be kept.

The standard rite performed on special occasions for the Dādāgurus is known as the *dādāguru baṛī pūjā,* which means the Dādāgurus' "great" (*baṛī*) rite of worship (*pūjā*). Its focus is an image or images of the Dādāgurus, and it is usually performed in a temple. The object of worship can be an anthropomorphic image of one of the Dādāgurus or foot images. The foot images are sometimes miniatures installed in little portable *chatrīs*; these may be placed atop a worshiping stand, just as a Tīrthankar's image is. The rite itself consists of a total of eleven ritual acts. The first eight duplicate the eightfold worship: The image (or foot image) is bathed, anointed with sandal paste, and then receives the usual offerings of flowers, incense, lamp, rice, sweets, and fruit. Then follow offerings of cloth, flags, and a final libation. The rite ends with the conventional lamp offering.

The manner in which the rite is performed is more or less the same as the procedure we have already seen in Pārśvanāth's five-*kalyāṇak pūjā*. This is a congregational rite, and there are two levels of participation: *Pūjā* principals perform the ritual acts while *pūjā* participants sing the ritual's text. As in other such rites, songs not included in the text are frequently added, and phrases from individual lines may be repeated for devotional effect. At the completion of the singing, a Sanskrit verse is recited by someone in the congregation followed by a Sanskrit formula of offering. At this point a gong is sounded and the appropriate ritual act performed. As with other rites of worship, ascetics may be present, and when they are they usually sing the Sanskrit couplet coming just before the offering formula, but never the offering formula itself. The same procedure is followed for each of the eleven parts of the rite.

The rite's text, which is easy for performers to follow, was written about ninety years ago by a *yati* signing himself "Ṛddhisār."[63] The text has been produced in many editions. Although I have seen a printed version of another Dādāguru *pūjā,* I have never seen any but Ṛddhisār's performed. Many devotees know it by heart.[64] Unlike the texts of the *snātra pūjā* and Pārśvanāth's five-*kalyāṇak pūjā,* Ṛddhisār's text does not tell a coherent story, although there is a rough chronological framework.

The rite begins with the sequence known as *sthāpnā,* which invokes the Dādāgurus' presence, and we should note that Ṛddhisār's text includes appropriate *sthāpnā* stanzas, which (as we saw earlier) are not included in the texts of rites for the Tīrthankars. The fact that Ṛddhisār included such verses in his text reflects the crucial idea that the Dādāgurus, in contrast to the Tīrthankars, can in some sense actually be invoked by worshipers.

After this preliminary, the rite properly speaking begins. The first two songs (preceding the image's bath) describe the line of spiritual succession (not given in its entirety) connecting the Dādāgurus with Sudharmā (called Saudharmā Munipati in the text). The text then goes on to mention the founding of the Khartar Gacch and some of its most illustrious early figures. The text refers to Vardhmānsūri, to Jineśvarsūri and his celebrated defeat of the Caityavāsīs in debate, and others too. These details are given in the rite's opening stanzas, and their point is to establish the Dādāgurus' position in a line of succession that includes the Khartar Gacch and that can be traced back putatively to the ultimate source of all sacredness, Lord Mahāvīr. Following this are brief references to the birth, parentage, and *gotra*s (clans) of the four Dādāgurus, plus allusions to some of their miracles. At this point the singing of the text ceases; the Sanskrit verse is then sung, after which one of the participants utters the formula of offering. At this point the image is bathed, which is the first of the eleven physical acts of the rite.

From this point on, the rite's text is mostly a compilation of the many miracles performed by the Dādāgurus. As best I can determine, most of the miracles mentioned in the rite's first eight sections (up to the offering of fruit) are, in legend, associated with the first Dādāguru, Jindattsūri. The three later Dādāgurus are more prominent in the later sections of the text, and in this sense the rite's organization is semihistorical. (The very last miracle mentioned in the entire text, however, is Jindattsūri's restoration of sight to a blind man in Surat.) From the organization of the text, I strongly suspect that it was originally designed as a rite of worship of the standard eight parts (that is, replicating the eightfold worship), probably dedicated to Jindattsūri. At some point other material was added. But what is important to devotees who sing this text today is the miracles themselves, and not the order in which they occurred, or even which Dādāguru was responsible for which ones. The basic idea is that this same miraculous power can work for the benefit of those who perform the rite.

The miracles mentioned by Ṛddhisār's text are many and are well known to most devotees. They are recounted in various hagiographies, and several have already been discussed in the Dādāgurus' biographical sketches given earlier in this chapter. Most devotees, however, know of these miracles not from the hagiographies but from the *pūjā* itself and also from popular art. Pictures of the Dādāgurus performing the best known of their miracles are conspicuously displayed at most *dādābāṛīs*. The exterior walls of the most popular Dādāguru shrine in Jaipur are covered with such pictures.[65] Anthologies of these pictures are also published from time to time (such as Kāntisāgar n.d.). The worshiper sings of miracles in the text and sees them depicted on the walls. The worshiper hopes for such miracles to come his or her way. This hope is the heart and soul of the Dādāgurus' cult.

## ASCETICS AS GODS

If we focus solely on the worshipers, there is hardly any difference at all between the worship of the Dādāgurus and the Tīrthankars. Here those who worship are the same lay men and women playing the same role as admirers and supporters of ascetics. We are dealing, that is, with the same basic ritual culture. But there is nonetheless a striking contrast. The Dādāgurus are in some ways very Tīrthankar-like.[66] However, because of their unliberated status, their relationship with worshipers is very different, as are the meanings that are assigned to that relationship. To put it otherwise, the cults of the Dādāgurus and the Tīrthankars are truly quite different in content and spirit, despite their formal similarities. For this reason, the cult of the Dādāgurus emerges as a subordinate and partially separate ritual subculture.

Perhaps the most striking difference is that soteriology is displaced by the miraculous fulfillment of worldly desires. As we have seen, normative interpretations of the eightfold worship stress the theme of liberation. The text of the Dādāgurus' worship, however, is focused on magic. As in the case of Chagansāgar, this is sanitized magic, legitimized in Jain terms. In the hagiographies the magic tends to be rationalized as a means of promulgating and protecting Jainism. In the cult of the Dādāgurus this same magic is refocused as a source of aid to individuals. Long ago the Dādāgurus came to the aid of Jains (or, as we shall see in the next chapter, Jains-to-be) in times of difficulty. The position of the worshiper now is analogous to that of those whom the Dādāgurus aided then; they too hope for the Dādāgurus' miraculous assistance. Typical phrasings from the hagiographies expressing this idea are *bhay se mukt karnā* (to liberate from fear) and *dukh se mukt karnā* (to liberate from sorrow). The term *mukt,* of course, can also mean "liberated" in the soteriological sense. It is therefore possible to say that liberation from worldly fears and problems replaces liberation from the world's bondage as a central theme in the Dādāgurus' cult.

The theme of world renunciation is also given a different context in the cult of the Dādāgurus. In the modern hagiographies the Dādāgurus' magical abilities are directly associated with asceticism; their power, for example, is called *yogbal* (power of *yoga*) or *tapobal* (power of asceticism).[67] Thus we see that their asceticism has been decoupled from direct association with the path of liberation and instead has been linked with magical power. This magical power, in turn is connected directly with the worldly well-being of those whom the Dādāgurus assist. This, indeed, is the whole point of their cult. While worship of the Tīrthankars tends to be rationalized as an act of renunciation (*tyāg*), worshiping the Dādāgurus is based on the desire for miraculous intervention in one's worldly affairs; it is about getting things, not giving things up.

All this rests on the base of a relationship between worshiper and object of worship fundamentally different from that obtaining in the cult of the Tīrthankars. The worship of the Dādāgurus is not reflexive; the benefits bestowed come from the object of worship, not from the worshiper himself or herself (as in the case of the eightfold worship).[68] As we have noted, this is possible because the Dādāgurus, unlike the Tīrthankars, are unliberated, and are therefore present in the world and available for transactions with worshipers. Their worldly presence is signaled in several ways in the rite itself. The inclusion of *sthāpnā* stanzas in the rite's text reflects the sense that they can actually be invoked at the site of a rite of worship. Moreover, although rice is offered to the Dādāgurus as it is to the Tīrthankars, there is a significant difference in the way it is offered. As noted already, in the case of the Dādāgurus the crescent and dot at the top of the diagram (standing for the liberated state) are omitted and replaced by a representation of a flag, an explicit acknowledgment of their unliberated state.[69]

The difference between the Dādāgurus and the Tīrthankars is most explicitly evident in the treatment of food offerings. As we know, when food is offered in the eightfold worship and in other rites directed at the Tīrthankars, it is never recovered by worshipers and consumed; according to the ambient ideology of the rite, the food is renounced, not offered in the expectation of transformation and return. In the case of the Dādāgurus, however, food offerings can be recovered and consumed. The only prohibition that seems to apply is that the retrieved offerings should not be consumed within the temple or shrine itself. Sometimes devotees simply take the offered sweets out of the temple at the end of a rite. At the end of major Dādāguru-*pūjā*s, edible offerings are often distributed at the temple gate as people leave. Experienced ritualists have told me that a more acceptable procedure is for only a small portion of the offering to be taken into the temple; some incense ash can then be taken from the Dādāgurus' altar and sprinkled on the larger portion remaining outside, which can be distributed to devotees. But however it is done, the crucial point is that the Dādāgurus belong to the same world of giving and taking as their worshipers. They can therefore engage in transactions and confer blessings through returned offerings.[70]

Indeed, so present are the Dādāgurus in their worshipers' world that individuals sometimes encounter them in person. Certain *dādābāṛī*s are reputed to be especially miraculous (*camatkārī*), and among these is the *dādābāṛī* at Mālpurā mentioned earlier.[71] This *dādābāṛī* originated in a miraculous fashion. According to one version, fifteen days after Dādāguru Jinkuśalsūri's death at Derāur (now in Pakistan), he miraculously appeared to a Brāhmaṇ at Mālpurā and indicated where a stone with his footprints was buried. He said that this place would be his principal place of worship and the place where his miracles (*camatkār*s) would occur. The *dādābāṛī* was then established with these footprints as the principal objects of worship, and the descendants of the Brāhmaṇ became the shrine's *pujārī*s.[72]

Jinkuśalsūri still frequents the vicinity. For example, at this same *dādābāṛī* a devotee told me of how he once got lost in the darkness while on a pilgrimage there from Jaipur. He was approached by a small boy, dressed in white, who pointed out the way; this was Jinkuśalsūri. Reports of such sightings are common, especially of Jinkuśalsūri, who seems to have a special propensity for visual manifestations.

The Dādāgurus are visualized as ascetics in their posthumous state. I have no survey data on visions of the Dādāgurus, but most informants seem to believe that when they appear they appear as ascetics.[73] The white dress in the above mentioned appearance suggests mendicant garb. In a frequently reproduced picture of Jinkuśalsūri's famous post-mortem rescue of devotees in a sinking boat (Kāntisāgar, n.d., illustration 22, and found in many other collections), the Dādāguru is portrayed as a mendicant, floating among the clouds in the sky with a beam of force emanating from his upraised right hand. And in one line of Ṛddhisār's text (*dhvaj pūjā*, verse 4), one of the Dādāgurus manifests himself in white clothes with a saffron mark on his forehead and wearing a garland of flowers. When I asked a knowledgeable friend about this latter line, he pointed out that this is simply what people see when they see the Dādāgurus' images—that is, images of ascetics with marks of worship—in temples.

At first glance these manifestations of the Dādāgurus as ascetics are puzzling. The Dādāgurus become gods after death, but gods, on first principles, cannot be ascetics. When I raised this issue with friends and acquaintances, they saw the point of my query, but they had clearly never given much thought to the matter. One friend remarked in response that the Dādāgurus "appear as we remember them," by which he meant to say that they are remembered as they were in life—as ascetics. It would seem, therefore, that in the imaginations of devotees, the Dādāgurus represent figures in whom the identities of ascetic and deity are somehow quite unproblematically fused. I suggest that this is an important fact.

What kind of beings are the Dādāgurus? We know that they are powerful ascetics to whom Jains (or Jains-to-be) can appeal for aid.[74] But in this they are not unique, for they are not the only powerful beings to whom Jains appeal directly for assistance in worldly matters. As we know, the Jain pantheon includes various deities who will also come to the aid of pious devotees. In this sense the Dādāgurus are simply part of a larger pantheon of unliberated deities. In fact, they are often called Gurudev or Dādāgurudev, the term *dev* meaning "deity." Frequently the term *devātmā* is used to describe the Dādāgurus in postmortem manifestations. Many of my informants compared the Dādāgurus directly to the Tīrthankars' attendant deities (*adhiṣṭhāyak dev*s) and to the Bhairavs who guard temple precincts.

But the matter does not end here. The cult of the Dādāgurus has a centrality in the religious life of Jaipur's Śvetāmbar Jains that other unliberated deities do not, and this is something that has to be explained. I suggest that one of the reasons for this is that although they are deities they are not *merely* deities like any others. The crucial difference is that they are beings who behave as deities but, because they are ascetics, belong to the category of beings who are (unlike deities) truly worthy of worship.[75]

The tendency of devotees to visualize the Dādāgurus, even in their present state, as ascetics is a significant datum. It indicates that, in the minds of devotees, the Dādāgurus' mendicant status is crucial to who they are. They are powerful beings who aid their worshipers. This power is partly legitimized in Jain terms by the fact that the paradigm for its exercise is the promulgation and protection of Jainism. This, however, is also true of other unliberated deities. More fundamental is the fact that their power is linked to their asceticism. Their asceticism, in turn, connects them—through a disciplic lineage (as Ṛddhisār's text asserts)—to Lord Mahāvīr, the last Tīrthankar of our region and era. The Tīrthankars are the very model of worship-worthiness. Thus, through the links of this chain, the Dādāgurus are beings in whom helpful powers and worship-worthiness are connected. This is not true of the other unliberated deities. The Dādāgurus therefore offer the possibility of pursuing worldly interests through a mode of worship that, because it is focused on them—that is, on them as ascetics—is consistent with the tradition's commitment to the idea that asceticism is at the heart of worship-worthiness.

It is sometimes said, often by Jains themselves, that the cults of the other helpful deities are simply Hinduistic add-ons: sops to the ignorant, and not truly Jain. Whether this is true or not, it points to the truly essential thing about the Dādāgurus' role in the tradition to which they belong. As beings in whom the attributes of ascetics and deities are fused, they provide a way of seeking worldly help from powerful beings that is fundamentally in tune with Jainism's dominant values, which are ascetic values.

## TIME AND THE DĀDĀGURUS

Another important difference between Tīrthankar-worship and the cult of the Dādāgurus is the temporal frame of reference. Consider the contrast between Pārśvanāth's five-*kalyāṇak pūjā* and Ṛddhisār's *pūjā* of the Dādāgurus. Each rite begins with what we might call its own "prehistory." This establishes a deeper temporal context for the events with which the rite is principally concerned. In the case of the five-*kalyāṇak pūjā,* this consists of Pāśvanāth's previous births, beginning with his first contact with Jain teachings and culminating in his acquisition of the *tīrthankar nām karm,* which he then carries (with one heavenly birth as a god intervening) into his final lifetime. In Ṛddhisār's *pūjā,* the structural equivalent of this is the establishment of a line of spiritual succession linking the Dādāgurus with Lord Mahāvīr, who is the ultimate source of their sacred power. It is of interest in this context that a succession of transmigratory existences is sometimes called a *paramparā,* a "tradition," which is the expression also used for ascetic lineages. The five-*kalyāṇak pūjā* of Pārśvanāth begins in "transmigratory time"; its equivalent is "historical/legendary time" in Ṛddhisār's *pūjā.* The transmigratory "lineage" of Pārśvanāth's soul becomes, in Ṛddhisār's *pūjā,* disciplic succession.

There is another parallel. There are of course no *kalyāṇak*s in Ṛddhisār's *pūjā,* nor can there be. Only the Tīrthankars have *kalyāṇak*s, which indeed are definitive of the status of Tīrthankar. In Ṛddhisār's *pūjā,* however, the functional equivalent of the *kalyāṇak*s is clearly the miracles. The Tīrthankars' *pūjā* celebrates *kalyāṇak*s; the Dādāgurus' *pūjā* celebrates miracles. And, as it turns out, both the *kalyāṇak*s and the miracles left significant traces behind. One can say that the Tīrthankars' *kalyāṇak*s still reverberate in the cosmos. The Tīrthankars are completely and utterly gone, but their *kalyāṇ*—a kind of beneficent power brought into being by their lives—remains, especially in the ascetic lineages that connect our time with theirs and transmit their teachings to us. The Dādāgurus, not so completely gone, have also left behind a miraculous power that is manifested as a benevolent force in the lives of their devotees.

There was, moreover, something else that the Dādāgurus left behind in parallel with the Tīrthankars: a Jain social order. This involves an aspect of the Dādāgurus' miracles that we have mentioned only in passing thus far. Many of these miracles involved the conversion of non-Jains into Jains. Ṛddhisār's *pūjā,* for example, tells of an incident in which Jindattsūri quelled a cholera epidemic in Vikrampur, which resulted in many conversions and initiations. He cured a prince of leprosy, the text says, and the king and ten thousand families then became Jains. He converted Cauhān, Bhāṭī, Pamār, Īndā, Rāṭhor, Śiśodiyā, and Solankī kings. He cured various diseases, and Brāhmaṇs, Kṣatriyas, and Maheśvaris became Jains. The text asserts—as do the hagiographies—that he created 130,000 laymen linked with the Khartar Gacch (as the text puts it, "130,000 *śrāvak*s of the Khartar Sangh").

It is clear that these conversions have a very special place in Ṛddhisār's text. Although the text is not very well structured, the section leading up to the offering of fruit differs from others. We have already seen that the offering of fruit plays a special role in Jain worship. It is the last act of the eightfold worship, and is said to represent liberation, the rite's "fruit." In Ṛddhisār's text, the section of the rite in which fruit is offered (*phal pūjā*) is exclusively concerned with conversions, and nowhere else in the text are references to conversions so abundant. By implication, Jain clans are the ultimate "fruit" of the Dādāgurus' endeavors. This is the subject of the next chapter.

CHAPTER FOUR

# Valor

## *The Transformation of Warrior-Kings*

It is a striking fact that most of the Śvetāmbar Jains of Rajasthan consider themselves to be—like the Tīrthankars, although in a different sense—transmuted warrior-kings. The Jains are identified by others, and identify themselves, as belonging to the Vaiśya *varṇa,* the ancient social category of merchants and traders. Nevertheless, almost all the Osvāl Jains—and members of other Jain castes as well, Śvetāmbar and Digambar—trace their descent to the Rājpūts. The Rājpūts are the royal and martial aristocracy of Rajasthan and are regarded as perfect exemplars of the Kṣatriya *varṇa,* the ancient social category of rulers and warriors.

The Jains and Rājpūts of Rajasthan have been in close contact for centuries, and their relationship is highly complex and in some ways contradictory. At one level, Rājpūt and Jain identities are radically opposed; at another level, they join. This chapter deals with Osvāl legends of their Rājpūt origin. These legends provide a culturally plausible account of Rājpūt-Jain connectedness. This account, in turn, draws deeply on images of kingship and kingly choice that are, as we have seen in previous chapters, central to the Jain view of the world. In this context, Jainism itself can be seen as a kind of origin myth for Jain social groups. To those who believe that Jainism is merely a soteriology, this will be a surprising development.

## KINGS WHO GIVE UP MEAT

Opposition between Rājpūt and Jain identity arises from the centrality to Jain life of the norm of *ahiṃsā,* nonviolence. *Ahiṃsā,* as we know, is a basic tenet of Jainism as a religious system. It is more than just a matter of religious doctrine, however, for *ahiṃsā* is also a cultural value that is embedded in many aspects of Jain life. Indeed, *ahiṃsā* is a crucial ingredient in the sense Jains have of who they are and how they differ from other communities. Jains are, or are at least supposed to be, strictly vegetarian, which differentiates them from nonvegetarian groups. But Jains also give their own distinctive modulations to vegetarianism, and this further distinguishes them from other vegetarian communities. As noted in Chapter One, observant Jains do not consume root vegetables (such as potatoes) because roots are believed to contain multitudes of souls; this is not true of vegetarian Hindu groups. Jains also contribute lavishly to Jain-sponsored animal welfare organizations and sometimes ransom goats to save them from the butcher's block. Bloodsports are naturally inconceivable for Jains. Jains avoid occupations that involve the taking of life, and the Jains themselves claim that this is why so many Jains are businessmen. Many other examples of the influence of *ahiṃsā* on Jain life could be given. *Ahiṃsā* is a value that expresses Jain piety and shapes a distinctively Jain lifestyle. It also establishes boundaries that separate Jains from other groups in Indian society, including other vegetarian groups.

The Rājpūts are the opposite of all this. Jains are the most vegetarian of vegetarians; Rājpūts eat meat. Jains rescue goats from the butcher; Rājpūts are renowned hunters. Indeed, hunting is as emblematic of Rājpūt values as vegetarianism is for the Jains. Jains abstain (or are at least supposed to abstain) from alcohol, while alcohol is an important element in Rājpūt hospitality. Rājpūts, above all, take pride in a heritage of warrior-kingship, while the Jains are deeply nonmilitary (although there have been, and are today, Jain military men). In this sense, Rājpūts and Jains represent true cultural opposites.

But at the same time there is a point at which Rājpūt and Jain identity merge, at least from the Jain perspective. Most of the Osvāl Jains of Rajasthan, and other Jain groups too, claim to be descended from Rājpūts who converted to Jainism and gave up Rājpūt customs centuries ago. This claim is frequently and vehemently made. It is true that the clan histories (of which more below) do include some accounts of

Jain clans of non-Rājpūt origin. And it is true, too, that it can be plausibly argued (within the assumptions of the system) that Jains, or any subgroup of Jains, sprang from "all" *varṇa*s and castes, because this in fact would be more consistent with the image of the Tīrthankar as a "universal" teacher (see Nāhṭā and Nāhṭā 1978: 11). This, however, is not the prevailing view among ordinary men and women with whom I discussed these matters. I have been told time and again by members of Jaipur's Śvetāmbar Jain community that the Jains are descended from Rājpūts or Kṣatriyas (the two words are synonymous in this context). Some individuals are reasonably well acquainted with their own clan histories; others have only vague ideas about such matters. Virtually everyone, however, takes as beyond dispute the general proposition that Jains were once Rājpūts.

The claim is made by Digambars as well as Śvetāmbars. Among Digambars, for example, the Khaṇḍelvāls (the largest Digambar caste in Jaipur) are believed to be mostly descended from a Cauhān (Rājpūt) king of Khaṇḍelā and his feudatory lords; they are said to have given up violent ways and embraced Jainism under the influence of Jinsenācārya, a famous Jain ascetic (Kāslīvāl 1989: 64–69).[1] An alternative version (K. C. Jain 1963: 103) holds that at that time eighty-two Rājpūts and two goldsmiths ruled eighty-four villages in the kingdom, and from these came the eighty-four clans of the Khaṇḍelvāls. The Agravāls, also prominent among Digambars, are likewise said to be of Rājpūt origin (Guṇārthī 1987: 55–56; Singh 1990: 151–53).

On the Śvetāmbar side, Rājpūt origin is claimed by both Śrīmāls and Osvāls. According to one version, the Śrīmāls are descended from the Kṣatriyas of the ancient city of Śrīmāl, who were converted to Jainism by an *ācārya* named Svayamprabhsūri (Śrīmāl n.d.: 3).[2] The Osvāl case, our main concern here, requires extended consideration. Two separate bodies of Osvāl origin mythology are relevant in the present context. One, which I shall call the "Osiyā legend," traces Osvāl origins to the town of Osiyā, north of Jodhpur. The other, a group of stories that I shall call the "Khartar Gacch legends," traces the origin of Osvāl clans to the proselytizing activities of past *ācārya*s of the Khartar Gacch.

Much of this material was apparently composed by Jain ascetics who, as Granoff has shown, functioned as the Jain equivalents of the caste bards and genealogists of the Rājpūts (Granoff 1989b: esp. 197–98). The composers' purpose was to cement ties between their own *gacch*s and particular exogamous patriclans (*gotra*s); the *gacch* of the monk responsible for a clan's original entry into the Jain fold would have a perpetual right to serve the ritual, spiritual, and record-keeping needs of that clan (ibid.: 200). As K. C. Jain (1963: 99–100) has shown, inscriptional evidence demonstrates that the consecration of images was a particularly important point of ritual connection between a given *gacch* and particular clans. The people of a given clan would utilize *ācārya*s of a particular *gacch* to perform image consecration ceremonies at their temples. Jain mentions several *gacchs,* now all extinct but two, as linked in this fashion with Osvāl clans: the Upkeś, Khartar, Maldhārī, Pallivāl, Ṣ[?]aṇḍerak, Bṛhad, Añcal, and Koraṇṭak *gacch*s. He lists the Gaṇadhara Copaḍā, Ḍāgā, Dosī, and Lūṇiyā clans as patrons of the Khartar Gacch. It seems possible that in the past there was a vast and complex network of ritual relations between clans and mendicant lineages among the Śvetāmbar Jains of Rajasthan. If this is true, then the clan origin mythology available today and the cult of the Dādāgurus may represent incomplete vestiges of what was once an arrangement of homologous and interlinked structures, an all-encompassing ritual-social order bringing the domains of spiritual and worldly "descent" together in a single system.

## OSIYĀ

These days Osiyā is a rather sleepy village, but legend proclaims it to have once been a large and flourishing city. Today it is an archaeological site of major importance, and it is also notable for two functioning temples.[3] One contains an image of Lord Mahāvīr. This temple dates from the eighth century C.E., and according to one writer (Dhaky 1968: 312) is the oldest surviving Jain temple in western India. The other temple, but a short distance from Mahāvīr's, is dedicated to a goddess known as Saciyā Mātā. Her main importance is that she is lineage goddess (*kuldevī*) to large numbers of Osvāl Jains. The town is accordingly an important pilgrimage center for Osvāls, and the volume of pilgrimage appears to have been increasing over the last three decades (Meister 1989: 280).

What I am calling the "Osiyā legend" is a myth of Osvāl origin that traces the caste's beginnings to ancient Osiyā. This story, a variant of which I was told by the *pujārī*s of the Saciyā Mātā temple at Osiyā, has been retold in its various forms by Māngīlāl Bhūtoṛiyā in his recent Osvāl history (1988: 67–72), and I shall be drawing heavily on his materials in the description and analysis to follow.[4] Let me hasten to add that this analysis is not meant as an endorsement of the idea that Jain clans originated as Rājpūt clans. The question of how Osvāl clans actually arose is completely beyond the ambit of this study. Our concern here is with Osvāl *images* of their origin and identity.

The story actually begins not in Osiyā itself but in the legendary ancient city of Śrīmāl. This city is said to have been the place of origin of the Śrīmāl caste, the other major Śvetāmbar caste in Jaipur, but it also figures centrally in the origin of the Osvāls. The roots of the tale go back to the life of Pārśvanāth, the twenty-third Tīrthankar with whose five-*kalyāṇak pūjā* this book began. Pārśvanāth's liberation is said to have occurred in 777 B.C.E., and of course after his departure the lineage of his disciples continued. Later came Lord Mahāvīr, and many of Pārśvanāth's followers joined Mahāvīr's congregation (*sangh*). According to this legend, however, many stayed on in Pārśvanāth's own disciplic lineage, which was known as the Upkeś Gacch.[5] It was Pārśvanāth's supposed fifth successor, an *ācārya* of the Upkeś Gacch named Svayamprabhsūri, who established the Śrīmāl caste (above).

At this point the story shifts to the city of Śrīmāl.[6] This city, now identified with the town of Bhīnmāl in Jalor District, was once a flourishing business center. At the time that Lord Mahāvīr walked the earth (as the tale goes), the city's monarchy was under the influence of *vāmmārgī* (tantric) Brāhmaṇs. Hundreds of thousands of animals were sacrificed in religious rites, and the people were much given to meat and liquor (*mās-madirā*) and lewd behavior of all kinds. Buddhism and Jainism had not yet arrived, and the whole region was given over to the worship of various gods and goddesses and the appeasing of ghosts and demons.

The king of Śrīmāl was a Kṣatriya named Jaysen. He had two sons: Bhīmsen and Candrasen. When the king died, Bhīmsen—who was a worshiper of Śiva—succeeded him, and he changed the name of the city to Bhīnmāl. He, in turn, had two sons: Śrī Puñj and Utpaldev (Upaldev).[7] On Bhīmsen's death Śrī Puñj became king. His minister's name was Suhaṛ, and Suhaṛ had a younger brother named Uhaṛ. Suhaṛ was a millionaire, and Uhaṛ was in need of a large sum of money. At that time in Bhīnmāl there were three separate sections of the city reserved for men of three different levels of wealth, and Uhaṛ apparently lacked the funds to live in a respectable area. When Uhaṛ asked his brother for the money, his wife (in this version Uhaṛ's wife; in other versions his brother's wife) taunted him.[8] Stung by this, Uhaṛ went to Utpaldev, and the two left Bhīnmāl together. On the road, Utpaldev bought some horses, and when at last they arrived at Delhi he gave the horses as a gift to the king there, whose name was "Sādhu." In return, the king gave him permission to establish a new kingdom on unused land.

The pair then went to Maṇḍor, and near there, at a spot thirty miles north of Jodhpur, they established a city. Thousands of people of all four *varṇa*s came from Bhīnmāl to settle there. This city was later to be known as Osiyā. Some say that it acquired this name from the term *oslā,* the Marwari term for "refuge" or "shelter"; others say that it was named for the "dewy" (*osīlī*) land upon which it was founded (Handa 1984: 8–9). Others still believe that the original name of the town was Upkeśpur, and that this name evolved into Osiyā (Bhūtoṛiyā 1988: 125).

According to the Osiyā legend, it was in this city, which later became large and flourishing, that the Osvāl caste was established. One version of how this happened is as follows.[9] Seventy years after Lord Mahāvīr's liberation (or 400 years before the *vikram* era)[10] a mendicant named Ratnaprabhsūri came to Upkeśpur (that is, Osiyā) with 500 ascetic followers. Ratnaprabhsūri was the sixth successor of Pārśvanāth (and presumably the immediate successor of Svayamprabhsūri, above), and had achieved the status of *ācārya* fifty-two years after Mahāvīr's liberation. At that time, King Utpaldev and his subjects were devotees of Cāmuṇḍā Devī (a meat-eating Hindu goddess), tantrics (*vāmmārgī*s), and completely ignorant of Jain ways. It was therefore very difficult for Jain ascetics to obtain alms, and Ratnaprabhsūri ordered his ascetic followers to leave. However, at the pleading of Cāmuṇḍā Devī herself he relented, and, sending 465 of his followers to Gujarat, he spent the rainy season retreat with the remaining thirty-five in Upkeśpur. At that time Utpaldev's companion, Uhaṛ, was still with him and had become his state minister. One day Uhaṛ's son was bitten by a snake and apparently died. Ratnaprabhsūri sprinkled the boy with water in which his own feet had been washed, and the boy was restored to life. All were overjoyed, and 184,000 Kṣatriyas became Jains.[11] These new Jains were later to be known as Osvāl from the name of the city in which this happened.

In another version of the tale, one that closely resembles the version I was told by the *pujārī*s of the Saciyā Mātā temple, Ratnaprabhsūri sent all 500 ascetic followers to Gujarat and stayed in Upkeśpur with but one disciple.[12] The disciple was at first unable to obtain alms, but he finally succeeded in getting some from an ailing householder whom he cured with medicine.[13] When he learned of this, Ratnaprabhsūri became angry (probably because *dān*, a religious donation, should never be gotten by exchange) and prepared to leave. Then Saciyā Mātā (that is, Cāmuṇḍā Devī by a different name) appeared and begged him to teach religion to the people. He thereupon transformed a roll of wool into a snake and gave it this order: "Do what will prosper the *dayā dharm* [Jainism]." The snake bit Utpaldev's son. King Utpaldev tried every remedy but to no avail; the prince appeared to die, and there were great lamentations in the city. The townspeople then began to take the corpse to the burning grounds. But, ordered to do so by Ratnaprabhsūri, the disciple stopped the procession and said that if the body were taken to his guru the prince's life would be restored. So they all went to the great monk and pleaded with him for the prince's life. The monk told the king that if he and his people would accept Jainism then the prince would be cured. They agreed, and by magical means the monk then called the snake. It came, removed all of the poison from the prince by sucking the bite, and disappeared. After hearing the teachings of Jainism from the Ratnaprabhsūri, the king and 125,000 Rājpūts then became Jains.

In yet another version,[14] King Utpaldev's daughter, Saubhāgya Devī, had married Uhaṛ's son, Trilok Singh. Trilok Singh was bitten by a snake and the daughter was ready to become a *satī*[15] when he was revived by the monk's footwashings. The conversions followed.

As are other castes—Hindu and Jain—the Osvāl caste is divided into exogamous patrilineal clans called *gotra*s. The Osiyā legend accounts for these by saying that there were originally eighteen Rājpūt clans in Osiyā, and that Ratnaprabhsūri changed these into the eighteen original Osvāl clans (*mūl gotra*s), which later differentiated into 498 subbranches. In his retelling of this, Bhūtoṛīyā (1988: 172–85) also lists clans founded by Ratnaprabhsūri at places other than Osiyā as well as clans founded by other *ācārya*s belonging to Ratnaprabhsūri's ascetic lineage (the Upkeś Gacch). He also lists clans founded by *ācārya*s of other ascetic lineages, but this he does not stress. As we shall see later, an emphasis on the conversions performed by *ācārya*s of other ascetic lineages reflects a somewhat different perspective on Osvāl origins.

## THE CONVERSION OF THE GODDESS

An Osvāl Jain acquaintance in Jaipur had been out of town for some days. When I asked him where he had been, he told me that he had gone to Osiyā to worship the goddess Saciyā Mātā, who is his lineage goddess (*kuldevī*). And why was that? To get rid of a *doṣ* (fault, blemish), he said, and to get "peace in the family." He never did explain the exact nature of the problem, but never mind; what is of interest here is the fact that, in addition to Tīrthankars and other lesser entities and deities, Jains also worship the tutelary goddesses (*devī*s) of patrilineages (*kul*s), who are believed to protect lineages and families.

The veneration of lineage goddesses is an institution shared by the Jains and Rājpūts of Rajasthan, and probably by most other caste communities as well.[16] Among Jaipur's Śvetāmbar Jains, they are found among Osvāls and Śrīmāls alike. Members of a lineage over which such a goddess presides should have their tonsure ceremonies (called *muṇḍan* and done for boys) performed at her temple. Also, a bride and groom should worship the groom's lineage goddess as a postlude to marriage. In essence, a woman changes her lineage goddess at the time of her marriage, although in some families she is invited (though not required) to attend rites of worship of her natal lineage goddess. Jain families in Jaipur commonly worship their lineage goddess annually or twice yearly. This usually occurs in conjunction with either or both of the twice-yearly Navrātrī periods (below), but this varies greatly. There is typically a physical epicenter for a given family's or lineage's goddess consisting of a temple which is a place of family pilgrimage and the preferred locale for tonsure rites and other special observances. In the household itself the lineage goddess is commonly temporarily represented for purposes of worship by a trident, *svastik,* or similar emblem executed in red on a wall. In rural areas households frequently keep permanent images of their lineage goddesses (Reynell 1985: 149), but this seems to be uncommon in Jaipur. These goddesses can also be (as we have seen) propitiated in times of trouble. One might make a vow to the goddess to go to her temple to take *darśan* and perform *pūjā* if the trouble is alleviated, a promise that must be kept at the risk of further troubles.

It needs to be stressed that attitudes and practices relating to lineage goddesses vary enormously in Jaipur. Some families have simply lost contact with these traditions, in most cases as a result of physical or social separation from their places of origin. In other cases the widespread feeling that there is something disreputable about lineage goddesses from a Jain standpoint has corroded patterns of lineage goddess worship. When this is so, the family can go to a nonlineage goddess temple or *dādābāṛī* for the tonsure rite. In the family of a Sthānakvāsī friend, the custom is to have the tonsure rite performed in a local Bhairav temple (a Hindu temple), and when he and his new wife were married they paid a postnuptual visit to a Jain nun instead of to a lineage goddess. Another friend took his bride to the Dādābāṛī at Mālpurā for this purpose.

The mother of the above Sthānakvāsī friend told me the following story of how her family (that is, the family into which she had married) lost their lineage goddess.[17] It seems that at some time in the remote past this family (belonging to the Botharā clan) lived in Bikaner, and once—at the time of Daśehrā—they and other families were about to worship their lineage goddesses.[18] While the food offerings were being prepared, a *yati* came around. He saw the preparations and angrily returned to the community hall where he was staying. There, by magical means, he drew to him all of the images of the lineage goddesses from the households in which they were kept and slapped his alms bowl over them. When the people began their *pūjā* they realized what had happened and went to the *yati*. He said, "If the goddess is more powerful than I am, then let her escape." He then threw the images into a well. From that time onward there have been no lineage goddesses for the Botharās (or at least in this branch of the Botharās).

Lineage goddesses vary in their degree of territorial or social inclusiveness.[19] Saciyā Mātā, for example, seems to be a generalized Osvāl lineage goddess; her votaries are widespread, and her image can even be seen in one of the principal Śvetāmbar temples of Ahmedabad.[20] Others are of far more local or socially parochial renown. Many, in fact, are *satī*s—that is, women who became deified after burning themselves alive on their husbands' funeral pyres; this is true of lineage goddesses in non-Jain castes as well. The essential idea in these instances is an amalgam of martial heroism and feminine purity. An illustrative example is provided by the story of a goddess named Satīmātā—despite the name, not a *satī* in the narrow sense—whose temple is located in Fatehpur (in Sikar District) and who is a lineage goddess for at least some lineages belonging to the Duggaṛ clan (of the Osvāl caste). Fatehpur, the story goes, was invested and overrun by the Mughals. A widow and her grown daughter fled the scene and retired to a certain place where they were protected from the searching Muslims by a mysterious power. In the end they died there, but with their womanly purity intact. They then became the goddess Satīmātā; here the term *satī* carries only its primary meaning of a virtuous and chaste woman. When

Satīmātā is worshiped by the Duggaṛs (which they do annually on Daśehrā), she is presented with a red and white cloth; the white cloth represents the widow, who is one-half of her composite persona.

A good example of a strong, functioning lineage-goddess cult is provided by a family of Osvāls I know who happen to belong to the Bhaṇḍārī clan. Although I initially came into contact with this family in Jaipur, their deepest roots are in Jodhpur. Moreover, as is the case with some Jodhpur Osvāls, this is a family located somewhere on the frontier between Jainism and Vaiṣṇavism; that is, their knowledge of Jainism is rather limited, and their religious practices are somewhat more Hindu in flavor than one would expect of knowledgeable and orthoprax Jains. Others told me that this is the case of a family that probably used to be unambiguously Jain but became Vaiṣṇavized under the influence of the local rulers whom they have served for generations.

Their lineage goddess is Durgā. She is housed in a temple located on the outskirts of Jodhpur next to a temple of Pārśvanāth. This temple is supported by a group of Bhaṇḍārī families of Jodhpur comprising about 400 individuals. When I was shown the temple, it was pointed out to me that the tiger on whom the image of Durgā sits faces east rather than west, and that this indicates that she is a "vegetarian" Durgā. A patriarch of the family said to me that when they were transformed from Rājpūts into Bhaṇḍārīs, they kept many Rājpūt traits: they "eat like Rājpūts," he said (though of course they are vegetarian), and they are "hospitable" like Rājpūts. And, he added, they continued to worship Durgā, who is the lineage goddess for many Rājpūts and an inheritance from their own Rājpūt days.

Among this family's numerous Jaipur connections was the marriage of one of their daughters into a Jaipur Osvāl family. Because of the rule of clan exogamy, her husband's clan is different from hers; it is Bhuraṭ. And his lineage goddess is different as well. His family considers their goddess to be Saciyā Mātā, and the Saciyā Mātā temple at Osiyā was where his tonsure ceremony occurred.

All of this is by way of introducing the fact that the Osiyā version of the origination of the Osvāls is more than the story of the conversion of Rājpūts into Jains; it is also about a goddess and the founding of a temple. The temple is the selfsame temple of Saciyā Mātā (often spelled Sacciyā Mātā and also known as Saciyā Devī) to which reference has been made. This is the temple where many Osvāls have tonsure rites performed for their male children, and of course pilgrims also visit this temple to pay homage to the goddess after marriage ceremonies. Special observances take place here twice per year on Navrātrī.[21] The story of the temple is extremely important, for it restates the symbolically central theme of warrior-kingship in a special frame of reference. Saciyā Mātā is not the lineage goddess of all Osvāl Jains. Still, she is an excellent representation of an important paradigm: the taming of the goddess as a concomitant to the conversion of Rājpūts into Jains.[22]

As retold by Bhūtoṛīyā (1988: 72–75), the story of Saciyā Mātā begins before the conversions of Utpaldev and the others. At that time (and as we have already learned) there was a temple of the goddess Cāmuṇḍā Devi in the town of Upkeśpur.[23] As is the Hindu practice, the sacrifice of goats and buffaloes was performed at this temple during the festival of Navrātrī. These practices are abhorrent to Jains, and so Ratnaprabhsūri put a stop to them. As a substitute for sacrificing animals, he instituted the practice of offering various sweets to the goddess. But the goddess was a meat eater and was infuriated by the deprivation of her customary sacrifices. In retribution she produced an ailment in Ratnaprabhsūri's eye. The monk, however, bore the pain with such fortitude that the goddess became fearful and asked him for forgiveness. She said that there would no longer be animal sacrifice in her temple and that thenceforth she would be known as "*saccī devī.*" Since then she has come to be known as Saciyā Mātā and what was previously the temple of Cāmuṇḍā at Osiyā came to be known as the *saciyā devī mandir.*[24]

The Hindu goddess Cāmuṇḍā is a sacrifice-demanding, meat-eating goddess, and is in fact one of the most ferocious of the goddess's many forms, created for the purpose of destroying the infamous buffalo demon, Mahiṣāsur. As such, her nature is in many ways identical with that of the Rājpūts, who are warriors and meat eaters themselves. The link between her character and that of the Rājpūts is explicit in the fact that meat-eating goddesses are commonly the lineage goddesses of the Rājpūts. Clearly, therefore, the story of the transformation of the goddess is a significant element in the Osiyā legend of Osvāl origin. The goddess Cāmuṇḍā is a projection of Rājpūt character. If this character is inimical to Jain vegetarianism—as it incontestably is—then a plausible account of how Rājpūts become Jains should include an account of how a meat-eating goddess becomes transformed into a goddess who is the vegetarian functional equivalent of the meat-eating Rājpūt lineage goddesses. To use Meister's apt phrasing (1993: 15), the "de-fanging" of Cāmuṇḍā is what the story of Saciyā Mātā is basically about, and it is a theme that is, as we shall shortly see, susceptible to many different elaborations.

## THE TALE OF THE BAHĪ BHĀṬS

There is another version of the story of Saciyā Mātā. This version Bhūtoṛīyā has drawn from the poetry of the Bahī Bhāṭs of Rajasthan. The Bahī Bhāṭs were so named because they recorded the genealogies of the Osvāls in *bahī*s (record books)[25] Their entire lives were passed in the service of Osvāl patrons, and at one time there were whole villages filled with them. More recently, their traditional calling seems to have fallen into desuetude and they have taken up other occupations. In addition to keeping genealogies, they also composed poetry in praise of the families of their patrons, and before they recited their genealogies they would recite their version of the history of the Osvāl caste. Bhūtoṛīyā provides a Hindi translation of a Bahī Bhāt account of the origin of the Osvāls (1988: 109–12) that provides interesting variations on the theme of the goddess's transformation. It runs as follows:

From a sacrificial fire pit on Mt. Abu, the tale begins, there emerged four Kṣatriya heroes, and from them came the Cauhān, Parmār, Paṛihār, and Solankī lines. A descendant in the Parmār line, Dhāndhūjī, was the ruler of Jūnāgaṛh (near Bāṛmer). He had two queens. The first was a daughter of Modha Singhjī Solankī and the second was a daughter of Jogīdāsjī, a Bhāṭī (Rājpūt) feudal lord. The first queen bore two sons: Upaldev (Utpaldev) and Jogā Kanvar. The second queen also bore two sons: Kāndh Rāv and Sānt Rāv. When Upaldev grew into young manhood he was married to a girl of the Kachvāhā Kṣatriya line.

One day Upaldev went out for an excursion with his friends. On the road he met a group of women water carriers who were bearing clay pots filled with water. The prince then played a thoughtless and unfortunate joke: He mocked and smashed their clay pots, spilling water over their clothing. The water carriers returned to their homes and bitterly complained about the incident. In accord with the saying, "Where the honor of daughters and sisters is not possible, in that kingdom one cannot stay," the elders of the community prepared to migrate elsewhere. Hearing of this, the king sent for them and gave his assurance that no such impropriety would occur again. Then, from the kingdom's treasury he gave them new metal pots.

Unfortunately, Upaldev and his friends had learned nothing from the incident, and they played a similar trick on the daughter of the *rājpurohit* (state priest). The offended priest also decided to leave the kingdom, and when the king heard of this he banished Upaldev.

Upaldev then wandered for twelve years. He rode a black mare and was accompanied by his wife and other relatives. One day his caravan of 300 vehicles came to Osiyā. That night Upaldev had a dream in which his lineage goddess gave "*parcā*" (a word commonly used in these materials to refer to a demonstration of a deity's or mendicant's powers). She said, "Don't leave this place. Start a city here." She added that the water problem (an obvious concern in the Rajasthan desert) could be solved by digging under his bed; there he would find a well that had been sealed by a certain King Sāgar, and sixty paces to the north he would find ninety-nine magical pots. In the morning he awoke to discover that a saffron mark had appeared on his forehead overnight and red marks on the foreheads of all the other members of his party. He dug under the bed and found the well. But the water was salty.

The next night the lineage goddess again appeared before him in a dream. She said, "You didn't make an offering (*caṛhāvā*) to the goddess (meaning herself), and that's why the water is salty. Now make the offering and the water will be sweet. And as many villages as you can encircle on your mare in a full day of riding, that will be the extent of your kingdom. First build a temple for the goddess, then your palace." He did exactly as she directed. First he built the temple, and because the goddess gave a *saccā* (true) *parcā,* she was called "Saciyā Mātā. The temple's foundation was laid in 127 C.E., and its construction took twelve years to complete.

After twelve years of exile had passed, Upaldev went to see his mother and father. He had married a second time in Osiyā, and both wives accompanied him. He halted at the border of his father's kingdom and sent a message ahead. His father's second queen, hearing the news, began to worry that Upaldev would acquire both Jūnāgaṛh and Osiyā, with nothing left for her sons, and so she devised a plan to take his life. She ordered the watchmen not to allow anyone into the palace with weapons. They made Upaldev leave his weapons outside, and when the defenseless prince entered the palace temple, assassins were able to sever his head.

When Upaldev's first wife heard the news, she ignored all modesty and got down from the carriage. She took burning coals in her hand as a test of truth, and cursed Dhāndhūjī's second queen and her line.

Kāndh Rāv was later attacked by the Rāṭhors and stripped of his kingdom (presumably as a result of the curse).

Upaldev's two wives then decided to become *satīs*, but because the younger queen turned out to be pregnant, she could not fulfill her vow. She then went to Osiyā and bore a son whose name was Bhagvān Singh. Some years later, the famed monk Ratnaprabhsūri came to Osiyā. For the entire rainy season retreat he was immersed in month-long fasts. His single mendicant follower, who was not fasting, was unable to obtain alms (as in the story given above). Finally, however, he was able to obtain food from a carpenter. When he returned the next day, the carpenter put an ax in his hand with which to cut dry wood in the jungle. When Ratnaprabhsūri finished his fasting he asked why his disciple was so weak, and the disciple told the whole story. Ratnaprabhsūri grew very angry. He first decided to destroy Osiyā by means of his *tapobal* (power of asceticism). However, at the entreaty of his disciple, and for the glorification (*prabhāvnā*) of Jainism, he decided on a different course. He made a roll of wool into a snake and sent it to the young king, Bhagvān Singh. The king was bitten, and when the people took him to the burning grounds they were stopped by the disciple, who took them to the venerable monk. Twelve feudatory lords pleaded with Ratnaprabhsūri to restore the king to life, which he did by means of his special powers. The king himself and these twelve lords then left the worship of Śiva (*śiv-dharm*) and became Jains. Thirteen main clans of the Osvāls resulted.[26]

Now these converts had given up violence. But Saciyā Mātā, who after all was the lineage goddess of the king, still had to have a blood offering of two goats. Ratnaprabhsūri himself took on the burden of this problem. For three days there was no *pūjā*, and the goddess became very angry. She came to the monk and demanded the sacrificial offerings (*mahābhog*, as she called it). The monk responded by decreeing that there would be no more animal sacrifice, and that she would receive only two kinds of sweets (*khājī* and *lāpsī*) and coconut, and this is in fact what is offered to her at the Saciyā Mātā temple in Osiyā today. The goddess, in response, uttered a curse. "Empty the village," she said, "in three days." Bhagvān Singh thereupon left Osiyā and settled in a place called Sāṇḍvā.[27]

This story is very similar to the version of the Osiyā legend of Osvāl origin related earlier, but there are interesting differences too, and by comparing the two we can separate variant and invariant themes. For example, we note that the line of Upaldev (or, as previously, Utpaldev) is crucial: This is the king who is the *ādi puruṣ,* the founding father, of the Osvāl line; whether it is he or his son who is converted seems not so important. We may surmise, moreover, that in the flux and flow of these stories as they were generated, told, retold, and modified by mendicants and genealogists over a period of centuries, the connection with the city of Bhīnmāl was, for some tellers anyway, not the essential thing. This connection was probably important for the then-extant Upkeś Gacch mendicants because it puts two very important Jain castes, the Osvāls and the Śrīmāls, into a single package, which is then tied to the activities of leading ascetics of the Upkeś Gacch. And it may also reflect the motives of those who, for whatever reason, wish to emphasize a special connection between Osvāls and Śrīmāls. But the essential thing is the focus on Kṣatriyas or Rājpūts. While it is sometimes said that those who converted to Jainism with Utpaldev came from all the *varṇa*s of Osiyā (ibid.: 71), the emphasis is on Kṣatriyas. As will be seen later, although some Osvāl clans trace their descent to non-Kṣatriya converts to Jainism, the Rājpūt or Kṣatriya convert is virtually archetypal in the tradition.

Another constant feature is the theme of miraculous intervention by a powerful ascetic. Someone is in trouble, either the minister's son or the king (or his son) himself. The theme of snakebite is a common thread, and turns out, as will be seen, to be very common in other stories belonging to the overall genre. Ācārya Ratnaprabhsūri's own involvement in the creation of the problem (in some versions) seems to be a side issue. The moral issue of a Jain ascetic causing harm (or apparent harm) to a living being is, in any case, covered by the rationalization that a Jain mendicant can act in very unmendicant-like ways in the interest of the protection or propagation of Jainism. Such variations aside, the basic narrative is simple. Trouble arises. Nothing avails. Only the power of the ascetic can solve the problem, and the conversions follow.

There is one matter more, and this is of very great significance. The tale of the Bahī Bhāṭs introduces us to the theme of the goddess's curse. As we shall soon see, this theme is important indeed to the concept of how Rājpūts could become Jains. It comes to the fore in the story of the nearby Mahāvīr temple.

## THE MAHĀVĪR TEMPLE

The other major attraction at Osiyā is the eighth-century temple of Lord Mahāvīr. It is, in fact, only a short distance from Saciyā Mātā.

One of the *pujārīs* of Saciyā Mātā's temple who showed me around the Mahāvīr temple kept referring to it simply as the "Jain temple." His implication seemed to be that Saciyā Mātā is a lineage goddess, whereas Lord Mahāvīr represents something that has actually to do with Jainism. However, the two temples are deeply interconnected, as we see from the following stories of the creation of Lord Mahāvīr's temple (drawn from ibid.: 72–74) which link this event to Saciyā Mātā and the creation of the Osvāl caste.

One version holds that the temple was created by the minister Uhaṛ.[28] The image of Mahāvīr was made by Cāmuṇḍā Devi from a mixture of sand and milk, and had to be dug up from the ground. Because it was excavated prematurely (that is, before the goddess said it should have been), it had two flaws (*granthi,* "knots") on its chest. As we shall see later, these flaws figure importantly in other stories, and this story resembles closely the story told by the *pujārīs* of the temple today.

According to another version—which Bhūtoṛīyā characterizes as "popular belief"—a wealthy person named Ahaṛ was at that time trying to construct a Mahādev (Śiva) temple. However, he had a big problem. As much of the temple as he built up during the day would be mysteriously torn down at night. In despair he went to Ācārya Ratnaprabhsūri, who suggested that he build a temple for Lord Mahāvīr instead. From this point on there was no obstacle, and the temple was built. Then arose the question of the image. For some time a cow had been letting its milk fall spontaneously on the ground at a place nearby, and all were amazed by this phenomenon.[29] Upon digging at this spot, the people found an image of a Tīrthankar. According to Ratnaprabhsūri, it was made of sand and milk. There were two knobs (flaws) on its chest, and the monk said that this was caused by the digging. Ratnaprabhsūri himself performed the installation ceremony of the image (while bilocationally doing the installation ceremony of another image elsewhere). The image later got the reputation of being filled with magical power.

Now, it is also said that 303 years after the establishment of this temple there was an important incident concerning the knots or flaws on the image's chest (this from ibid.: 76). It seems that some zealous laymen, thinking the two knots to be unsightly, tried to remove them. The goddess was enraged by this and created a great disturbance (*updrav*) that affected the whole city. Here we recognize Saciyā Mātā acting in the standard role of a guardian deity to Lord Mahāvīr's image. In a version of this story told to me by the Saciyā Mātā *pujārīs* (below), milk and blood flowed from the image.

Disturbed by these frightening events, the community invited an *ācārya* named Kakksūri, who was the thirteenth successor to the leadership of the Upkeś Gacch, to come and quell the disturbance. He had a *snātra pūjā* performed for the image, and in this *pūjā* the eighteen clans of the Osvāl caste (often referred to as the "*mahājan vaṃś*" in these accounts) were the *pūjā* principals. Nine clans poured the liquids from one direction, nine clans from the other. The disturbance stopped, but because of the goddess's curse the Osvāls had to leave the city. This was the great Diaspora of the Osvāls. After they fled Osiyā, theorizes Bhūtoṛīyā, the name "Upkeśīya" must have come into currency for these people, which in time became Osvaṃśīya. In any case, in time the city became deserted, and so it nearly is today.[30]

## THE PUJĀRĪS' TALE

The *pujārīs* of the Saciyā Mātā temple gave me a somewhat different version, but thematically it comes to the same thing. The tale begins in 170 C.E. when there was a marriage of a boy of Osiyā to a girl from another village. When it was time to return to the boy's family (in Osiyā) after the marriage ceremony, the bride said that she would neither eat nor drink without her Durgā, for it seems that there was a temple for Durgā in her native village. So when they brought her to her conjugal village they made a Durgā temple for her, which is the present Saciyā Mātā temple. The goddess then came to the girl in a dream and said that an image for the temple would emerge. The mountain split and the image came out—one leg in, the other out, riding a lion.

The tale (as I paraphrase what was told to me) now turns to Rājā Upaldev. He and his people all had a dream that at a certain location would be found 900,000 gold coins. They went to that spot, which is 2 kilometers from the temple, and there was a stone with a copper pot under it with the 900,000 golden coins. That's why the name of the place is "nine hundred thousand pond" (*navlākh talāb*). The king then founded the temple (that is, he built it on the site of the previously existing shrine). The goddess was non-vegetarian. The population of Osiyā was then 380,000.

At this point, along came Ratnaprabhsūri, and now we find ourselves on familiar ground. He went to the jungle, sat in the forest, and made a snake out of a roll of cotton which he enlivened by means of his special powers. He then sent it to bite the king's only son. The prince sickened and died, despite the best efforts of magicians and physicians. As in the version of this tale given above, the ascetic restored the prince to life; he made another cotton snake that sucked the poison out, and the king and the people became Jains.

Now, because the king and his people had converted to Jainism, the sacrifice offered to the goddess had to stop, and this made the goddess very angry. As it happened, at this time the people were building a Vaiṣṇava temple. These people were all Vaiṣṇavas—the *pujārī* says—before they become Jains.[31] Each day they would build it a little higher, and each night the angry goddess would tear down what they had built. So they went to the monk for advice, and he said, "I'll tell you tomorrow." That night he went to the goddess's temple and prayed to the goddess Durgā. She said to the monk that she was angry because the people had stopped giving her meat and liquor. She said that if she was to become a Jain goddess, then the temple being built should be a Jain temple, not a Vaiṣṇava temple. So the next day the monk told the people to build a Jain temple, which they began to do, and the construction went ahead with no further trouble.

But when the temple was finished there was no image. Now, the king's chief minister had a cow, and this cow started going to a particular spot three times daily and dropping her milk on the ground. When asked for the meaning of this, the monk said, "I'll tell you tomorrow." He then went to the goddess at midnight. She said, "I knew you'd come to me," and then went on to say that an image was being made from milk and soil under the ground and that it would be complete in seven days. The next day the monk told this to the people. But they were impatient and dug up the image—which of course was an image of Lord Mahāvīr—before the seven days had elapsed. As a result, the image had a tumor on its chest. They installed the image in the temple, and the monk performed the consecration.

But then the people, unwilling to leave well enough alone, tried to remove the tumor on the image's chest by hitting it. The people who did this died on the spot, and a mixture of milk and blood flowed in a river from the wound on the image and brought various diseases to the people. Thousands died. So, as usual, the people went to the monk and asked him what to do. "I'll tell you tomorrow," he said. He went to the goddess at midnight. She was still angry from being denied her meat and liquor. He said, "You'll get sweets but not meat." She replied with recriminations. The people had pulled the image out too soon, and had hit it—and this was the image she had made. She said that she would punish the whole village, but she also said that she would come to the aid of whoever gave her sweets and had faith in her. Because of her curse the people had to leave the village, which they did within three days. The goddess then established the following rules: 1) that after a marriage the bride and groom must come and honor her at the Osiyā temple, 2) that her followers must also perform the tonsure rite at this temple, 3) that her followers should go to the temple for *darśan,* and 4) that they must worship her as their *kuldevī* (lineage goddess). Because of the curse, no Osvāls can live in Osiyā (or at least not, the *pujārī* added, "with families").

## LINEAGE GODDESSES

We see, then, that the Osiyā legend is not a single tale but a whole complex of tales. There are many versions, refracted through the sensibilities of various tellers, but thematically they all show a remarkable consistency. They center on three basic matters: the conversion of Rājputs into Jains; the taming (or Jainizing) of a meat-eating, sometimes angry, and curse delivering goddess; and the relationship between the Osvāl caste and the image of Lord Mahāvīr. This latter relationship is a complex one: Osvāls venerate the image, but are cursed to stay at a distance. And this complexity, in turn, echoes an ambivalence in the goddess's own character. She is a vegetarian lineage goddess for Jains, but she is nonetheless never quite tamed.

The physical juxtaposition of the two temples—Saciyā Mātā's and Lord Mahāvīr's—is emblematic of these issues. How is it possible, we may ask, for Rājpūts to become Jains? At the level of the logic of ritual symbolism this can be transmuted into another question, namely, how is it possible to bring these two physical structures into a viable relationship? The answer seems to be, in part, that a meat-eating goddess must become vegetarian, and must also become the servant and protector of Lord Mahāvīr. This formulation is of particular interest because not only does it reach deeply into the heart of Osvāl identity, but it also provides a wider Indic context for this identity. This is because the goddess is an Indic figure, not a specifically Jain figure. Cāmuṇḍā, who is the original goddess whose nature is transformed, is a manifestation of the transregional Hindu goddess in her warlike form. According to the stories we have examined, she was the lineage goddess of Utpaldev. She then became a lineage goddess for Osvāl Jains. This suggests the need for a closer examination of the phenomenon of lineage goddesses among the Rājpūts.

The lineage goddess complex is, in fact, central to Rājpūt cultural and social life, and we are fortunate indeed that this complex has recently been subjected to a searching ethnographic description and analysis by Lindsey Harlan (1992). What follows is based on her account.

Among the Rājpūts, lineage goddesses are associated with patrilineages (*kul*s) or their subdivisions (which, though branches of *kul*s, are frequently confused with *kul*s). *Kul*s, in turn, are considered segments of the three great clans (*vaṃś*) of the Rājpūts, the sun, moon, and fire lines. The *kul*s are traced to founding ancestors who, as Harlan notes, "typically left a homeland ruled by an older male relative or conquered by a foreign invader" (ibid.: 27). The goddesses are seen as protectresses of the lineages with which they are associated, and this function is typically demonstrated when the goddess in question manifests herself at critical junctures in order to come to the aid of Rājpūts who are in danger of some kind. "In most cases," Harlan writes, "she reveals herself to their leader and inspires him to surmount whatever problems he and his followers face. Often she first manifests herself in an animal form. Afterward she helps him establish a kingdom, at which point he and his relatives become the founders of a kinship branch (*kul* or *shakh*) with a discrete political identity" (ibid.: 32). Subsequently she continues to manifest herself at times of crisis to render aid. We have already encountered, in a Jain context, the theme of aid in kingdom establishment in the tale of the Bahī Bhāṭs.

The theme of protection is fundamental to the entire ritual and mythical complex surrounding lineage goddesses among the Rājpūts. The goddess possesses power, *śakti,* which she uses on behalf of the group over whom she exercises guardianship. In Harlan's materials the myths concerning the first manifestations and miraculous interventions of lineage goddesses involve such protective acts as saving endangered princes (and thus the lineage), reviving exhausted and wounded warriors on the battlefield, and aiding in conquests and in the establishment of kingdoms.

Kingship and the battlefield are tightly intertwined in the imagery surrounding lineage goddesses. These goddesses are, above all, protectresses on the battlefield. Rājpūt men are warriors; they fight for glory and to expand their kingdoms. The lineage goddess appears at crucial moments to aid them in this endeavor. She also protects the kingdom through the figure of the king. The king is her chief devotee, and by protecting him she protects the kingdom as a whole. Thus, she is not only an embodiment of the identity of the lineage, but her worship also legitimizes the king's rule.

The public buffalo sacrifice occurring on Navrātrī is, as Harlan shows (ibid.: 61–63), the perfect exemplification of this principle. The lineage goddess is identified with the Sanskritic goddess Durgā, the slayer of the buffalo demon Mahiṣāsur. As the sacrificer, the king is identified with the goddess. But he is also identified with the sacrificial victim, who is himself a king. "Thus," says Harlan, "the blood he offers is also his own. The demon Mahish, liberated by death from his demonic buffalo form, becomes the Goddess's foremost devotee. The king, also represented as the *kuldevi*'s foremost devotee, offers her his death to assure her victory over the enemies of his kingdom" (ibid.: 63). These ideas resonate deeply with the image of the king-warrior who sheds his blood in battle; his blood "nourishes the *kuldevi* who protects the *kul* and the kingdom" (ibid.).

Saciyā Mātā is also closely identified with Durgā. Before her transformation she was Cāmuṇḍā, who is one of Durgā's forms. The *pujārī* of the Saciyā Mātā temple told me that the "form" of Saciyā Mātā is Mardinī Durgā, and Handa (1984: 16) concurs that Saciyā is a manifestation of Durgā Mahiṣamardinī (that is, the goddess as "Destroyer of the Buffalo Demon"). It is of interest to note that R. C. Agrawala (n.d.: 19–20) reports that images of Mahiṣamardinī are actually still being worshiped in some Jain temples in western India. The *pujārī* of the temple added to the above statement that just as the Rājpūts have their Durgā, the Osvāls have Saciyā. He is, of course, exactly right. Saciyā is, in effect, a vegetarian Durgā, suitable for Osvāls. She is a generalized Rājpūt lineage goddess, sanitized in such a way that she becomes an appropriate lineage goddess for those who once were Rājpūt but have now become Jains.

It should be noted that the vegetarianization of a meat-eating goddess is not a purely Jain phenomenon, for there is a prominent Hindu example as well. The famed Hindu goddess Vaiṣṇo Devi was in all likelihood once a meat-eating goddess herself, who became "tamed" in accord with values deriving from the Hindu Vaiṣṇavas.[32] Her name derives from the term *Vaiṣṇava,* and the Vaiṣṇava tradition is strongly vegetarian; indeed, the term *Vaiṣṇava* can mean, simply, "vegetarian."

Vaiṣṇo Devī thus appears to be another transmuted goddess, tamed in submission to the vegetarian imperative of a non-Jain ritual culture.

## AMBIVALENT GODDESSES

The Hindu goddess—that is, the goddess of the wider South Asian religious world outside the ambit of Jainism in the strict sense—is a very complex figure. Many analysts have noted an apparent conflict between what seem to be two very different, even contradictory, sides of her nature. When she takes the form of such manifestations as Lakṣmī she embodies fertility, prosperity, and well-being. As Kālī and in other similarly fearsome or martial forms, however, she is associated with bloodshed and death. As David Kinsley (1975) has pointed out, this is not necessarily a contradiction. When seen in the context of wider Hindu views about the nature of the cosmos, prosperity *is* destruction, and birth *is* death. It seems possible that these transformations of the goddess's character have something to do with marriage (see Babb 1975: 217–29; but for a contrary view see Erndl 1993). Her more combative forms are often represented as unmarried, or at least marriage is unstressed, whereas her more peaceful manifestations seem to be associated with the married state.

These issues emerge in an extremely interesting way in Harlan's materials. The lineage goddess has two sides or facets among the Rājpūts. For men, she is a protectress of the lineage and the kingdom. For women, on the other hand, she is primarily a protector of the household. These two functions are associated with radically different images of the goddess: unmarried versus married. As household protectress she frequently appears to women in dreams or visions, and when she does she appears in the form of a "lovely *suhagin,*" a married woman (Harlan 1992: 65). The battlefield protectress, often appearing in animal form, is directly associated with unmarried Durgā, "whose very power derives from her status as a virgin unrestrained by male control" (ibid.: 71). As household protectress she is linked with the ideal of the *pativrat,* the dutiful wife; here her protective function is wifely and maternal. Indeed, to be a *pativrat* is to emulate the lineage goddess who is the archetypal protectress that an ideal wife should be.[33] Moreover, in the worship of the lineage goddess in her domestic manifestation, which is primarily a women's activity, *fasting replaces blood sacrifice* as the central ritual motif (ibid.: 86–88).[34]

The Rājpūt lineage goddess, moreover, is not merely an *emblem* of the identity of the group with which she is linked; she is an *embodiment* of that identity in a way that seems to involve a linkage of substance. As Harlan points out, fluid imagery is very important in this context. She is associated with the blood her warriors shed on the battlefield; when the king or warrior dies, his death is a sacrifice to her that "nourishes" (ibid.: 62) her. But other myths portray her as a milk-giver (ibid.: 55–56), an image that seems to come to the fore in the domestic contexts of her worship (ibid.: 69–70). In these fluid transactions the lineage goddess emerges as custodian not merely of a lineage's power and renown but of its very substance. In this connection, it is surely significant that, according to one version of the tale, when the people of Osiyā undertook their ill-advised project of repairing the Mahāvīr image, the goddess's anger is manifested as a flow from the image of a lethal mixture of milk and blood, two powerful symbols seemingly associated with the essential nature of any lineage goddess, Rājpūt or Jain.

From the standpoint of the goddess, when Rājpūts become Jains the issue is sacrifice. And what is at issue is not merely what the goddess eats, although that is an important aspect of the matter. More fundamentally, and as we see in Harlan's material, the very symbolism of the sacrifice itself is central to the notion of who Rājpūts are. Rājpūts *are* those who offer themselves on the battlefield as the goddess's sacrificial victims. The Navrātrī buffalo sacrifice resonates with this idea. Thus, when Rājpūts become Jains the sacrifice must go. As in the Rājpūt myths—myths that associate the lineage goddess with a crucial event in the formation of a group and the establishment of its identity—the transformation of Cāmuṇḍā into Saciyā Mātā is associated with the formation of the Osvāl caste. Crucial to this event is Cāmuṇḍā's giving up of sacrificial victims. She becomes vegetarian, in parallel with the transformation of meat-eating Rājpūts into Jains, which is central to the myth of Saciyā Mātā's temple.

However, in this transformation she does not lose all of her former functions or character. She remains a protectress, but she also seems to retain a certain vindictiveness. In Harlan's materials the lineage goddess can be punitive (ibid.: 68–69), punishing her devotees for their own good. The punishment is frequently imaged as a deprivation of fluids; cows dry up or her victims' bodies are dessicated by fever. Often she does this "because her worship has been neglected in some essential way. She warns that unless her worship is performed properly, various undesirable consequences will ensue" (ibid.). We see the same tendency in the myths of Saciyā Mātā's curse. In the tale of the Bahī Bhāṭs her anger arises from the omission of an essential element of her ritual culture, namely animal sacrifice. In the myths of the Mahāvīr temple a Jainization of her bad temper has occurred; here her anger is not inspired by neglect of her ritual needs but by mistreatment of Mahāvīr's image.

It is of interest that, in an apparent inversion of the Rājpūt imagery, in the *pujārī*s' tale Saciyā Mātā's punishment of the Osvāls is manifested as too much fluid, not too little. This rather surprising reversal may have the function of preserving—within the context of an encompassing idea of the goddess's punitive inclinations—a clear distinction between Jain and Rājpūt goddesses.

But we must note, finally, that in a sense the Jain version of the Rājpūt lineage goddess is not really "transformed" at all, because even the Rājpūt lineage goddess has a "Jain" side to her character—that is, there is a side to her character of which Jains can approve. We see this in the distinction between the Rājpūt lineage goddess in her martial and *pativrat* forms—the lineage goddess of the *mardānā* (men's quarters) versus the lineage goddess of the *zanānā* (women's quarters) respectively. The Rājpūt lineage goddess does indeed possess an unwarrior-like form, which is her domestic manifestation. And it is surely significant that when the domestic lineage goddess is stressed (as is the case in women's worship), not only does the Navrātrī buffalo sacrifice recede into the background, but on the all-important occasion of Navrātrī the votive fast (*vrat*) moves to the fore (ibid.: 88).

The imagery of the domestication of Saciyā Mātā, I suggest, can be seen as an assertion of the domestic subtradition of Rājpūt lineage goddess worship, a subtradition with an ascetic bias. In a tale of Rājpūts becoming Jains, it makes sense for sacrifice to be pushed aside, allowing asceticism to assume the central role in religious practice. Saciyā Mātā becomes the servant and protector of ascetic Lord Mahāvīr, which is emblematic of the fact that the fast, not blood sacrifice, has become the defining ritual act.

## KHARTAR GACCH LEGENDS

Because of its putative time-depth, the Osiyā legend might be considered the most "inclusive" account of Osvāl origin. From the perspective of Jaipur, however, the Osiyā myth seems to recede into a nebulous background. In this city, the dominant influence is the Khartar

Gacch, and the most relevant Osvāl origin mythology emphasizes the role of this mendicant lineage in the creation of Osvāl clans. I will refer to this body of material as the Khartar Gacch legends. Because the Khartar Gacch did not come into existence until the eleventh century C.E., the putative time frame of the Khartar Gacch legends is much later than that of the Osiyā legend.

Lest we lose the thread of our overall argument, it must be emphasized that the Khartar Gacch legends stress, as does the Osiyā legend, the claim of Rājpūt/Kṣatriya origin for most Osvāl clans. In a history of the Osvāl caste that adopts the Khartar Gacch perspective (Bhansālī 1982; see chart on pp. 217–22), out of the eighty-one major clans listed, a total of sixty-five are (by my reckoning) traced to Rājpūt/Kṣatriya clans or lineages.[35] Six are held to be of Maheśvarī (a business caste similar to the Osvāls) origin, but the Maheśvarīs themselves are said to have been Kṣatriyas originally. The remainder (including two clans of Brāhmaṇ origin) can be regarded as special cases that do not disconfirm the main trend.

These accounts may be considered to be expressions of a coherent general theory about the origin of the community of Osvāl Jains. This is a theory that was shared by most of those with whom I discussed these matters in Jaipur. Some were hazy about the specifics, but the general view that Osvāl clans were created when Rājpūts were converted to Jainism by distinguished ascetics—mostly Khartar Gacch ascetics—was quite widespread (see Figure 12 for an illustration of this belief). The Khartar Gacch legends themselves are less focused on the origin of the Osvāl caste as a whole than on the separate origins of Osvāl clans. As articulated to me by Jaipur respondents, the underlying theory holds that the Osvāl clans were created by Jain monks. These monks then encouraged their converts to marry only their co-religionists. In this way, the exogamous clans became knit into the encompassing Osvāl caste.

In what follows I draw heavily on two volumes that were placed in my hands by knowledgeable Jains in Jaipur. One is a history of the Osvāls (cited above) authored by Sohanrāj Bhansālī (Bhansālī 1982). The other is a short anthology of materials on *jatis* (castes) and clans putatively converted by Khartar Gacch monks (Nāhṭā and Nāhṭā 1978). Each of these books brings together large amounts of material gleaned from traditional genealogists, and together they are a rich source of material on Osvāl origins from the Khartar Gacch point of view.

Figure 12. Jindattsūri pointing to the names of clans created by him. Picture on the wall of the *dādābāṛī* at Ajmer.

## THE QUALITY OF MIRACLES

A survey of these tales of conversion and clan formation reveals that thematically they are very much like the Osiyā legend; the major differences are in the details. As in the Osiyā legends, the theme of an ascetic's miraculous power is central. The convert-to-be, usually a king of some kind, finds himself in serious difficulty. A Jain mendicant overcomes the difficulty in a miraculous fashion, and the conversions follow.[36] The following examples will provide an idea of the range of the difficulties and miraculous interventions involved in these tales.

The difficulty is often the bite of a snake. For instance (this from Bhansālī 1982: 67–72), the Kaṭāriyā (or Ratanpurā) clan came into being when a Cauhān (Rājpūt) king was bitten while resting under a banyan tree. Dādāguru Jindattsūri,[37] who just happened to be nearby, cured the king by sprinkling *mantrit jal* (*mantra*-charged water). The king offered him wealth, but Jindattsūri explained that mendicants cannot possess wealth. Jindattsūri then spent the rainy season retreat in the king's city (Ratanpur). The king came under the influence of his teachings, with the result that he and his family became Jains.

The miraculous cure of an illness is also a major theme. A good example is the story of the Bāvelā clan (ibid.: 117). The Cauhān king of Bāvelā suffered from leprosy. As in all these tales, no cure could be found. However, in 1314 C.E., Śrī Jinkuśalsūri (the third Dādāguru) came to the kingdom and told the king of a remedy that had originated with the goddess Cakerśvari (a Jain goddess). The remedy was tried, and in seven days the king recovered. He then converted to Jainism, and his descendants became the Bāvelā clan.

Another example of a clan originating with the cure of an illness is the Bhansālī clan (ibid.: 149–50). This is in fact one of the most illustrious of the Osvāl clans. In the tenth to eleventh century a Bhāṭī (Rājpūt) king named Sāgar ruled in what is now the famous pilgrimage town of Lodravā (near Jaisalmer). He had eleven sons, of whom eight had died of epilepsy. One day, Ācārya Jineśvarsūri[38] came to the town. The king and queen went to him and pleaded for him to do something to save their remaining three sons. Jineśvarsūri said all would be well if they gave the kingdom to one son and allowed the other two to become Jains. The king agreed, and Jineśvarsūri initiated the princes in a *bhaṇḍśāl* (a barn or storage building), which is how the clan got its name.

Considering the warlike nature of the Rājpūts, it is hardly surprising that victory and defeat in battle are issues on which these conversion tales sometimes hinge. An example is the story of the origin of the Kānkariyā clan (ibid.: 1982: 72–74). It so happens that in 1085 one Bhīmsen, the Kṣatriya lord of Kānkarāvat village, was summoned by the king of Cittauṛ. He refused to obey, and the king of Cittauṛ sent an army to fetch him. Bhīmsen took the "shelter" (*śaraṇ*) of Ācārya Jinvallabhsūri,[39] who happened to be visiting the village at that time. The monk said that he would help if Bhīmsen became his *śrāvak* (lay Jain). After Bhīmsen had accepted Jainism, Jinvallabhsūri had a large quantity of pebbles brought. He rendered them *mantrit* (that is, infused them with the power of a *mantra*), and, in accord with his instructions, when the Cittauṛ army came they were met with a shower of these pebbles. The invaders panicked and fled. The clan got its name because of the role of these pebbles (*kankaṛ*) in its founding.

The Khīmsarā clan began as a result of defeat in battle (ibid.: 76–78). In a place called Khīmsar lived a Cauhān Rājpūt named Khīmjī. One day, enemy Bhāṭīs plundered his camels, cows, and other wealth. With some of his kinsmen he pursued the thieves, fought them, and was defeated. While returning to his village he met Ācārya Jinvallabhsūri and told him the sad story. The monk said that if Khīmjī would give up liquor, meat, and violent ways, then all would be well. Khīmjī and his companions accepted. The monk then repeated the *namaskār mantra* according to a special method designed to subjugate enemies and then gave his blessing. Because of the influence of the *mantra* the mental state of Khīmjī's enemies changed; they begged for mercy and returned all their plunder. This story further tells of how these converts maintained marriage relations with Rājpūts for three generations. But in the end, troubled by "derision" (whose is not clear), Bhīmjī (a descendant of Khīmjī) brought the problem before Jindattsūri when he happened to visit the village. The monk imparted his teachings, and then joined this clan to the Osvāl *jāti* (caste). They then began to marry within the Osvāl caste.

The Gāng clan (ibid.: 80–82) is another example of a clan created because of an ascetic's intervention in battle. Nārāyaṇsingh was the Parmār (Rājpūt) ruler of Mohīpur. There he was besieged by Cauhāns. The Parmārs began to run low on resources, and things looked grim. Nārāyaṇsingh's son, however, reported that Ācārya Jincandrasūri "Maṇidhārī" was nearby, and suggested that this very powerful ascetic might help them out of their difficulty. The son disguised himself as a Brāhmaṇ astrologer and sneaked through the enemy lines and came to the monk. The monk taught him the *śrāvak dharm* (the path of the lay Jain), and, on the son's promise that he would accept Jainism, repeated a powerful *stotra* (hymn of praise) for getting rid of disturbances. The goddess of victory appeared with a powerful horse. On this horse the son rode back to Mohīpur. Because of the influence of the *stotra,* when the enemy army saw him they thought they were seeing a vast army that was coming to aid the besieged Parmārs. They fled, and in the end all sixteen of the king's sons became Jains, which is the origin of the sixteen subbranches of this clan.

Some conversions result from a lack of male issue. The Bhaṇḍārī clan (ibid.: 163–64) is an example. In the tenth to eleventh century there was a Cauhān ruler of Nāḍol village (in Pali district) named Rāv Lākhan. He had no sons. One day, Ācārya Yaśobhadrasūri[40] came to the village. The king told him about his trouble and asked for a blessing. The monk said that sons would come, but that one of them would have to be made into "my *śrāvak*." The king's twelfth son became a Jain, and because he served as the kingdom's treasurer (that is, keeper of the *bhaṇḍār*) the clan became known as Bhaṇḍārī. A descendant of this son came to Jodhpur and settled in 1436. Previously this family had been known as "*jainī cauhān kṣatriya*," which means that they were Jains who were still Rājpūts. At this point they became Osvāl Jains as a result of the teachings of a Khartar Gacch *ācārya* named Bhadrasūri.

## CONVERSION AND SUPERNATURAL BEINGS

In parallel with a similar pattern that we have seen already in the story of Saciyā Mātā, in these tales the work of conversion is sometimes associated with the "Jainizing" or taming of non-Jain supernaturals. As Granoff points out (1989b: 201, 206), the ascetic in these tales often works his conversion miracle through the agency of a clan deity, usually a goddess, a theme that is certainly present in the Osiyā materials surveyed earlier. "In these stories," Granoff points out, "monks are often powerful because they can command a goddess to do their bidding and aid their devotees or potential devotees" (ibid.: 201–2).[41] Granoff's survey of clan histories discloses another common pattern, that of the *vyantar* who is in fact a deceased kinsperson and who has come back to trouble his or her former relatives; the malignant spirit is then pacified by the monk and becomes a lineage deity (ibid.: 211). Most of these ideas are also present in the Osvāl materials I have surveyed.

For example, converts-to-be sometimes suffer from demonic possession. An alternative story about the Bhansālī clan (this one from Nāhṭā and Nāhṭā 1978: 36) again focuses on King Sāgar. One day a *brahm rākṣas* (a kind of demon belonging—the demon himself says in the story—to the "*vyantar jāti*") afflicted his mother.[42] Nothing could induce it to leave her. Finally, in the year 1139, Ācārya Jindattsūri arrived in Lodravā and was asked to remove the demon. When he ordered it to go, it responded by saying, "The king was my enemy in a previous birth; I taught him about nonviolence, but this wicked devotee of the goddess wouldn't accept it and killed me. After I died I became a *brahm rākṣas* and I have come to destroy his family in revenge." The monk taught the demon Jain doctrine and made his vengeful feelings subside. The demon then left the mother, and Sāgar became a Jain in the *bhaṇḍśāl* as before.

In fact, the Bhansālī clan seems to have had special problems with vengeful supernatural beings. According to another story (Bhansālī

1982: 158–59; see also Granoff 1989b: 214–15), there was once an inhabitant of Pāṭaṇ named Ambar who hated the Khartar Gacch. When Jindattsūri's disciple came to Ambar's house to obtain food and water for the guru's first meal after a fast, Ambar tried to kill Jindattsūri by providing poisoned water. At Jindattsūri's instructions, a Bhansālī layman, who happened to be in the community hall at the time, mounted a hungry and thirsty camel to fetch a special ring that would remove the poison. When the ring was brought and dipped in the water, the influence of the poison abated. Then this entire unfortunate matter became known throughout the city, and the king summoned Ambar, who admitted his guilt. The king gave the order for Ambar's execution, but Jindattsūri had the order cancelled. After that, Ambar began to be called "*hatyārā*" (murderer), and upon his death he became a *vyantar* and began to create various kinds of disturbances (*updravs*).[43] He vowed that he would not become peaceful until the Bhansālī line was destroyed. In the end, Jindattsūri thwarted this *vyantar* by waving his *oghā* (broom) over the Bhansālī family ("*parivār,*" but apparently referring here to the entire Bhansālī clan). This is how the Bhansālīs acquired their reputation of being second to none in their devotion to gurus (*guru bhakti,* and referring specifically to devotion to the Dādāgurus).

An example of the involvement of a goddess in the origin of a clan is provided by the story of the Rānkā-Vānkā clan (Nāhṭā and Nāhṭā 1978: 38–9). The two protagonists, Rānkā and Vānkā, were descended from Gauḍ Kṣatriyas, who had migrated from Saurashtra; they lived in a village near Pālī where they were farmers. One day Ācārya Jinvallabhsūri came and declared that Rānkā and Vānkā were destined to have an encounter with a snake within a month, and that they should refrain from working in the fields. Despite the warning they continued to go to the fields, when finally, as they were returning one evening, they stepped on the tail of a snake. The angry snake pursued them, and they had to take refuge in a temple of the goddess Caṇḍikā (a meat-eating Hindu goddess) where they slept that night. In the morning, they saw the snake still lingering near the temple. They then began to praise the goddess in hopes of eliciting her aid. The goddess said, "Because of the *sadguru*'s (Jinvallabhsūri's) teaching I have given up meat eating and the like, and you people must give up farming and become the 'true lay Jains' (*sacce śrāvaks*) of Jinvallabhsūri." She called off the snake, told them that they would acquire *svarṇsiddhi* (the ability to make money), and sent them home. Later, Ācārya Jindattsūri visited that place and

Ranka and Vanka began to attend his sermons. They were "influenced," became pious lay Jains, and later prospered greatly.

The Jain goddess Padmāvatī is important to the story of the origin of the Phophliyā clan (ibid.: 49–50). The story begins with King Bohitth of Devalvāḍā, who founded the Botharā clan (a very well known Osvāl clan) after being converted to Jainism by Jindattsūri. At the time of his conversion, his eldest son, whose name was Karṇ, remained a non-Jain and succeeded his father to the throne. Karṇ, in his turn, had four sons. One day he was returning from a successful plundering expedition when he was attacked and killed. His queen then took her sons to her father's place at Khednagar. One night the goddess Padmāvatī appeared to her in a dream, and said, "Tomorrow because of the coming to fruition of your powerful merit, Śrī Jineśvarsūrijī Mahārāj will come here; you should go to him and accept Jainism, and you will obtain every kind of happiness." The four sons all became Jains. They made an immense amount of money in business, and were assiduous in doing the *pūjā* of the Tīrthankar. At the instruction of Jineśvarsūri, they sponsored a pilgrimage to Śatruñjaya, and while on the way they distributed rings and platters full of betel nuts (*pungīphal*) to the other pilgrims. For this reason the eldest son's descendants become known as the Phophliyā clan.

Even the Hindu god Śiva was once used by a Jain monk as an instrument of conversion (ibid.: 42). It seems that the Pamār king of Ambāgaṛh, whose name was Boraṛ, wanted to see Śiva in his real form, but was never successful.[44] When he heard about Ācārya Jindattsūri he went to him and asked if he could arrange such an encounter. The great monk said that he would arrange the vision, but only if the king agreed to do whatever Śiva instructed him to do. The king agreed, and went with the monk to a Śiva temple. Standing before the *linga* (the phallic representation of Śiva), the monk concentrated the king's vision, and amidst a cloud of smoke trident-bearing Śiva himself appeared. Śiva said, "O King, ask, ask (for a boon)!" The king said, "O Lord, if you are pleased, then give me *mokṣ* (liberation)." Śiva said, "That, I'm afraid, I don't have in my possession. If there's anything else you want, then say so, and I'll give it to you, but if you desire eternal *nirvāṇ*, then you must do what this Guru Mahārāj says." After the god left, the king worshiped Jindattsūri's feet and asked how to obtain liberation. The monk imparted the teachings of Jainism, and the king accepted Jainism in 1058. His descendants are the clan called Boraṛ, so named for their royal ancestor.

## WARRIOR-KINGS TRANSFORMED

If one looks over the conversion stories as a group, it is possible to see that the interventions by Jain ascetics often have certain interesting common features. The cure or rescue is usually accomplished by means of the ascetic's personal supernormal power, which is often mediated by substances or deities. However, and importantly, such magical power is accompanied by something else. It is not enough for a convert-to-be to be overawed by an ascetic's miraculous power; a vital ingredient is a transformation in the convert-to-be's outlook. Whether or not it is made explicit in the narrative, the assumption is that this is accomplished by means of the ascetic's *updeś,* his teachings. The ascetic is usually said to "awaken" (*pratibodh denā*) the convert. The convert thereby becomes "influenced" (*prabhāvit*) by the ascetic's teachings. He then comes to "accept" (*angīkār karnā*) the Jain *dharm* (Jainism).

The social and cultural personae of such converts are completely transformed. Awakened converts give up meat and liquor (*mās-madirā*) and violence toward other beings (*jīv hiṃsā*). As Nāhṭā and Nāhṭā put it, they abandon "meat-eating, hunting, animal sacrifice, liquor, those foods that are not to be eaten, and other things that tend toward violence and sin" (1978: 2). They lay down the sword and take up other occupations.

Sometimes the new Jains get rich. But although business is mentioned as an occupation taken up by new Jains, it does not seem to be especially stressed. These conversion accounts are mainly about how Rājpūts became *Jains,* not about how they became businessmen. The emphasis in the clan histories is on giving up violence and coming under the protection of Jain ascetics. Their business life seems to be regarded as a kind of unintended (or not directly intended) by-product of Jainism, a method of obtaining a livelihood that does not involve violence.

How are we to interpret such tales? Taken together, they say—among other things—something like this: "We were not always as you see us now; once we were warrior-kings." And in saying this, they provide a general cultural context for a particular kind of Jain identity. It must be plainly stated again that the historicity of such claims is not at issue here; what matters is the role these assertions play in the social and cultural self-image of Osvāl Jains. It is true that other, non-Jain groups claim Rājpūt origin too; given the historical role of the Rājpūts in the region, this should not surprise us.[45] The Osvāls (and Śrīmāls too), however, assert the claim of Rājpūt origin within a specifically Jain frame of reference, and thus for them it is a claim that establishes a specifically *Jain* identity. They see themselves as those who, *under the influence of Jain ascetics,* renounced the violent ways of warrior-kings.

The Osvāl Jains (and many Śrīmāls too) see themselves as a community of intermarrying, once-royal but ritually-still-kingly clans who came to be as they are by means of the ascetic powers of Jain *ācāryas*. They are ex-Kṣatriyas who were transformed by ascetics and who are, above all, supporters of ascetics. They are also (as we saw in Chapter Three) still under the protection of ascetics—in general terms, the protection of the very ascetics who converted their ancestors to Jainism.

When told from a Jain perspective, a tale of a warrior-kingly past has plenty to resonate with, as we have seen. In a discussion of the Rājpūt origins of the Osvāls, an Osvāl friend in Jaipur once reminded me of the Tīrthankars: They, he said, "were Rājpūts too." Of course he was right, and on more than one level. The spiritualization of martial valor is central to Jainism's message. The Tīrthankars, the ego-ideals of the tradition, were also of royal origin, and they, too, renounced their royal heritage. The image of such a transformation is thus an open mythical paradigm, available *as a plausible model of how groups might come to be Jains.* That it is also an attractive model no doubt stems from the immensely high prestige of the Rājpūt/Kṣatriya aristocracy, particularly in Rajasthan.

Because this symbolism of Osvāl origins draws so heavily on Jain images of kingship, the renunciation of kingship, and asceticism and the powers of Jain ascetics, we may say that in this context Jainism itself has become the most widely "encompassing" origin myth of the Osvāl Jains: a belief system that—among many other things—invests the origin myths of particular Jain groups with their widest significance.

## AMBIGUOUS IDENTITY

It remains to be said that the Tīrthankars' example of the transformation of hero-prince into hero-ascetic cannot, as it stands, provide a symbolic foundation for the social identity of an actual Jain community. Such a community can indeed be one of ex-warrior-kings, and so the Osvāls have seen themselves. However, it cannot be one of hero-ascetics for the simple reason that it must be a self-reproducing community of men and women who make their way in the world. Asceticism exercises a powerful influence on Jain conduct. Ascetic practice can be pursued as a permanent condition of life, as it is for monks and nuns. Or it can be temporary and circumscribed, as it is for the many ascetic exercises, especially those involving fasting, for which Jain lay religious custom is renowned. These practices have a deep legitimacy conferred by the tradition's bias toward the ascetic *mokṣ mārg*. But sustained realization of ascetic values is not an option for most lay Jains.

Still, if a Jain community cannot be a community of hero-ascetics, then there is another thing it *can* be: a community of ex-warrior-kings who are not themselves ascetics but who respect and worship Jain ascetics. This is indeed how Osvāl origin mythology portrays Osvāl identity.

How, then, is the identity of those who worship ascetics to be conceived? Out of what symbolic materials is it to be constructed? To take the case of the Osvāl Jains, such respecters and worshipers of ascetics obviously cannot be warrior-kingly on the Rājpūt model (or on any other), for they have shed the culture of violence.[46] Nonetheless, they can retain at least one kingly attribute, for they are supporters of holy personages and religious institutions. The model for this role is provided by the Indras and Indrāṇīs who are divine kings and queens and who are also the archetypal supporters and worshipers of Jain ascetics. Those who have been "influenced" and "awakened" by Jain ascetics can never again participate in the culture of warrior-kingship as represented by groups like the Rājpūts. But royal identity can be expressed in the more limited domain of ritual contexts (as well as other domains such as philanthropy). Ritual culture thus emerges as an arena in which the symbolism of worldly kingship—the choice *not* taken by those who bear the tradition's highest values, the Tīrthankars—is allowed explicit expression.

The sociocultural identity of lay Jains can be said to be poised between two unreachable poles. One pole is heroic asceticism, but this is fully available only to the world renouncer. The other is worldly kingship, but this has been renounced and thus is available only in ritual settings. By default, perhaps, the only truly stable and available platform for a sense of what it means to *be* a lay Jain is *ahiṃsā* itself. Therefore, a Jain laity must be deeply, passionately vegetarian. Such a laity, moreover, must be more vegetarian than other vegetarians, and in all departments of life. Ex-Rājpūts who respect Jain ascetics thus become the cultural "others" of Rājpūts.

## IDENTITY AND THE DĀDĀGURUS

These same dilemmas and ambiguities are directly reflected in ritual culture. In an earlier chapter we have seen that there is an inherent instability in the dominant ritual culture of the image-worshiping Śvetāmbar Jains. At one level, the identity of the worshipers of the Tīrthankar gravitates powerfully in the direction of kingship. Momentarily they become the kings and queens of heaven who are the models for the veneration of ascetics. Such worshipers might even hope to become "actual" gods and goddesses in a future birth. For those worshipers who see themselves as ex-Rājpūts, moreover, the rite is also a movement backward in symbolic time; it recalls their own lofty origin. The gods, in this context, represent a past paradise, and a possible future one, for ex-kings who respect ascetics. But even in ritual culture, these images seem vulnerable to challenge. The fact that asceticism is the central value of the rite acts as a powerful corrosive on the royal image of the worshiper. Therefore, in a regnant interpretation of the meaning of worship, the image of kingly generosity gives way to that of the ascetic's giving up.

In the ritual subculture focused on the Dādāgurus, however, the pressure of ascetic values is relaxed. Chapter Three showed that these figures are Jain ascetics who can be worshiped as gods who will aid their devotees in worldly matters. In other words, they provide a method for lay Jains to pursue worldly values through ritual, but ritual of a sort that is nonetheless indisputably Jain.

In this chapter we see how the aid rendered by the Dādāgurus is rooted in a paradigm of Jain social identity. The Dādāgurus, as noted before, are basically generic figures. They really stand for *all* the great ascetics of the socially significant past. The Dādāgurus' worshipers belong to a community that sees itself as having come into existence when warrior-kings learned to respect Jain ascetics by being healed or aided in other ways by such mendicants. From that time forward, the two roles became frozen: Warrior-kings exchanged the protection of the swords they had laid aside for the protection of powerful ascetics. The Dādāgurus represent that formative moment. Therefore, when devotees stand before the Dādāgurus, they reclaim the magic of those far-off days. They are kings and queens in need of healing, and are invoking an old bargain. These roles are the basis of the ritual subculture associated with the Dādāgurus.

As we have reiterated frequently in this book, Jains worship ascetics. Unlike the cult of the Tīrthankars, however, the cult of the Dādāgurus does not impose ascetic values on the worshiper. The Dādāgurus are genuine Jain ascetics, but the very basis of the ritual relationship between them and their devotees is very different from the relationship between Tīrthankar and worshipers. The Dādāgurus are helpers; the worshiper's object is not emulation but connection. When the cult is examined in relation to caste and clan origin mythology, we see that the identity it imposes on devotees coincides with their social identity as members of a Jain caste. Here the ambiguities associated with the worshiper's identity seem much less acute than in the worship of the Tīrthankars.

We may now return to Ṛddhisār's *pūjā*—the principal rite of worship for the Dādāgurus—and examine it in a more general context. When we do, we see it links the present, through history and transhistory, to eternal principles. Devcandrajī's *snātra pūjā* is located in eternity; the events it enacts have existed always and will always exist through infinite time. The *pūjā* of Pārśvanāth's five *kalyāṇak*s connects eternity with manifested sacredness. Pārśvanāth's career on earth—and this is true of all the Tīrthankars' earthly careers—causes eternity and "history" to touch. His was a particular career, different from that of all other Tīrthankars, except with respect to the five *kalyāṇak*s. These crucial five events, though always exactly the same, bring forth beneficial power at particular times, power that lingers on in the cosmos even after its source has departed. The worship of the Dādāgurus, in its turn, connects this beneficial power—manifested last in the career of Lord Mahāvīr—to the identity and vitality of a living Jain community.

When Jains worship the Tīrthankars they are in contact with eternity. The actions performed and the roles taken have always existed, and will always exist, in the beginningless and endless repetitions of cosmic time. At this level the tradition is focused on the timeless predicament of the unliberated soul's wanderings in *saṃsār.* When Jains worship the Dādāgurus these acts and roles are duplicated, but on a different plane; they are brought into connection with the world in which worshipers actually live. The Tīrthankars create, and eternally recreate, the fourfold order of Jain society. By contrast, the Dādāgurus were the creators of historical Jain clans.[47] Those who worship the Tirthankars are archetypal Indras and Indrāṇīs, the kings and queens of the gods. Those who worship the Dādāgurus are the sons and daughters of kings who became Jains when powerful monks came to their aid.

The cult of the Dādāgurus is a ritual subculture that enlarges the religious tradition to which it belongs in very important ways. It utilizes standard features of Śvetāmbar ritual culture, but reinterprets them and changes their context radically. In so doing, it bridges the gap between the tradition's highest values—ascetic values oriented toward liberation—and the material and social landscapes inhabited by men and women who remain in the world.

CHAPTER FIVE

# Giving and Giving Up

A ritual culture supports and is supported by the roles assumed by those who are the actors in ritual performances. From this standpoint, a ritual of worship can be seen as a theater of identity staged within a particular symbolic milieu. Participants in rituals of worship play roles, and in so doing take on identities of various kinds. These ritually enacted identities are built out of—and in turn give life to—ideas, values, and images that are available in the symbolic surround within which the rites in question occur.

This book has been an exploration of the implications of this idea in a Jain frame of reference. Among image-worshiping Śvetāmbar Jains we have discovered a ritual culture that is manifested in a distinctive pattern of interaction between worshipers and the sacred. At its core is the most fundamental fact of all about Jain ritual culture—often reiterated here—that Jains worship ascetics. All religious traditions must deal with inner tensions and ambiguities; in the case of Jain ritual culture, these arise largely from the asceticism of the object of worship. Within the domain of Śvetāmbar ritual culture, the central question is always that of how the relationship between a worshiper and an ascetic object of worship is to be defined, and, correlatively, how the identity of the worshiper is to be conceived. The issue of the worshiper's identity is of course a transposition of the question of how it is possible to be a lay Jain, expressed in ritual terms. In the Jain ritual culture with which we have been concerned, we have found the identity of the worshiper to be defined at three identifiable levels.

On one level we find what we might call "soteriological" identity.

Here the worshiper imitates the object of worship; in so doing, he or she enacts a hoped-for liberation, to be achieved by means of an ascetic shedding of the world. This interpretation of the worshiper's identity directly reflects the values and aspirations of the *mokṣ mārg*, the Jain path of liberation, and it is most favored by ascetics and those who adopt the ascetic point of view. Who is the worshiper according to this interpretation? He or she is someone headed for liberation, however long the wait may have to be.

At the second level is what we might call "royal" identity. Here the worshiper is identified with Indra or Indrāṇī, the king or queen of the gods. This image is the negative other of that of the Tīrthankar—one who, as we have seen, gave up earthly kingship to become a king of the spirit instead. It is also highly resonant with the notion of the worshiper as one who prospers in the world, as do the kings and queens of the gods. Such a worshiper admires and supports ascetics, and reaps the material rewards of doing so; he or she defers, though in no sense disclaims, the actual seeking of liberation. Who is the worshiper according to this interpretation? He or she is someone who is certainly on the road to liberation, but who is headed down a detour of worldly felicity along the way.

This image of the worshiper is in deep tension with the soteriological image, and because of the tradition's profound bias in favor of world renunciation, the most prestigious interpretations of worship tend to favor the image of the worshiper as a world renouncer. In the case of Śvetāmbar Jains associated with the Khartar Gacch, this tension is resolved in the ritual subculture of the cult of the Dādāgurus. In this cult the pressure to define the worshiper as an ascetic who emulates the object of worship is relaxed. Here the worshiper is imaged as a seeker of worldly assistance engaged in transactions with powerful ascetics, ascetics who can and do intervene in his or her worldly affairs. Asceticism, as it were, is sequestered by projecting it entirely on the role of the object of worship, and of course the asceticism of the object of worship is, finally, flawed by comparison with that of the Tirthankars. These transactions are nonetheless invested with Jain legitimacy by stressing the ascetics' membership in a spiritual lineage connecting them with the Tirthankar, by associating their powers with Jain ascetic praxis, and by insisting that current interventions in the affairs of their devotees are latter-day manifestations of the Dādāgurus' historical efforts to protect and elevate Jainism. Thus, their worshipers are free to pursue worldly felicity with minimal twinges of conscience.

The third level is that of social identity. In the Rajasthani materials we have surveyed, we have seen that at this level the focus on the worshiper's identity as Indra or Indrāṇī is shifted somewhat; the worshiper still adopts the role of Indra or Indrāṇī, but superimposed over that role—and deeply consistent with it—is the identity of the worshiper as the lineal descendant of the medieval warrior-kings of Rajasthan. Who is the worshiper? He or she is a person of warrior-kingly lineage who has come before a powerful ascetic seeking help as his or her ancestors did long ago. That is, he or she is an Osvāl Jain—or indeed a member of any of the many Jain groups who consider themselves to be the descendants of Kṣatriyas, who were long ago converted to Jainism by powerful ascetics.

Two facts unite these three projections of the worshiper's identity. The first is the centrality of asceticism itself. It must be remembered always that Jains worship ascetics, and this is crucially true of each of the three levels of lay identity that we have discovered in Śvetāmbar ritual culture. The other common element—profoundly related to the first—is the metaphor of kingship. Tīrthankars are kings-who-might-have-been, who chose to renounce the world instead of to rule it. Those who worship the Tīrthankars face the same choice that they did. They are either ascetics, in imitation of the Tīrthankar, or they take on the identities of the kings and queens of the gods. For worshipers of the Dādāgurus this latter identity grades into the identity of the sons and daughters of earthly kings.

## VARIATIONS

Thus far we have considered a Jain ritual culture in relative isolation. While we have alluded from time to time to its wider context, both in the Jain world and even beyond, our object has been to map its internal terrain, not its location on broader landscapes. In this chapter we turn from the tradition itself to its wider context in South Asian religion, with a particular emphasis on other South Asian ritual cultures. Doing so discloses a surprising result. Seen purely as a system of ideas embodying a strategy for achieving liberation—which is the view often taken of Jainism—Jain traditions seem radically different from the "Hindu" traditions that form their cultural surround. This sort of comparison seems to vindicate the familiar image of Jainism as "heterodoxy." If, however, we shift the focus to ritual culture we discover that Jainism is far less "other" to other South Asian traditions than is commonly supposed. From this perspective it represents a variation—perhaps an extreme variation—on common South Asian ritual themes. At this level, Jain ritual culture itself might be seen as a subculture of a more generalized South Asian ritual culture.

The crucial issue, as we shall see, is that of exchange. A consideration of who gives what to whom in situations of worship turns out to be a powerful technique for tracing essential similarities and differences between religious traditions.

## VAIṢṆAVAS

A Śvetāmbar Jain friend from Jaipur once suggested to me that, to understand why *prasād* is not distributed to the Tīrthankar's worshipers, one must see things from the Vaiṣṇava point of view. Vaiṣṇavas are those who worship the major Hindu deity Viṣṇu and his manifestations. To the Vaiṣṇavas, my friend went on to say, God is a creator and a giver; he is wealthy. The Tīrthankar is obviously not wealthy, he added, so how can he be a giver?

This was an extremely acute and interesting observation. To begin with, it pointed to the truly essential thing about Jain ritual culture: the asceticism of the object of worship. Jains worship ascetics. This book has been largely devoted to tracing the implications of that bedrock fact. But there is more, for the remark was revealing in another way. It is highly significant that my friend did not use the word *Hindu* in formulating his suggested comparison. This shows us that, to an insider's sensibility, *Hinduism* is not necessarily the right entity with which to compare Jain traditions; more logical, to my friend at least, would be the Vaiṣnavas.[1] He almost certainly had in mind the Puṣṭimārg, a Vaiṣṇava sect that is extremely influential in Rajasthan and has many followers within the general merchant class to which Jains belong.

If we follow my friend's advice—that is, if we forget about Hinduism and concentrate on the Puṣṭimārg and its ritual culture—then we make an interesting discovery. It is probably true that many of the elaborations and flourishes of major Jain *pūjās* have been influenced by Vaiṣṇava patterns. At a deeper level, however, the ritual culture of the Puṣṭimārg is very different from that of the Jains; in a sense, it is Jain ritual culture precisely inverted.

The Puṣṭimārg was, in effect, invented as a ritual culture. According to the sect's own account of its origin (Barz 1976: 22–29; Bennett 1983: 152–53), a bent arm made of black stone miraculously appeared out of the ground on the top of Mt. Govardhan in Braj in 1410 C.E. This object was in fact (or was later held to be) a portion of an image of Kṛṣṇa as Śrī Govardhannāthjī,[2] but because the image was discovered on Nāg Pañcmī day (a snake festival), the local people worshiped it with milk as snakes are worshiped. In compliance with instructions received from Kṛṣṇa in a vision, Vallabhācārya—the founder of the Puṣṭimārg—went to Braj in 1494 and revealed the image's true identity. He then established proper procedures for its regular worship (known as *sevā*), which have been central to the sect's praxis ever since. The image, now at Nāthdvāra, is the sect's physical epicenter. In the same year, Kṛṣṇa also revealed a conversion formula to Vallabhācārya. It expresses one of the sect's core ideas: that all that the devotee possesses—mind, body, and wealth (*man, tan, dhan*)—should be offered to Kṛṣṇa before use; in this way the soul can be cleansed of faults (*doṣa*s) and redeemed.

If we compare the ritual culture of the Puṣṭimārg to the cult of the Tīrthankars, its most striking feature is the strong emphasis it places on exchanges between worshiper and worshiped. Readers will recall that worshipers do not engage in transactions of any kind with the Tīrthankars. The Puṣṭimārg reverses this. If much of the actual content of Jain ritual culture is shaped by the transactional *absence* of the object of worship, in the Puṣṭimārg Kṛṣṇa is seen as *present* to the highest degree and thus can engage in exchanges. If Jain worship is transactionally *null,* worship in the Puṣṭimārg is transactionally *dense.* This contrast is most clearly seen in ritual transactions in the medium of food.

The Jain and Puṣṭimārg traditions take opposite views of the whole matter of food and eating. While feasting certainly plays a role in Jain life (especially on such auspicious occasions as marriage ceremonies), in the final analysis—as we know—food has a bad reputation in the Jain world; it is the basis of bodily existence, and thus a primary ingredient of bondage. It is precisely because of the spiritual hazards of eating that fasting is so central to both lay and monastic religious practice among Jains. A Jaipur Śvetāmbar friend once remarked to me, only half ironically, that (as she put it in English) "In Jainism you're not supposed to eat." An Ahmedabad friend, with no intention of irony at all, said to me that one should eat with tears in one's eyes for the creatures that had to die that one might eat.

It is in this context that the meaning of food offerings in Jain ritual has to be understood. Food is dangerous, poisonous stuff; it is the world of bondage in concentrated form. Thus, in rites of worship of the Tīrthankars, the offering of food is interpreted not as a gift of nourishment but as a symbolic renunciation of eating. But far from being spiritually hazardous, food is a powerful positive value in the Puṣṭimārg. Here the very concept of *nourishment*, radically devalued in Jainism, is central to the relationship between worshiper and deity. The term *Puṣṭimārg* means the "road" or "path" (*mārg*) of *puṣṭi*. The latter term carries the meanings of "nourishment," "strengthening," or "support," and in this context it refers to Kṛṣṇa's grace (*anugraha*) that nourishes and supports the devotee (Barz 1976: 86).

This idea is manifested in a food-exalting ritual culture. Food offered to Kṛṣṇa is called *bhog*, "enjoyment." Kṛṣṇa "enjoys" the food offering and, through his enjoyment, transforms it. The recovered offering becomes his *prasād*, his grace, by which devotees are "nourished" (Bennett 1990: 199; also Toomey 1990: 167–68). The Puṣṭimārg's alimentary emphasis is vividly expressed in the festival of Annakūṭa, the "mountain of food" (Bennett 1983: 295–307; 1990: 199–200). Occurring on the second day of Divālī, it commemorates the famous episode in which the people of Braj ceased giving sacrifice to Indra and started worshiping Mt. Govardhan instead. They made a mountain of food as high as Mt. Govardhan, and Kṛṣṇa, assuming the form of the mountain, ate it all.[3] Worshipers give their own mountains of food symbolizing their overflowing devotion; Kṛṣṇa is "both receiver and redistributor, the repository of an overflowing store of devotion and the source of boundless grace" (ibid.: 200).

The idealized personae of worshipers are also very different in Jainism and the Puṣṭimārg. The Jain worshiper becomes Indra or Indrāṇī. These regal divinities support and admire the Tīrthankar, and even bathe the infant Tīrthankar lovingly. It is obvious, in fact, that many human worshipers feel their contact with Tīrthankar images to be truly intimate, and a feeling of devotional closeness between worshiper and object of worship is unquestionably an important dimension of the ritual experience of Jains. Such intimacy, however, is challenged by its symbolic and ideational context, for the relationship between Indras and Indrāṇīs and the Tīrthankar cannot, in the end, be described as intimate. Rather, the kings and queens of heaven acknowledge a superior sovereignty, the spiritual kingship of he who is a victor (*jina*) over attachments and aversions. And, as we have seen, the Jain emphasis on asceticism decisively separates worshiper from worshiped in the final analysis. The connection between worshiper and worshiped ranges from metaphorical to analogical; it cannot be tangible or substantial. Closure between worshiper and the Tīrthankar is brought about only by a tightening of metaphor into analogy; what results is *resemblance,* not *contact,* and the worshiper becomes a world renouncer in imitation of the object of his or her devotion.

The Puṣṭimārg stresses intimacy. Here the connection between worshiper and worshiped is not metaphorical but, within the world of the ritual, "real." This tradition recognizes four principal emotional attitudes (*bhāv*s) that the devotee can assume in his or her relationship with Kṛṣṇa: that of servant to master, friend to friend, parent to child, and lover to beloved (Barz 1976: 87–91; Bennett 1983: 141–42).[4] The servant-master relationship, with its implications of rigid hierarchy, is downplayed as inconsistent with the desired intimacy between devotee and deity. Of the other emotions, the most important is that of parent to child (*vātsalya*) (Barz 1976: 88; Bennett 1983: 214), and in ritual the worshiper's favored role is that of Yaśodā, Kṛṣṇa's foster mother (Bennett 1983: 249; Toomey 1990: 167–68). The food offering is full of mother's love-as-nourishment; what returns is Kṛṣṇa's "nourishing grace."

The key point is that Kṛṣṇa, in contrast to the Tīrthankar, is a highly transactional being. Vallabhācārya taught that souls are burdened with faults or impurities, and that these must be cleaned away by offering all that one has to Kṛṣṇa—mind, body, and wealth (Barz 1976: 16–20).[5] Kṛṣṇa himself would accomplish this, for only he "could remove the impurities which darkened the soul" (Bennett 1983: 88). The agency of this transformation was Vallabhācārya (and his successors), who was an incarnation of Kṛṣṇa appearing precisely for this purpose (ibid.: 89). In this role, Vallabhācārya was associated with Agni (the Vedic god of fire) and the sacrificial fire that "burns away" impurities (ibid.: 93–94). Thus, the first step toward redemption is a transaction; in effect, the offerer gives himself, and a purified self is returned.

Having been thus purified, initiates are "fit" to approach Lord Kṛṣṇa more directly. Now the transactional gateway between deity and devotee opens widely; intimate transactions, tending toward complete consubstantiation, become possible. Food offerings are the highest ritual expression of this intimacy. From a worldly (*laukik*) point of view, fine foods are given in abundance, and the remnants of Kṛṣṇa's meal are eaten by devotees. From a spiritual (*alaukik*) standpoint—which is the perspective of realized devotees—the transaction is emotional. The offered food embodies the devotee's feelings of love; Kṛṣṇa's "enjoyment" infuses the offerings with his "bliss" (*ānanda*), which is returned to devotees as his *prasād* (Bennett 1983: 246–61).[6] The transaction thus actualizes the devotee's primordial identity with Kṛṣṇa, which is one of the tenets of Vallabhācārya's theology of *śuddhādvaita* (Barz 1976: 56–79).

The ritual cultures of the Jains and the Puṣṭimārg are true opposites. Kṛṣṇa takes and enjoys mountains of food. In his liberated condition, the Tīrthankar—"eatingless" in his very nature—takes and enjoys nothing. The Puṣṭimārgī devotee gives *everything* to Lord Kṛṣṇa—his mind, body, and wealth—and then keeps giving. The Jain worshiper gives, but gives nothing *to* the Tīrthankar; what he gives, he "gives away" in an act of symbolic renunciation.[7] Lord Kṛṣṇa is a *giver*, a bestower of overflowing grace. The Tīrthankar gives nothing, and *can* give nothing; the benefits the worshiper receives he generates himself. All this is consistent with a basic soteriological difference. The Puṣṭimārg asserts that redemption (*uddhār*) cannot be achieved without Kṛṣṇa's grace (ibid.: 1976: 60), whereas the Jains say that liberation can only be achieved on one's own.[8]

We may note finally that Kṛṣṇa's ritual persona seems to utilize a different image of kingship than we see in the case of the Tīrthankar. The Tīrthankar is a royal figure: He *could* become an earthly emperor, but chooses the path of a spiritual sovereign instead. The emphasis is on spiritual conquest, his victory over attachments and aversions. In Kṛṣṇa's case the accent is on royal generosity. While it is true that the Puṣṭimārg strongly downplays hierarchy between worshiper and worshiped, Kṛṣṇa's role nevertheless seems to reflect, if only in part, an image of the king as the focus of a redistributive network (see Bennett 1983: 268–307). In Jain tradition, the attribute of regal generosity is shifted away from the Tīrthankar and assigned to the gods instead.[9]

## ŚAIVAS

The Puṣṭimārg is considered a Hindu sect. Have we, then, discovered an essential difference between Jainism and Hinduism? Not quite, for it turns out that Jain ritual culture has close parallels in what is generally regarded as the "Hindu" world. An example is Śaiva Siddhānta. Let me stress that a comparison of Jain and Śaiva ritual culture is not suggested—as is our Jain-Vaiṣṇava comparison—by close regional and social juxtaposition. Rather, in this case comparison finds its rationale in the existence of structural similarities. These similarities raise serious questions about the validity of the conventional Jain-Hindu boundary and may also point to structural unities underlying South Asian ritual cultures.

Similarities between the ritual cultures of Jainism and Śaiva Siddhānta are quite striking, especially in the treatment of food offerings. From the fine recent account of Richard H. Davis (1991) we learn that the Śaiva worshiper makes offerings to Lord Śiva, but they are not afterwards consumed by the offerers.[10] Instead of being reclaimed by worshipers, the forbidden leftovers, called *nirmālya,*[11] are offered to a fearsome deity named Caṇḍa who seems to function as a kind of temple guardian. Afterwards, the now twice-offered materials of worship are burnt, buried, submerged, or given to animals.

What are we to make of this? When we look more closely at Śaiva ritual culture, we see an overlay of themes reminiscent of the Puṣṭimārg. We also see, however, what appears to be a deeper affinity with Jain ritual culture. Let me say that it is not my intention to characterize Śaiva Siddhānta as an entire ritual tradition; I am concerned, rather, with the admittedly narrow issue of ritual exchanges. What interests me is that, from this perspective, it is almost as if Śaiva ritual culture is Jainism in a "Hindu" guise.

As in the Puṣṭimārg, in Śaiva ritual the deity is a transacting "presence." Śiva is believed to "descend" (Davis 1991: 128–33) into the *linga,* which is seen as a "physical support" for his presence (ibid.: 122). Moreover, Śiva actually does receive the offerings, which provide him "with pleasurable sensory experience while he is embodied and present in the shrine" (ibid.: 150). As in the Puṣṭimārg, the offerer even offers himself; he moves from giving other substances to "giving his own inner constituents to Śiva, ending with his most essential part, the soul" (ibid.: 153).

But we must also note strong echoes of themes that we have encountered among the Jains. To begin with, the Śaivas seem to share with the Jains the notion that worshiper and worshiped do not "merge." In this respect both traditions contrast similarly with the Puṣṭimārg. As among the Jains, the relationship between worshiper and worshiped postulated by the Śaivas seems, at least in some respects, more *metaphorical* than tangible. In accordance with the well-known formula, " 'Only a Śiva can worship Śiva' " (ibid.: 52), the Śaiva worshiper metamorphoses his body into a Śiva-like form. But actual merger is not the goal of Śaiva ritual; one seeks not to become *Śiva,* but to become *a* Śiva (that is, just as a Jain should become *a siddha*). "A liberated soul," says Davis, "does not merge into divinity or become united with him, as some other systems of Hindu philosophy assert. Nor does it enter again into the manifest cosmos. Rather, it remains as *an autonomous theomorphic entity,* separate from Śiva but with all his powers and qualities" (ibid.: 83; my italics). The central goal of the ritual act is to transform the actor into a Śiva-like state by means of what is called *ātmaśuddhi,* soul-purification; the ultimate aim is to achieve this condition permanently. *Ātmaśuddhi* purifies the soul by means of a ritual transformation of the body, and this is viewed as a "rehearsal" for the ritualist's final liberation (ibid.: 101).

Furthermore, as do the Jains, the Śaivas emphasize ritual reflexivity. Although the Śaivas state that Śiva's grace is a necessary precondition for the removal of binding fetters (ibid.: 28–29), the logic of ritual is based on the idea of self transformation. The Śaiva worshiper, Davis says, "exercises his own capacities of self-transformation, both rehearsing his final liberation and at the same time gradually bringing it about" (ibid.: 101).[12] Śaiva ritual therefore also echoes the Jain theme of ritual emulation. The ultimate goal of the ritual act is the purification of the soul in emulation of Śiva's own qualities.

What, then, becomes of the unrecovered offerings? Between the Jains and the Śaivas the basic practice is the same, but there are apparent differences. Among the Jains, the nonreturnability of offerings has to do with the asceticism of the object of worship and the worshiper's reflexive asceticism. The offering is unrecovered because it bears *negative* value that cannot be transmuted into something positive. Among the Śaivas, however, the issue seems to be "purity," a positive value. "Contact with Śiva," says Davis, "has rendered the *nirmālya* immaculate, yet human worshipers continue to inhabit bodies infested with *mala* and so are not able to bear contact with so much pureness" (ibid.: 156). Śiva says (in one *Purāṇa*) that to consume his leavings is equivalent to a Śūdra studying the Vedas, and will lead to the consumer's destruction. Thus, because it is *too* positive to be borne by humans, the leftover offering has to be given to Caṇḍa instead. "In contrast to humans," Davis says, "Caṇḍa is able to bear the intense purity of *nirmālya,* presumably by means of his own ardent character" (ibid.: 157).

There is, however, another possible angle on this issue. Davis says, "Worshiping Caṇḍa has a second purpose as well. Not only does it present the *nirmālya* to an appropriate recipient, it also removes any faults (*doṣa*) the priest may have committed while worshiping the linga. . . .

Like Śiva's own power of reabsorbtion, the fierce Caṇḍa removes and absorbs a host of things: the afflictions of his devotees, mistakes made in worshiping Śiva, and Śiva's too-pure leftovers" (ibid.: 157).[13]

Now it is not for us to tell the Śaivas what they mean. But if we bracket the "too pure" formula and instead emphasize the possibility that offerings carry, or at least resonate with, negativities—faults, afflictions, and so on—then we can make good sense of the pattern, for it bears a strong resemblance to the pattern we have called "Jain." Offerings of food, for the Jains, carry negative value; in harmony with the prevailing ascetic outlook, they are *shed* in the context of the ritual encounter. It seems possible that the Śaiva offering also carries a negative burden. In this context it may be significant that, as do the Jains, the Śaivas see the act of making offerings as a form of "abandonment" (*tyāga*) (ibid.: 159).

What actually transpires between Śiva and any offering-borne negativity? We know that Śiva consumes only that portion of the offering that has (by ritual means) been infused with his nature (*śivatva*), not the physical part (ibid.: 154). Can "faults" be made into Śiva? I think the answer is no; I suspect this precisely because the negativities seem to be passed along to Caṇḍa, who must then deal with them somehow. When the Śaivas say that the offering is "too pure" to be recovered by the offerers, this may cover a deeper idea that Śiva, unlike the Puṣṭimārg's Kṛṣṇa, is not a deity who transforms and returns, but a being who—like the Tīrthankar—presides over ritualizations in the reflexive and emulatory mode.

Similarities between Jain and Śaiva ritual patterns make theological sense. Unlike the "wealthy" deity of the Vaiṣṇavas, neither Tīrthankar nor Śiva is a very good candidate for dense transactional relationships with worshipers. The Tīrthankar is an ascetic. So is Śiva. The Tīrthankar is entirely nontransactive. Śiva seems minimally so. He *does* in some sense receive the offering, but in the end it, or at least the physical part of it, is passed to another being. Whatever their differences, Jain and Śaiva ritual cultures seem to be shaped in similar ways by the worship of divine beings who transact thinly, not thickly, with devotees.

## BUDDHISTS

Jainism and Buddhism are often classed together as anti-Vedic "heterodoxies." Leaving aside the question of whether or not such a label makes much sense, the fact remains that a comparison at the level of ritual culture reveals striking similarities between these two traditions. In Theravada Buddhism, as in Jainism, "presence" is an issue (cf. Parry 1986: 462).[14] The Buddha has achieved *nirvāṇa* and in theory no longer exists. Neverthless, his images are worshiped. What, then, can such worship be?

In the Sinhalese tradition—to which I shall confine my brief observations—the dilemma is apparently mitigated to some degree by conferring continued existence on the Buddha. Obeyesekere suggests that the Buddha's own shelving (as spiritually irrelevant) of the question of whether the *arhat* is living or dead leaves an opening for the notion of a nonextinguished *nirvāṇa*-realized being (1966: 8). He goes on to say that the presence of Buddha relics in Buddha temples provides a conceptual bridge to the idea that the Buddha images contain the Buddha's "essence." Gombrich likewise reports that the Buddha is regarded as "in some sense present and aware" and "numinously present" (1966: 23; for an extended discussion of this issue, see Gombrich 1971: 103–43).

Still, there are also indications that as an object of worship the Buddha's character is far closer to the Tīrthankars than to, let us say, the Puṣṭimārg's Kṛṣṇa. To begin with, although the lesser deities of the Sinhalese pantheon intervene directly in the affairs of their worshipers, the Buddha does not. The lesser gods and goddesses are directly propitiated in prayer, whereas prayer directed to the Buddha is "commemorative" (Obeyesekere 1966: 5). Recitation of the Buddha's attributes repels malign supernaturals, but they are deterred out of respect for the Buddha and his teachings, not by any "active force" emanating from him (Gombrich 1966: 23).

Moreover, offerings to the Buddha have a special status. Michael Ames characterizes such offerings as "nonreciprocal." By this he means that they are not given in the expectation of divine favors, but simply to express reverence for the Buddha and his teachings. They have no effect on their recipient; rather, by representing the offerer's "renunciation" they improve the offerer's own "virtues," while nothing is actually "bestowed" by the Buddha (Ames 1966: 31). Also, offerings to the Buddha are not recovered as *prasād,* although *prasād* is indeed taken from the altars of deities. Food offered to the Buddha belongs to the same category as food offered to the *sangha* (the ascetic community), an idea echoed in the Jain materials we have seen, and "no self-respecting Buddhist would touch it" (Gombrich 1971: 119; see also Seneviratne 1978: 70, 176 f.n.). Normally, offerings to the Buddha are simply thrown away, given to beggars, or given to animals, especially dogs or crows (H. L. Seneviratne, personal communication; Gombrich 1971: 108, 119).

These materials seem to indicate that there are significant formal similarities between Tīrthankar-worship among Śvetāmbar Jains and Buddha-worship in Sri Lanka. In the Sinhalese tradition, too, we seem to be dealing with a ritual mode that is essentially monopolar and reflexive. There is no transactional closure; instead of forming the basis for intimate reciprocity with a divine other, the act of giving is a ritualization of what are conceived to be autonomous spiritual strivings. "Ego gives and alter receives," says Ames; "Alter's reaction, whatever it may be, is not necessary to validate ego's original act of giving. All alter has to do is accept the prestation" (1966: 31). To this might be added only the observation that the expulsion of the gift from the community—and even from the human world—suggests that it is, in ritual logic as well as physical fact, accepted by no "alter" at all.

We are, of course, unsurprised by the obvious similarities between Jain and Theravada Buddhist ritual cultures. These ritual cultures are associated with very similar ritual roles. Jains worship ascetics, and the highest worship is reserved for a personage so ascetic that he is beyond the reach of worship. Most of what is distinctive about Jain ritual culture follows from that fact. Buddhist worship is likewise focused on an ascetic being who is incapable of transactions with worshipers. Theological differences aside, Jainism and Buddhism are close siblings at the level of ritual culture.

## HOT POTATOES

What, we may now ask, has become of the boundary between Hinduism and Jainism (or, for that matter, between either and Buddhism)? The materials presented in this book suggest that to see such boundaries as rigid or impermeable is problematical. Of course to those who regard themselves as "Hindu" or "Jain" this distinction is obviously meaningful and is certainly real. But if we take a somewhat more analytical stance, and if we focus on ritual culture, then we see that the real division in the materials we have seen is not between Hindus and non-Hindus but between traditions emphasizing transacting versus nontransacting or minimally transacting objects of worship. It is true that Jainism and Buddhism emerge from our comparison as strikingly similar, but it is also true—at least at the level of ritual culture—that

Śaivism has more in common with Jainism and Buddhism than with its fellow "Hindu" tradition Vaiṣṇavism.

It therefore seems logical to ask if there might be some ordering principle other than the division between Hindu and non-Hindu that we can apply to these ritual cultures. I think there is. An important clue to what it might be is contained in recent studies of a class of South Asian ritual prestations known as *dān* (or *dāna*). Normally this term is translated as "charitable gift" or "alms" in English. Ideally it is a gift given to some highly meritorious receiver; in turn, it produces merit for the giver, but it should be given disinterestedly and without any thought of return. *Dān,* I suggest, provides further evidence of structural unities between ostensibly very different ritual traditions.

## RITUAL GIFTING

On the basis of his study of Brahmaṇ priests and other ritual specialists of Banaras (1986, 1994), Jonathan Parry has shown that in this milieu *dān* is conceived as a material vehicle for the transmission of donors' "sins" to priestly recipients. Such priests become "sewers" for the "moral filth" of their patrons, and because they are unable to ameliorate the evil, or pass it to others, they must suffer it themselves (1994: 123). The "sewer," says Parry, becomes a "cess pit," filled with the accumulated sins of others (ibid.). As a result, the priest "is liable to contract leprosy and rot; to die a premature death vomiting excrement, and to suffer the most terrible torments thereafter" (ibid.: 124). The priest would avoid all this if he could, but unfortunately the necessity of earning a livelihood requires his acceptance of *dān.* The principle underlying these ideas is that the gift of *dān* carries something of the giver with it—and not the best of the giver. Parry suggests that these ideas are rooted in the symbolism of the ancient Vedic sacrifice. *Dān* is a substitute for sacrifice in the current degraded era. In the sacrifice, offering and sacrificer are identified; the sacrificer is "reborn" and vanquishes death by "transferring the burden of death and impurity to the priest through his gifts" (ibid.: 132–33). The sacrificial identity between victim and sacrificer is, in the case of *dān,* transmuted into an identity between gift and giver; the gift carries the "sins and impurities" of which the giver wishes to rid himself, transferring them to the unfortunate recipient (ibid.: 133).

Similar priniciples are disclosed by Gloria Raheja's analysis (1988) of the ritual culture of villagers of Saharanpur District. In the village she studied, *dān* is seen as a material vehicle for the transmission of "inauspiciousness" (*nāsubh*) from donors to receivers.[15] The giver of *dān* is considered the *jajmān,* the sacrificer. Depending on the context, the receivers (*pātras*) may be married daughters and sisters or their husbands, or individuals acting in caste-specific roles in relation to donors. The donor is said to have a "right" (*haq*) to give *dān,* and the receiver the "obligation" (*pharmāyā*) to further the welfare of the donor by taking it.

A good example of the pattern is a class of rites known as *vrats*, "votive fasts." Most *vrats* occur in two phases. The first is the performance of some kind of asceticism. Raheja interprets asceticism as "disarticulative"; it results in "heating," which loosens inauspicious or harmful qualities preparatory to their removal. Then follows the critical transfer, which occurs in a final ritual phase called *udāpan.* Certain materials (called *caṛhāpā* or *pujāpā* in this context) are passed to specified recipients as a form of *dān.* The *dān* has absorbed the disarticulated inauspiciousness, which it then carries to the receiver.

When a deity happens to be involved (and deities are not involved in all *vrats*), the materials (foodstuffs, clothing, ornaments) are first offered to the particular deity presiding over the rite. This deity is usually thought to be the source of the difficulty (often afflicting brothers, sons, or husbands of female performers) the rite is designed to ameliorate. Having been presented to the deity, the offering is passed on (*āge denā*) to a specified human recipient, the ultimate receiver of the inauspiciousness or difficulty.

An example of such a performance is the *śanivār* (Saturday) *vrat* (ibid.: 81–82). The *kathā* (the story of the *vrat,* which Raheja takes from a locally available manual for the performance of such rites) tells of how an astrologer once predicted that King Daśarath would be afflicted by inauspicious Śani (Saturn) because this planetary god was about to move into a particular asterism. Having heard the prophecy, the king ascended to the world of asterisms and blocked Śani's way. Impressed by the king's bravery, Śani offered him a boon, and the king asked that he not enter the asterism in question. This Śani granted, and then taught the king the *vrat.* In the *vidhi* (method) provided with the *kathā,* the performers of the *vrat* are instructed to bring the offerings (mustard oil, a black cloth, and various black grains) into contact with the afflicted person and then offer them to Śani. At the conclusion of the rite they are offered as *dān* to an appropriate recipient. It is not clear in the *kathā*'s text who appropriate recipients might be, although a Brāhmaṇ is said to be the right recipient for a black cow. In village practice, however, the *dān* of the *vrat* is received by Dakauts (a caste of "very low" Brāhmaṇs) (ibid.: 115).

According to Raheja, in such rites "the deity himself does not assimilate the inauspiciousness but acts only as an intermediary between the *jajmān* and the *pātra* [recipient]. . . . " (ibid.: 82). There is an identity between the deity and the human recipient: The recipient is seen as belonging to a class or group of people who resemble the deity responsible for the trouble.[16] When the offering is given to an appropriate human recipient, this seems to enable the deity to receive the offering while the inauspiciousness is actually passed to the human recipient (ibid.: 70). Instead of a deity, a specified kinsperson, also seen as the "source of the inauspiciousness," might receive the offering first before it is passed on to an ultimate recipient (ibid.: 71).[17]

This is a pattern reminiscent of one we have seen before. Although the *content* is certainly different, the *structure* of this series of acts is paralleled in Śaiva ritual. The Śaiva offering is positively, not negatively, valued, but it seems to be associated with negativities nonetheless. Śiva accepts the offering (or part of it)—but the offering is then passed on not to the human offerer but to a quasi-divine entity who absorbs negativities. Caṇḍa is thus the structural equivalent of the human recipients of *dān*-borne inauspiciousness in Raheja's village. It is of interest, therefore, that at least one Śaiva author characterizes the offering as *samarpaṇa* and *dāna* (Davis 1991: 137).

Let us be as clear as possible about what is being said and not being said. There are obviously fundamental differences between the ritual cultures discussed previously in this chapter and this book and that described by Raheja, and we are certainly not saying that they are the same. Śaiva ritual culture is soteriological in its basic thrust in that it is concerned with the soul's final deliverance, not with the worldly goals inherent to the rites Raheja describes. The same is true of Jain, Buddhist, and Vaiṣṇava ritual traditions. All these traditions stress the view that the attainment of worldly benefits is—at most—a kind of by-product of ritual action that should have the supreme goal as its true aim. But it is surely significant that, when ritual transactions are abstracted from their theological matrixes, we find that there are indeed structural similarities between such ostensibly different ritual cultures as Śaiva Siddhānta and Raheja's village traditions. Leaving aside all justifications and rationales, in both cases the offering carries negativities that are borne past the presiding deity and deposited with a third party.

The same pattern can be seen in Jain (and, for the same reasons,

Buddhist) ritual; the only difference is that the Jains push the logic to its furthest limits. From the encompassing ascetic perspective, a central theme in Jain worship is "shedding"; morally and spiritually dangerous materials are gotten rid of by passing them on, ultimately to a non-Jain human receiver. The ultimate point of the rite is renunciation, "getting rid" of the world. There is no ambiguity in the matter of the gift's return; the Tīrthankar is completely nontransactional, and there can be no question of the offering's becoming—as in the Puṣṭimārg—a vehicle for the return of a deity's grace or blessing. Thus, as in Raheja's village, the gift cannot return. The non-Jain recipient, usually a temple *pujārī*, becomes the structural equivalent of Śaivism's Caṇḍa.

These points seem to suggest that the principles underlying *dān*-type transactions can help us understand Jain ritual culture as part of a wider South Asian world. We must start with the fact that among the Jains, worship (*pūjā*) is sometimes said to be a form of *dān*.[18] *Dān*, of course, is also given to living mendicants. Now, Jains certainly do not see *dān*-giving as a transfer of "sins" (Parry) or "inauspiciousness" (Raheja). Nonetheless, the gift *does* have certain negative associations. Certainly this is true of food, which is perhaps the most important gift received by mendicants from laypersons. Food fuels the calamity of bodily existence, and is also associated with the sins inevitably occasioned by its production and preparation. As we saw in Chapter One, ascetics are protected from these negativities by the strategy of taking food from households randomly and consuming it—at least ideally—without any sense of enjoyment. The Tīrthankar represents the perfection of this principle. If the living mendicant takes without really taking, the worshiped Tīrthankar takes nothing at all. The worshiper, as we have seen, therefore "gives" nothing; what he gives he "gives up."

The logic of the situation is reminiscent of the dilemma of *dān*-style gifting to Brāhmaṇs as analyzed by Trautmann (1981: 285–88). Because of its implication of dependency, to accept gifts—even from kings, and perhaps especially from kings—compromises the Brāhmaṇ's sense of his own superiority. This anxiety is transmuted into the idea that such gifts are spiritually dangerous; the Brāhmaṇ who accepts the fewest gifts is the most worthy and powerful, for the acceptance of gifts erodes the Brāhmaṇ's *tapas* (austerity). The greatest merit is therefore gained by the donor who gives to the Brāhmaṇ who is least inclined to take (on this point, see also Parry 1994: 122). Trautmann concludes:

> Only the purest, most disinterested brahmin can accept gifts without danger to himself. But the purest brahmin does not solicit gifts or, better yet, will not accept. Pushed to its logical extreme, the gift finds no recipient. The brahmin, having rejected reciprocity in favor of an asymmetrical, hierarchical form of exchange as a basis on which he deigns to be a party to the social contract, abandons even this one-sided exchange for the individualistic self-sufficiency of the ascetic. The theory of the gift tends toward its own destruction. (ibid.: 288)

Although he is certainly no Brāhmaṇ, the Tīrthankar represents the full realization of the same logical involution. The ritual culture of Jainism reflects the exigencies of worshiping a being who apotheosizes asceticism; the greatest benefit results from gifting to one who cannot take gifts at all. The worshiper therefore cannot connect; he can only emulate.

## SACRED OTHERS

We have two basic patterns of ritual gifting before us. In one the gift returns; in the other it does not, as in the case of *dān*-type prestations. They seem very different. Some ritual offerings, those that are not returned, take negative qualities away and keep them away. Others serve as media for intimate reciprocity between deity and devotee. Still others may fall somewhere in between. In this final section I would like to propose that there is a relationship between them; using Raheja's materials as a background of reference, we can see them as variations on a theme.

Offerings made in the Puṣṭimarg are not called *dān,* nor are they *dān* in any sense whatsoever. Nor is there anything at all negative about food offerings to Kṛṣṇa; indeed, they represent the offerer's best feelings and best self.[19] Nonetheless, the theme of offering-borne negativity is to be found in the Puṣṭimārg, although this notion seems to be sequestered off from the normal routines of worship. We see it in the initiate's vow to sacrifice "mind, body and wealth" to Kṛṣṇa, which, cleansed by him of faults, are restored to the offerers. Purified by him, worshipers then comingle with him in ritual acts that express the devotee's highest ideal, which is consubstantial identity with him. Kṛṣṇa emerges as a being who is both highly transactional and transformative.

But when offerings are made to a nontransactional or minimally transactional being, negativities cannot be destroyed. The logic of the ritual encounter then becomes different. Negativities must be passed onward; reciprocity becomes problematic. The crucial difference is in the character of the ritual "other," the sacred being.

Raheja's *vrats* do not actually require the presence of sacred beings at all. But when such beings are involved they seem to function as *antagonistic others.* They are the source of troubles and afflictions, and the troubles they bring seem to emanate from their intrinsic nature as entities; the affliction somehow participates in the nature of its source. The ritualist's goal is getting rid of trouble; the affliction is disarticulated, loosened, and shed onto others. Because of the association between the affliction and the nature of the deity, there is a sense in which the ritual is a shedding, a getting rid of the deity. Trouble is sent back to its source, although ultimately it is passed on to designated human others. Perhaps this is because the final human recipient stands in for the deity (for they are supposed to resemble each other), or possibly the gift appeases the god while the inauspiciousness it bears is passed onward; on present evidence it is difficult to say. But in any case, what *is* clear is that the offering bears negativity, that the negativity is associated with the deity, and that the act of giving is a passing on of the negativity to others.

The ritual culture of the Puṣṭimārg is more familiar to students of what is called Hinduism. Here the deity possesses transformative power. Here, too, the goal of the devotee's encounter is self-transformation, but it is not a shedding of negative qualities emanating from an antagonistic other, but rather a reciprocal exchange with a being who is an object of devotion. Such a deity functions as an *intimate other.* If negativity is involved, it is ameliorated through his sacred power. Given the deity's transactional and transformative nature, the gift can and should be returned to the giver. Intimate other is thus divine counter-giver, and reciprocity becomes the dominant theme of ritual.

The Tīrthankar represents "pure" otherness—otherness, one might say, without presence. The same seems to be true of the Buddha, at least as he is venerated in the Sinhalese Theravada tradition. That the Tīrthankar is really an "other" cannot be seriously doubted, for his image is seen, touched, anointed, addressed in prayer. And it certainly seems possible to say that he is in some sense "present" in the hearts of his devotees. But what separates the Tīrthankar from the Puṣṭimārg's Kṛṣṇa and Raheja's godlings alike is that he is not a *transactional* presence. Transactionally he is an "absence" surrounded by a field of transactional negation—the perfect embodiment of what McKim Marriott, in a general analysis of South Asian transactional patterns, has called the "minimalist" strategy of "symmetrical nonexchange" (1976: 122, 127).[20]

The Tīrthankar's worship is indeeed transformative, but not because worshipers share his nature and grace, or because they send misfortune back to its source. Rather, one might say that his image serves as an *occasion* for reflexive (and intransitive) ritualizations. His persona—disengaged and completely nontransactive—represents a condition the worshiper hopes to achieve. This condition is itself nontransactiveness, and in the very nature of the case, the quality of nontransactiveness cannot be transmitted by means of transactions. Therefore, the Tīrthankar is, as he must be, an *exemplary other.* He is the target only of love and emulation, but not of gifts. This is what comes of worshiping an absolute ascetic; the connection cannot be tangible, but only metaphoric or analogical.

The ritual subculture of the Dādāgurus presents us with a mixed case. In some respects the Dādāguru is an intimate other; transactions between Dādāguru and worshiper do indeed occur, and blessings are indeed conferred. But we are struck by the hesitancy and relative exiguousness of these transactions by comparison with the all-throttles-open transactions of the Puṣṭimārg. Furthermore, the role of the Dādāguru as transacting other is in need of special legitimization. The miraculous power of these figures is portrayed as specifically Jain in nature and its deployment is justified as needed for the protection and glorification of Jain teachings. Because the object of worship is a Jain ascetic, and also because the historical context and supporting ideology are clearly Jain, it would not seem egregiously wrong to say that the Dādāgurus cult is a ritual subculture of one branch of Śvetāmbar "Jainism," not a form of "Hinduism" grafted onto a Jain base. That is, its informing spirit is that of a particular type of exemplary other, the Tīrthankar.

The materials on Śaiva worship present us with another mixed case. In its structure, Śaiva worship recalls Raheja's *dān* pattern, with Caṇḍa designated as the ultimate offering-recipient. But Śiva is no antagonist. Indeed, his grace is required for liberation, and he even receives the offerer's self; to this degree he resembles an intimate other. And yet we also see that his contact with the offering is minimal, and that he himself is minimally transformative, which is why the offering must be passed on to the demon-like Caṇḍa. This is in keeping with Śiva's character as an ascetic, and in this respect the pattern seems more reminiscent of Jainism than of the Puṣṭimārg. It may be that we are dealing here with a Tīrthankar-like exemplary other whose patterns of worship have been overlain with a more classically devotional rationale. Perhaps this is an instance of disjunction between ritual role structure and ritual culture—in this case a structure of transactional minimalism and a culture that includes some elements of devotional intimacy. But whatever the case, Śaiva ritual culture raises serious questions about the status of interreligious boundaries in the Indic cultural region.

If we combine the Jain materials with other data we have surveyed, we find three ideal-typical interactional patterns between parties to ritual relationships. A ritualist's transactions with Raheja's godlings may be characterized as *one-way:* Negativity is sent back to its source, and then beyond the source to a destination identified with the source. The Puṣṭimārg specializes in *two-way* transactions: By means of intimate exchange devotee and deity become sharers in each other. Offerings given in the Tīrthankar's name represent the limiting case of transactional analysis: The ultimate recipient is defined only negatively, for the sole requirement is that whoever takes the offering not be a Jain. These gifts are *zero-way.* Destinationless, untransformed, and spiritually unwholesome offerings are expelled from the universe established by the ritual, carrying their burden to the non-Jain world beyond. As we see, these distinctions have little to do with boundaries between such reified "isms" as Hinduism and Jainism; the patterns are neither Hindu nor Jain but variations on a deeper structure that is simply South Asian.

## JAINISM IN AND OUT OF CONTEXT

We began this book by asking what it would mean to worship beings who are believed to be completely beyond the reach of worship. This is the central question in the study of Jainism from the standpoint of ritual. We find that to understand the matter fully it is necessary to look beyond as well as within the Jain tradition. At one level the nonaccessibility of the object of worship is a deeply formative fact of Jain ritual culture; at another level it turns out to be a particular logical permutation of general transactional possibilities, one with close analogues elsewhere in South Asian religions. One might even go further to suggest that evidence of similar transactional possibilities might be discovered in ritual cultures beyond the South Asian region.

However, in the final analysis the tradition we have explored has to be understood on its own terms. From within it is a complete world, one that has a strong claim on our attention on its own account. Readers may have suspected that a focus on ritual culture would encourage a narrow view of a rich religious tradition. I hope this book has dispelled that idea, for our concern with ritual roles and symbols has turned out to be a wide net that pulls great realms of cultural detail into view and also into intelligible patterns.

Let there be no mistake on one point. The quest for liberation, the *mokṣ mārg,* is central to Jain traditions. It just will not do to suggest that this is an arcane interest, confined to ascetic virtuosi, somehow imposed or inflicted on the laity. It is true that most lay Jains of Ahmedabad and Jaipur are theologically unsophisticated. This is also true of many Jain ascetics. And it has to be said as well that—although we cannot truly know what is in others' hearts—most Jain laymen with whom I discussed the matter seemed to have little, if any, sense of liberation as in any meaningful way in prospect for them. Nonetheless, the ideal is seriously held as an ideal, and its influence on ritual symbolism and exegesis is pervasive. Asceticism is the key to liberation, and Jains, as we have said, worship ascetics.

Nonetheless, this seemingly constricted emphasis on ascetic values turns out to be consistent with a surprisingly complex and inclusive view of the world. The tradition utilizes a rich sociopolitical symbolism as a way of providing a connecting point between the world renouncer and those who must remain in the world. The idea of warrior-kingly valor transmuted is at the very heart of the ritual construction of the ascetic. The ascetic's lay worshiper becomes the ascetic's symbolic other—the king/deity who remains in the world to support and admire the ascetic and his projects, and to prosper and flourish while doing so. This same symbolism, in turn, ramifies into an image of how Jain communities came to be and where they fit in the social and cultural worlds of Rajasthan. More than the mere soteriology it is often thought to be, the Jain tradition, even in its ritual dimensions, can be seen as a unifying vision of the cosmos and our human and creaturely destiny.

# Notes

## INTRODUCTION

1. This word is apparently derived from the term *śrāvak,* meaning a lay Jain.

2. Although the Osvāl caste is the dominant Śvetāmbar caste in Jaipur, there is also a group known as the Multānī Osvāls who are Digambar Jains. They come originally from Multan, now in Pakistan; at the time of partition they migrated to Delhi and Jaipur (see Kāslīvāl 1989: 55–56). In Jaipur they are concentrated in the Bīs Dukān area.

3. Details of Jain cosmology and cosmogony are given in Chapter One.

4. In all probability Pārśvanāth, the twenty-third Tīrthankar, was also a historical figure.

5. Tradition avers, however, that Mahāvīr changed Jainism's format somewhat by adding a fifth vow (celibacy) to the then-existing four vows for initiated ascetics (nonviolence, truthfulness, not taking what has not been freely given, and possessionlessness) (Dundas 1992: 27).

6. This point has been persuasively argued by Laidlaw. See 1995, Part III, esp. Ch. 7.

7. The same issue has also been addressed in two outstanding recent works dealing with Śvetāmbar Jains, John Cort's "Liberation and Wellbeing: A Study of the Śvetāmbar Mūrtipūjak Jains of North Gujarat" (1989; see also 1991c) and James Laidlaw's *Riches and Renunciation: Religion, Economy, and Society among the Jains* (1995), and I draw heavily on the insights of both these authors. Cort's work, centered in Gujarat, is the first true ethnographic study of Jainism and also the first major work to recognize and analyze the role of auspiciousness in the Jain tradition. Laidlaw's study, based on data collected in Jaipur, asks how it is possible to live by values (the soteriological ones) that seem to be at war with life and provides a rich and comprehensive answer. These works are in some ways less narrowly focused than this study and are also much more detailed in certain areas, such as

ascetic praxis and interactions between laypersons and ascetics. On the other hand, I explore areas that Cort and Laidlaw do not, especially royal symbolism in ritual and the relationship between Jainism and the origin mythology of contemporary Jain communities. I have also been instructed by Caroline Humphrey's and James Laidlaw's *The Archetypal Actions of Ritual* (1994), a fascinating and provocative book that proposes a general theory of ritual utilizing the Jain *pūjā* as its empirical base and point of departure. Readers of both my study and theirs will see that I am somewhat more inclined to attribute meaning to ritual than are they. Another excellent recent study of Śvetāmbar Jains is Marcus Banks's *Organizing Jainism in India and England* (1992), which deals primarily with the social organization of a religious community (in both India and England).

8. I specify rituals of worship because ritualized ascetic practices are also important elements in Jain life. The emphasis in this book is decisively on the former. Ascetic rituals are treated in detail in Laidlaw (1995).

9. This general view echoes the distinction between cultural and social systems suggested by Talcott Parsons and his colleagues some decades back (see Parsons and Shils 1962, esp. Ch. 1), a distinction that entered the anthropology of religion primarily via the writings of Clifford Geertz (e.g., 1973b). The approach utilized here, however, is different from Geertz's. When Geertz deploys these concepts in the analysis of religion, the context is "religion" writ large—"religion as a cultural system" (1973a). I focus more narrowly on the ritual milieu as the "system" to be analyzed.

10. This is an issue I have attempted to address at greater length in *Redemptive Encounters: Three Modern Styles in the Hindu Tradition* (Babb 1986).

11. According to one source (Śrīśrīmāl 1984 [addendum]: 78), in the early 1980s the total Śvetāmbar population of Jaipur was 13,992. Of the 2,363 families listed, 745 were Sthānakvāsī, 581 were Mandirmārgī, and 320 were Terāpanthī; 717 listed less specific affiliations—such as "Jain"—or no affiliation. Although the Śvetāmbar community in Jaipur is basically a business community, this is not true of Śvetāmbar groups in other areas of Rajasthan. In particular, many of the Osvāl families of Jodhpur and Udaipur have been in service to the Mahārājās for generations.

12. On caste in Śvetāmbar communities, see Banks (1992), Cort (1989), Ellis (1991), Reynell (1985), Sangave (1980), and Singhi (1991).

## CHAPTER ONE

1. The full *namaskār mantra* is as follows (from P. S. Jaini's translation; 1979: 162–63):

> I bow before the worthy ones [arhat]—the Jinas;
> I bow before the Perfected beings [siddha]—those who have attained mokṣa;
> I bow before the [mendicant] leaders [ācārya] of the Jaina order;
> I bow before the [mendicant] preceptors [upādhyāya]
> I bow before all the [Jaina] mendicants [sādhu] in the world

This fivefold salutation, which destroys all sin, is preeminent as the most auspicious of auspicious things.

2. I use the term *ascetic* (or *mendicant*) to refer to individuals who have taken

initiation (*dīkṣā*) as full-time world renouncers. It should be understood, however, that lay Jains also engage in ascetic practices, and it is believed that lay Jains can even—in rare cases—achieve liberation directly from the householder state. I use the terms *monk* and *nun* to refer to male and female ascetics (*sādhus* and *sādhvīs*).

3. Successful completers of major fasts are, in fact, publicly feted.

4. Only Mallināth, the nineteenth Tīrthankar of our region and cosmic period, was female. The Digambars maintain that a Tīrthankar can never be female. See P. S. Jaini 1991a.

5. Rāma is a form of Viṣṇu and one of the most important Hindu deities.

6. This temple is known as the Kesariyānāthjī Temple.

7. Mahāvīr's career represents a partial exception to this pattern because his descent into the womb departed slightly from the norm. Because of a slight karmic residue, he first entered the womb of a Brāhmaṇ woman, and because a Tīrthankar can only be born in a high-ranking Kṣatriya family, Indra had to transfer him to the womb of a Kṣatriya mother. I have heard this event referred to as a "sixth *kalyāṇak*."

8. Before his final lifetime on earth, a Tīrthankar-to-be usually exists as a heavenly deity. Very occasionally, however, a Thīrthankar comes from hell.

9. The liturgical manual (*Vṛhat Pūjā-Sangrah*) used in the two temples I frequented most in Jaipur included *pūjās* of this type for Ṛṣabh, Śantināth, and Pārśvanāth, as well as a larger *pūjā* for Mahāvīr that also celebrates his five *kalyāṇaks*.

10. This is a standard pattern followed in most elaborated Śvetāmbar *pūjās*.

11. I am indebted to John Cort for this insight.

12. The *siddhcakra* is a sacred figure portraying nine essential elements of Jainism: the five *parameṣṭhins*, the "three jewels" of right faith, understanding, and conduct, plus right austerity. In the description to follow (and in a description of the *snātra pūjā* in Chapter Two) I designate both the Tīrthankar's image and the *siddhcakra*—which are treated alike—as "the image."

13. This is preceded by a rite known as *snātra pūjā,* which is the standard opening for all major *pūjās*. The *snātra pūjā* will be described in detail in the next chapter. In the present case, there were very few participants present for the *snātra pūjā*. This is common. The rite is a mere preliminary, not the main event, although it may be performed as the main event on other occasions.

14. The twenty spiritual observances and activities (*bīs sthānaks*) that generate the type of *karma* that leads to rebirth as a Tīrthankar.

15. The full list of dreams is as follows: an elephant, a bull, a lion, the goddess Śrī (Lakṣmī), a garland, the moon, the sun, a flag, a vessel filled with water, a lotus lake, a milky ocean, a celestial palace, a heap of jewels, a fire.

16. These are the lowest of the five types of knowledge (*jñān*), of which omniscience (*kevaljñān*) is the highest. *Avadhijñān,* clairvoyant knowledge, is normally possessed only by deities and the denizens of hell.

17. On whom see Sharma 1989.

18. Nemināth was the twenty-second Tīrthankar of our period and region of the world.

19. The Śvetāmbar Jains believe that the gods give all Tīrthankars their ascetic garb. The Digambars, of course, hold that the Tīrthankars were nude.

20. Some say that afterwards the births before liberation become "countable."

21. My account is based on conversations with knowledgeable individuals in both Ahmedabad and Jaipur as well as on written sources. Particularly helpful was Pt. Hīrālāl Jain's edited version of Śāntisūri's *Jīvvicār Prakaraṇ*. This book was placed in my hands by an educated Jain friend specifically to answer my queries about cosmology, cosmography, and biology. I will cite this and other sources on specific points.

22. Śāntisūri 1949: 156. Caillat and Kumar, presumably using Digambar sources, give the following definition of a *rajjū:* the distance covered by a deity flying for six months at the rate of 2,057,152 *yojan*s per second (1981: 20).

23. Because of its location midway between the top and bottom of the cosmos it is called the middle world (*madhya lok*); it is also known as the world of humans (*mānuṣya lok*).

24. There are, in addition, fifty-six small inhabited islands in the first ocean (known as *antardvīp*s).

25. This zone is also known as "the upper world" (*ūrdhva lok*).

26. Also known as "the lower world" (*adho lok*).

27. J. L. Jaini's commentary on Umāsvāmi's *Tattvārthādhigam Sūtra* (1974: 83, 89–90). It should be noted that varying accounts exist and that most ordinary people have rather inexact ideas of these matters. What most people know is that these spans of time are exceedingly great.

28. Hīrālāl Jain, in his commentary on Śāntisūri's *Jīvvicār Prakaraṇ* (1949: 147–48), gives the duration of a complete cycle as twenty *sāgaropam,* and defines a *sāgar* as equal to a *koṛākoṛī* of *addhāpalya.* He defines (with some ambiguity) an *addhāpalya* (or *addhāpalyopam*) as the time it would take for the fine hairs of a seven-day-old *yugliyā* (below) to be removed, one every hundred years, from a pit of the same size.

29. Also known as Ādināth, the "first lord."

30. What follows is based on materials in Hastīmaljī (1988) and Lalvānī (1985).

31. Lalvānī suggests that the fourteen *kulkar*s are comparable to the fourteen Manus of the Hindu tradition (1985: 21).

32. The Jain account is somewhat similar to the elective and contractarian theory of the Buddhists, on which see Tambiah 1976: 13–15.

33. Although the Brāhmaṇ class was created by his son, Bharat.

34. There are, however, Tīrthankars currently in other areas of the cosmos. Sīmandhar Svāmī, a figure sometimes worshiped by Śvetāmbar Jains, is teaching in Mahāvideh at the present time. Some believe that it is possible to obtain liberation now by being reborn in Mahāvideh.

35. There are fifteen different types of liberated beings, but these are of little importance and need not detain us. I will be omitting many details in what follows.

36. All unliberated beings are also either *paryāpt* or *aparyāpt. Paryāpt* refers to the capacity of a soul fully to develop the characteristics of the body into which it is born; those who are *aparyāpt* die too quickly after incarnation to do this.

37. An alternative view, one that I have heard more than once from lay Jains, is that although potatoes are forbidden because of the large numbers of souls they contain, onions and garlic are forbidden because, being *tāmsik* (imbued with *tamas,* the quality of darkness and ignorance), they increase sexual desire.

38. Aruṇvijay classifies the *nigods* as belonging to the *sukṣam* subclass of the *sādhāraṇ* class of plants (n.d.: 24); Hīrālāl Jain does not classify them.

39. There are inconsistencies in the materials I have seen about the content of the *tiryanc* class. The chart provided in Hīrālāl Jain's annotated edition of Śāntisūri's *Jīvvicār Prakaraṇ* includes only five-sensed animals in the *tiryanc* category. Other sources regard it as a more inclusive category (See, e.g., Jaini 1979: 108–9; Stevenson 1984: 97). Aruṇvijay seems to treat the *tiryanc* class as including all animals and plants except *nigods*.

40. For example, in the edition (1949) of a Hindi version of Śāntisūri's *Jīvvicār Prakaraṇ* cited in this book there are pictures showing the hunter being devoured by tigers in hell, the driver of an overloaded cart being driven by a whip-wielding demon, the butcher being butchered, and so on. Such illustrations of punishments have apparently been popular for centuries. See Caillat and Kumar 1981: 80–81.

41. In the technical terminology of the system, they are *aparyāpt.*

42. These latter details are from Johnson (1931: 401).

43. The game metaphor used here was originally inspired by McKim Marriott's game of "*samsara*" (Marriott 1984), an instructional game devised for the Civilizations Course Materials Project, Social Sciences Collegiate Division, University of Chicago. The version I have seen is dated 4-2-84. I subsequently came to know, however, that there exists a Jain version of the game of snakes and ladders called *jñān bājī.* See Pal 1994: 86, 257.

44. Or at least this seems to be true of five-sensed animals. Earlier in the chapter we have seen how a cobra, having been spiritually awakened by Pārśvanāth when he was a Tīrthankar-to-be, became the god Dharṇendra. We have also seen how sins committed in animal incarnations (by the archvillain Kamaṭh) led to sojourns in hell.

45. Relevant materials are found throughout the book, but especially on pp. 30–35 and 41–44. Rainy season discourses are the sermons delivered by distinguished monks during the period of the rainy season retreat (below).

46. This is the author's first mention of sin (*pāp*) as a factor in the soul's situation. Again, it is of interest that an animal is here seen as capable of sin.

47. What follows is summarized specifically from pp. 41–44.

48. Students of Hindu traditions will recognize this as a familiar point. The notion that one who does not take advantage of a human birth to seek liberation will fall back into the "eighty-four *lākh*s (8.4 million) *yoni*s" seems to be common coin in South Asian religions.

49. Excellent accounts of ascetics and ascetic-lay relations among Śvetāmbar Mūrtipūjak Jains can be found in Cort (1989) and Laidlaw (1995). For a more inclusive discussion of Jain mendicancy, see Cort 1991b.

50. For a description of this relationship, see Cort 1989: 333–36.

51. For a fine account of *gacch*s and *gacch* organization, see Cort 1991b: 549–69.

52. Lest it be thought that nuns were unimportant before modern times, it should be pointed out that Jindattsūri, certainly one of the most distinguished of all past Khartar Gacch ascetics, was brought into mendicancy by nuns. See Chapter Three.

53. For a far more extensive discussion of mendicant discipline, see Dundas 1992: Ch. 6. On the life routines of Śvetāmbar Mūrtipūjak Jains, see Cort 1989: 308–11.

54. A nun was once at great pains to point out to me that this practice should not be confused with the wearing of mouth-cloths by laypersons while performing *pūjā*. The reason for the latter practice is to avoid breathing impurities on the image. I do not know how widespread this distinction is.

55. For detailed descriptions, see Banks (1992: 177–84); Cort (1989: 157–85); Folkert (1993: 189–211); Laidlaw (1995: Ch. 12).

56. The same dreams, of course, are seen by the mothers of all Tīrthankars.

57. I have heard the view that ascetics cannot perform worship because of their bathlessness. However, although it is true that bathing is required for those who actually touch the images, ascetics are also barred from performing what is called *agra pūjā* (see Chapter Two), which involves making offerings without having actual contact with the image.

58. Among Digambars this idea is accentuated by the ideal that, before going out to eat, the ascetic vows to eat at a house of some quite arbitrary description; if no such house is found, he returns without eating.

59. Among Śvetāmbars the food is never consumed in the presence of the donors (among Digambars it is), or indeed within the sight of any nonascetic.

60. On this point, see Cort 1989: 91, n. 5.

61. In Jaipur, however, I found that mendicants did not like the word *dān* to be used in this context. The objection was to its implications of charity.

62. Thus, in a sense, it is the householder who is begging. A householder who wished to give a gift of clothing to a mendicant, for example, might say, "*mujhe kapṛe kā lābh dījiye*" (Please give me the benefit [*lābh*] of clothing." That is, it is the giver who benefits, not the recipient.

63. For descriptions of these patterns, see Babb 1986.

64. Among Digambars, however, *prasād* is indeed sometimes taken from mendicants.

## CHAPTER TWO

1. John Cort, personal communication.

2. By this I mean merely that I have been challenged on this point when entering Digambar temples. I have never had this experience entering a Śvetāmbar temple.

3. In Ahmedabad some *pujārīs* identified themselves as Brāhmaṇs or Rājpūts. Most, however, seem to come from middle-ranking Hindu castes, especially the Mālī (gardener) caste. Members of the so-called Untouchable castes are barred from this role, as are nonvegetarians. In Jaipur many *pujārīs* said they were Brāhmaṇs, though it is hard to know how to evaluate this claim.

4. For a complete description of *caitya vandan*, see Cort 1989: 348–57; also Ratnasenvijay 1995.

5. These details are taken from Umrāvcand Jargaḍ's (1959a) account.

6. My account of the rite is based on numerous observations of its perfor-

mance as supplemented by Umrāvcand Jargaḍ's *sārth* version of the text (1959b). I also consulted two ordinary *snātra pūjā* manuals (*Snātra Pūjā* 1979 and n.d.), which I read through as I observed performances of the rite. These booklets include both the text of the rite and brief instructions for its performance. All Jain temples are well supplied with manuals of this sort for various rituals.

7. The objects of worship are the same as in Pārśvanāth's five-*kalyāṇak pūjā*. As before, I shall refer to the two objects of worship together as "the image."

8. Nor is such a mantra included in Vīrvijay's Tapā Gacch *snātra pūja* (Jitendravijayjī 1986). *Sthāpnā mantra*s are included in Digambar *pūjā*s I have witnessed. When queried about this, Digambar informants stressed the purely figurative meaning of the gesture. This, however, is a matter that needs further investigation.

9. For the list, see Chapter One, n. 15.

10. On on the *Śakra-stava,* see Cort 1989: 351–52.

11. This is the only time at which dwellers in hell have the experience of seeing light.

12. The place where Tīrthankars from the continent of Bharat are given their first bath. It is located on a terrace at the peak of Mt. Meru.

13. Most of the details to follow come from Hīrālāl Jain's commentary on Śāntisūri's *Jīvavicār Prakaraṇ* as supplemented by discussion with knowledgeable individuals.

14. A Terāpanthī monk told me that they cannot obtain liberation because "they have no desire for it." He meant that they are too happy to wish for liberation.

15. This appears to be a more common practice in Tapā Gacch-influenced Ahmedabad. It is seen less commonly in Jaipur. But the identification it symbolizes is common to both traditions, and indeed is universal in the Jain world.

16. This is not a uniquely Jain pattern. Hindu businessmen also enter into partnerships with Hindu deities.

17. Determined by auction.

18. The Hindi version includes a small picture of Bhairav with brief identifying captions; the English version includes the same picture and notes (as the Hindi version does not) that many pilgrims come to Nākoṛā who yearn for "wealth, position and worldly desires."

19. It should be noted that the Buddha was also a potential *cakravartin.* See esp. Tambiah 1976.

20. Living ascetics, however, do indeed engage in worship in a more general sense. They can perform *bhāv pūjā* and can also participate in congregational worship as observers and singers. But *dravya pūjā* is barred.

21. *Sāmāyik* is conceptualized as a temporary state of being under full ascetic vows. Conversely, mendicants are seen as being under lifelong vows of *sāmāyik* (Cort 1989: 248; Laidlaw 1995: 201–2).

22. For a particularly good description of *pratikramaṇ,* see Laidlaw 1995: 204–15.

23. Cort (1989: 301–305) has described the motives of fasters in detail.

24. Excellent descriptions of this rite and its variations can be found in Cort (1989: Ch. 7) and Humphrey and Laidlaw (1994: Ch. 2)

25. In Gujarat, water from *jal pūjā* is also used to purify the ground traversed

by Jina images when they are taken out of temples in procession. See Cort 1989: 182–83. I have not seen this done in Jaipur.

26. In this and in the following instances of verses, I am providing my translation of Muktiprabhvijay's own rendering of the verses into the vernacular.

27. Exactly the same verses for all these rites are provided by Hemprabhāśrījī in her layman's manual (1977: 34). I do not know their ultimate source.

28. *Jñān-darśan-cāritra* are the three jewels of knowledge, insight, and right conduct; the *pañcācār* are these three plus *tapas* (austerity) and *vīrya* (fortitude).

29. There are, however, differences of opinion about where the dividing line is between these two categories. The inclusion of *jal pūjā, candan pūjā,* and *puṣpā pūjā* in the *ang pūjā* category seems to reflect the general view (and is given by Hemprabhāśrījī [30]). Muktiprabhvijay, however, includes *dhūp pūjā* in the *ang pūjā* category. See also Humphrey and Laidlaw 1994: 32–33.

30. Muktiprabhvijay also provides lines for recitation while making the *svastik,* which I have omitted in the interest of space. The theme of these lines is that the worshiper has been wandering through the four classes of beings (symbolized by the arms of the *svastik*), and that the worshiper wishes to have the eight kinds of *karma* destroyed so that liberation can be attained.

31. For Śvetāmbar Jains, Dīvālī commemorates Mahāvīr's liberation, but this is a rather unobtrusive part of the overall Dīvālī celebrations..

32. Gombrich's well-known distinction between cognitive absence and affective presence (1971: 142), applied originally to Buddhism, would seem to be relevant here.

33. Digambar Jains do not use this term; they call leftover offerings *nirmālya* (see Chapter Five), the consumption of which they likewise forbid. Some Digambars maintain that if, during *pūjā,* one accidentally touches the platter into which one is depositing offerings, one should wash one's hands before resuming worship.

34. A ritually expert friend told me that if the *pujārī* happens to be Jain, then he must be paid out of the temple's general account and not from items offered in *pūjā.* It should probably be added that another reason Jains are hardly ever *pujārī*s is simply that few Jains would be willing to engage in such a low-prestige occupation.

35. At one Jaipur temple there is an attached hall that is frequently used for wedding dinners. At such a dinner I once saw platefuls of food taken into the temple and deposited before the main image (but only in the main hall, not in the inner shrine) and also in front of images of Bhairav and Ghaṇṭā Karṇ Mahāvīr (two deities). They were not, however, taken back out, but were left (I was told) for the *pujārī*s. That is, the food did not become a recovered offering.

36. He is said to be one of fifty-two demigods known as *vīr*s. He resembles the Hindu deity Hanumān somewhat, and is sometimes said to be the "Jain Hanumān."

37. For further discussion of this rather vexed question, see Cort 1989: 405–25.

38. A Digambar acquaintance offered a similar explanation. He said that the Tīrthankar's omniscient state attracts a vast inward flow of merit (*puṇya*). But because the merit does not adhere to the Tīrthankar, it becomes generally available—in fact for hundreds of *yojan*s around. His implication was that worship somehow taps into this flow.

39. The adjective usually used for such powerful images is *camatkārī.*

40. I have never personally seen it drunk, but a Jaipur friend told me that he

has seen it done "out of ignorance." He went on to say that those who make this mistake do so because they are "more used to going to Vaiṣṇava Temples," where such practices are acceptable. This is quite plausible.

41. On the superordination of *bhāv pūjā,* see also P. S. Jaini 1979: 207.

42. This entire issue is richly described and discussed in Laidlaw 1995: Ch. 4.

## CHAPTER THREE

1. Its dating is uncertain, but it is certainly not very old. As far as I am aware, the earliest inscriptional date in the temple is 1803 C.E., which is given as the date of the consecration of a foot image of Jinkuśalsūri. I thank Surendra Bothara for this information.

2. Śānti Vijay's image and the various foot images of other ascetics are given full rites of worship daily by the temple's *pujārī* on his normal morning rounds. Vicakṣaṇśrī's image is worshiped less formally.

3. See Granoff 1992 for an extended discussion of the mortuary dimension of Jain worship.

4. I have insufficient data to address the question of whether there are phenomena analogous to the cult of the Dādāgurus among Tapā Gacch-affiliated Jains.

5. Who—as the inclusion of *sūri* in his name indicates—achieved the status of *ācārya,* which his guru never did.

6. Mahāvir's birthday, which occurs on the thirteenth of the bright fortnight of the lunar month of Caitra (March/April).

7. His full name and title as given in the biography: *sacce sukhõ ke sāgar rūp paramguru dev gaṇādhīśvar śrī śrī sukhsāgarjī mahārāj.*

8. However, Manjul Vinaysāgar Jain (1989: 48) says that his initiation was given by Bhagvānsāgar. Although Sukhsāgar died in 1885 (to be succeeded by Bhagvānsāgar), his death did not occur until some months after Chagansāgar's initiation.

9. These are the twelve "lesser vows" that, in theory, a truly serious layman or laywoman should undertake.

10. From his account we also learn that the author came from a non-Jain family belonging to the Jāṭ caste. We also learn that Bhagvānsāgar was his (the author's) paternal uncle (*cācā*) in secular life (*gṛhasthāvasthā mẽ*).

11. Manjul Vinaysāgar Jain (1989: 48) says that he created 68 nuns. He does not give a figure for monks.

12. More correctly, perhaps, I should say that he predicted the end of the drought. He and Bhagvānsāgar had been blamed for the drought. He responded by saying "Hey, isn't rain on its way? Why are you blaming me?" Sure enough, the rain came, and the people considered it a miracle.

13. A periodic *pratikramaṇ* occurring at four-monthly intervals. One of them occurs at the beginning of the rainy season retreat.

14. See Cort (1989: 159–60) for details on this issue.

15. This is a conventional formula. It is also conventional in these materials not to say simply that an individual "died," but to state that he or she attained *svargvās* (a "heavenly abode").

16. Nonetheless, his death anniversary, which is noted in the Khartar Gacch al-

manac, is given as the sixth of the bright fortnight of Bhādrapad. This is because in a normal year both Paryuṣaṇ and his death would have occurred in Bhādrapad, not in Śrāvan.

17. For an enlightening discussion of these monuments, see R. L. Mishra 1991: Ch. 6.

18. At the time of my research these observances were no longer being held in Jaipur. A knowledgeable respondent told me that his death anniversary would be likely to be noted and observed only by ascetics. Special observances continue to be held, however, at his memorial shrine in Lohāvaṭ. Most of my friends and acquaintances had never heard of Chagansāgar.

19. I know of no cases of nuns possessing similar powers. In principle, however, there is no reason why they should not.

20. This is by no means unusual in Jain hagiography. For example, we have already seen that the birth of Devcandrajī, author of the *snātra pūjā,* was heralded by a dream in which his mother saw sixty-four Indras performing the birth ablution of a Tīrthankar's image on Mt. Meru.

21. On the Dādāgurus, see also Laidlaw 1985. The term *dādā* means "paternal grandfather"; *guru* means "spiritual preceptor."

22. An early precedent for the Dādāgurus' cult may have been the cult of Gautama (Mahāvīr's foremost disciple and usually called Gautam Svāmī by Śvetāmbar Jains), which had emerged among Śvetāmbars by medieval times and was, as is the Dādāgurus' cult today, associated with worldly prosperity (Dundas 1992: 33–34). Unlike the Dādāgurus, however, Gautama has achieved liberation. For an excellent description and analysis of Gautama's role in contemporary Śvetāmbar ritual, see Laidlaw 1995: Ch. 17.

23. The latter can be easily distinguished from images of the Tīrthankars by the usual presence of three symbols: the *muhpattī, oghā,* and book. The *muhpattī* is the cloth that ascetics hold before their mouths when speaking to avoid harming small living things in the air; the *oghā* is the moplike implement that ascetics use to brush surfaces free of small life-forms before sitting or lying. The book symbolizes the teaching function of ascetics.

24. There is nothing uniquely Jain in the emphasis on feet. From early times the Buddha was represented by footprints. Ritual attention to the feet of important persons, deities, and ascetics is a pan-Indian theme. See Babb 1986, esp. Ch. 3, for Hindu examples.

25. Other temples in which the Tīrthankar is represented by feet rather than by an anthropomorphic image are rare. The best known example is at Pāvāpurī, where Lord Mahāvīr is said to have achieved *nirvāṇ.*

26. On the formation of the Khartar Gacch, see especially Dundas 1992: 120–22; also 1993. Variations exist in the accounts available. The narratives and biographies to follow are based on materials drawn from Vinaysāgar 1959 and 1989. Vinaysāgar 1959 was a particularly valuable source and will be cited specifically in relation to particular points.

27. In some accounts, however, Vardhmānsūri is not present at this debate. See Dundas 1992: 121.

28. For translated accounts of this debate, see Granoff 1990b: 172–78.

29. This is my translation of the Hindi translation given in Vinaysāgar 1959: 8.

30. According to the account given in Vinaysāgar, the Caityavāsīs all later found various pretexts to return and begin living in temples again (1959: 10–11).

31. According to Dundas (1992: 121), this name is associated particularly with Jinvallabhsūri.

32. The following accounts of the lives of the Dādāgurus are based on A. Nāhṭā (1988), A. and B. Nāhṭā (1939, 1971), Vidyut Prabhā Śrī (1980), and Vinaysāgar (1959, 1989). For an English version of Jindattsūri's life translated from the *Khartargacchbṛhadguruāvalī,* see Granoff 1993.

33. This incident is retold in Vinaysāgar (1959: 32).

34. This incident is reported in each and every account of Jindattsūri's life that I have seen.

35. The miracle of the book at Cittauṛ is also attributed to Siddhasena, another distinguished ascetic. Here, too, the monk obtains magic powers from the book (or books). See Granoff 1990: 265–66

36. The miracles described here and also for the other Dādāgurus are described in virtually all accounts of their lives. In many temples and *dādābāṛīs* they are portrayed in vivid illustrations on the walls. In addition, they are described in the text of the Dādāgurus' most important rite of worship (to be discussed later in the chapter). Most devotees of the Dādāgurus know them well.

37. On the five *pīrs*, see William Crooke 1978: 202–3, 206. He suggests that they are possibly Muslimized versions of the *Mahābhārata*'s five Pāṇḍavas.

38. A similar story is told of the great fourteenth-century Khartar Gacch leader, Jinprabhasūri (see Granoff 1993: 25). Sixty-four *yoginīs* attended his discourse disguised as laywomen. He cast a spell on them and they were unable to rise from their seats. They then begged for forgiveness.

39. In these materials the term *updrav* is used for such disturbances.

40. A remarkably similar story is told of Jineśvarsūri. See Vinaysāgar 1959: 12–13.

41. A mountain and famous pilgrimage site in Junagadh District, Gujarat.

42. This is apparently the same pilgrimage party that experienced the miraculous rescue from the bandits, but this is not completely clear in the sources I have seen.

43. To devotees this is a perfect example of how the Dādāgurus always fulfill wishes (the word for which is usually *manokāmnā,* one's "heart's wish").

44. This incident is reported in Vinaysāgar 1959: 49.

45. A period sacred to the goddess.

46. I asked many people about this, but nobody seemed to know or care. I was and remain somewhat surprised by this apparent indifference, because the "*maṇi*" is obviously an important element in this figure's identity.

47. Which Vidyut Prabhā Śrī identifies specifically as an Osvāl *gotra* (1980: 19).

48. The version presented here is taken from Vinaysāgar (1989), but these events are described in most histories of the Dādāgurus.

49. This detail from Vinaysāgar (1959: 155). The author says that Jindattsūri came from heaven to witness the ceremony.

50. An alternative date for his demise is Phālgun *amāvasyā.* See Vidyut Prabhā Śrī 1980: 23.

51. Identified as Osvāl by Vidyut Prabhā Śrī (1980: 24).

52. One of the most important of the early figures in the Khartar Gacch lineage.

53. It should be pointed out that other Jain mendicants are credited (by other sources) with similar influence over Akbar. Most importantly, Abū'l Fazl's *Ā'īn-ī-Akbarī* lists three such mendicants among "The Learned Men of the Time." They are Hīrvijaysūri and his disciples Vijaysensūri and Bhānucandra Upādhyāy (V. Smith 1917: 265, 267), all three belonging to the Tapā Gacch. Jincandrasūri is not mentioned by Abū'l Fazl. Hīrvijaysūri is actually credited with the conversion of Akbar to Jainism (ibid.: 267). According to an inscription at Śatruñjaya (dated 1593), Hīrvijaysūri persuaded Akbar to ban the slaughter of animals for six months per year, to abolish confiscation of the estates of the dead, to abolish the tax on non-Muslims, and so on (ibid.: 272–75). See also Bhatnagar 1974. According to Bhatnagar, Vijaysensūri was sent to Akbar in 1593 by the Tapā Gacch in order to counter the influence of Jincandrasūri.

54. Of course Jindattsūri subdued the five *pīr*s (above), who are Muslim entities. In an apparent echo of this theme, Jincandrasūri is said to have subdued the *adhiṣṭhāyak dev*s of the five rivers at Akbar's orders in 1595. These terms would suggest non-Muslim supernaturals. On the other hand, in the introduction to Jośi (presumably written by A. and B. Nāhṭā) these *dev*s are identified as five *pīr*s (illustration facing p. 29). In any case, the theme of Jain/Muslim opposition is a good deal stronger in accounts of Jincandrasūri's life than in accounts of the other Dādāgurus.

55. This story is also told of the fourteenth-century figure Jinprabhasūri. See Granoff 1993: 25–26, 34.

56. It is, however, rare for Digambars to visit their shrines. I was told that "even Muslims" worship the Dādāgurus. This seems improbable to me, but expresses the Jains' own sense of ecumenism regarding the Dādāgurus.

57. I think this may have reflected a desire to give the foreign investigator a "correct" version of Jainism, which in the minds of many Jains would definitely have nothing to do with such material benefits as wealth. It also may have reflected a diffidence about beliefs known to be regarded as unmodern and "superstitious" in the West. Peace of mind (in Hindi, *man kī śānti*) seems to be a generic respectable and reasonable religious goal in South Asia.

58. Unlike the Tirthankars, too, they were never omniscient.

59. For a description of the routines at a typical *dādābāṛī*, see Laidlaw 1985.

60. Gopāljī, n.d. This text was composed by someone named Gopāljī of Bikaner in 1951. I do not know whether he was a *yati* or a layman. It is pretty clearly a Jain imitation of the Hindus' famed *Hanumān Cālīsā.* (I thank Philip Lutgendorf for confirming this point.) The Dādāgurus are praised as *sankaṭ mocan* (one who liberates from dangers and difficulties), which is an epithet of Hanumān, and the text is to be recited 108 times in the morning, as is the *Cālīsā.* Most imporant, both texts focus on worldly benefits to be gained by the worshiper and conferred by the object of worship.

61. In Ahmedabad I was told that the anointing of the nine points on the image's body should be done exclusively to Tīrthankar images. Images of deities should receive only a mark on the forehead. This, I was told, is because in actuality they are the worshiper's fellow-worshipers. Jaipur Jains seem less fussy about this.

62. In this respect, however, there is variation in the practices of Jaipur Jains. I

have seen diagrams with the crescent and dot made even before images of Bhairav, which from the standpoint of orthopraxy is even less acceptable than making such images before the Dādāgurus.

63. Ṛddhisār was a prolific author. A Jaipur friend possessed several books on Ayurvedic medicine, Osvāl history, and other religious materials authored by this man.

64. Many people know the *snātra pūjā* text by heart as well. But the language of Ṛddhisār's *pūjā* is definitely easier.

65. This temple is owned by the Śrīmāl community, not by the Osvāls. The Śrīmāls of Jaipur are staunch devotees of the Dādāgurus.

66. The idea of the Dādāguru as a Tīrthankar-like figure is sometimes expressed quite overtly. For example, Vinaysāgar's edited history of the Khartar Gacch describes Jindattsūri as "like a Tīrthankar" (*tīrthankar ke samān*) (1959: 37), and states that Jindattsūri responded to laymen's questions "in the manner of the omniscient one" (ibid.: 38). It refers to Jindattsūri as a *dharm cakravartī* (ibid.: 152, 156). This expression means "universal spiritual monarch," and obviously resonates with the image of the Tīrthankar as the spiritualized king.

67. Sometimes also it is called *jñānbal* (power of knowledge).

68. It is true that devotees stress that positive results will come only to those who worship with the appropriate devotional spirit (*bhāv*); results will come to the "faithful" (*śraddhālu*), it is sometimes said. Nonetheless, the actual aid comes from the Dādāgurus themselves.

69. On various occasions I have seen worshipers err by forming the conventional crescent used in Tīrthankar worship. I have also witnessed such erring worshipers being corrected by others.

70. On many occasions informants have told me explicitly that the reason returned food offerings (*prasād*) can be taken from the Dādāgurus but not from the Tīrthankars is that the Dādāgurus "have not achieved liberation (*mokṣ*)." This is a matter I raised repeatedly with informants and I am satisfied that this formula represents a general view.

71. The *dādābāṛī*s at Ajmer and Mehraulī are also reputed to be highly miraculous.

72. I was told this version orally at Mālpurā. In the version reported in Jośī (1962: 124) the recipient of the vision is identified only as a "disciple" (*śiṣya*). I was also told that the descendants of the Brāhmaṇ are no longer *pujārī*s of the temple, having been displaced when the temple's management was shifted from Mālpurā to Jaipur some years ago.

73. A Mālpurā *pujārī*, however, hinted that Jinkuśalsūri has manifested himself in the form of a snake. While I am sure that other examples of such reports can be found, they do not accord with what seems to be the general view that the Dādāgurus manifest themselves in ascetic form (*sādhu rūp*).

74. In fact, it is usually held that the Dādāgurus will assist anyone, of whatever religion, who comes to them with a sincere heart.

75. The question of possible functional equivalents of the Dādāgurus among Tapā Gacch-affiliated Jains or in other Jain traditions is not addressed here for lack of sufficient evidence. Nor do I find it possible to speculate about possible cause-and-effect relationships between the cult of the Dādāgurus and the low number of monks in the Khartar Gacch. Does the cult of the Dādāgurus flourish because of

the absence of monks, or has the presence of the Dādāgurus' cult in some way inhibited or discouraged the initiation of ascetics—or, indeed, is there any relationship at all? I am unable to answer these questions on the basis of the materials at hand.

## CHAPTER FOUR

1. There are many Hindus as well as Jains among the Khaṇḍelvāls and also the Agravāls. There are Hindu Osvāls as well.

2. I was unfortunately unable to obtain sufficient materials to investigate Śrīmāl clan origin mythology. During the period I was in Jaipur, Bhūtoṛiyā's Osvāl history had recently appeared, and in this volume he makes the assertion that the Śrīmāls are a branch of the Osvāls (1988: 186–93). This obviously contradicts the view of many Śrīmāls that their caste emerged earlier, and infuriated a local Śrīmāl notable and author whose opinions were of great interest to me. But I was unable to obtain sufficient data to pursue these issues. An enlightening and concise discussion of the Śrīmāls can be found in Lath 1981: 105–9.

3. On these temples, see Dhaky 1967, 1968; Meister 1989.

4. For a useful discussion of Osvāl origin myths in English, see K. C. Jain 1963: 94–100.

5. The source for this appears to be the *Upkeś Gacch Paṭṭāvali,* written in 1306 C.E. For an English translation, see Hoernle (1890).

6. Bhūtoṛīyā takes these details from a book called *Jain Sampradāy Śikṣā* that was authored by a Khartar Gacch *yati* by the name of Śrīpālcandrajī and published in Bombay in 1910. This version is very close to the one in the *Upkeś Gacch Paṭṭāvali.*

7. One of Bhūtoṛīyā's sources, Yati Rāmlāljī's book *Mahājan Vaṃś Muktāvalī* (published in 1910), maintains that the king had three sons, and that the king was of Parmār (Rājpūt) lineage (1988: 68); Bhūtoṛīyā believes it unlikely that the king was Parmār and thinks that this view arises from a confusion of Utpaldev of Bhīnmāl with a ninth- to tenth-century Parmār ruler of Abu who had the same name.

8. In another version, Uhaṛ had "99 *lākh*" (9.9 million) and his older brother "18 *kroṛ*" (180 million). Uhaṛ lived outside the fort. He asked his brother for a loan of one *lākh* to enable him to live in the city (Bhūtoṛīyā 1988: 69). In yet another version (Handa 1984: 9), Puñj drives Utpaldev away by his taunts.

9. This version is apparently based on the *Upkeś Gacch Caritra,* a text written in Sanskrit verse and dating, according to Bhūtoṛīyā (1988: 156), from the thirteenth to fourteenth century.

10. The caste genealogists, however, seem to prefer the date of v.s. 222 (Bhūtoṛīyā 1988: 113).

11. There is, however, at least one version in which a rich Brāhmaṇ's son is the one bitten; Brāhmaṇs and Baniyās then convert to Jainism (Handa 1984: 13). However, virtually all versions I have seen state that the Osvāls are (or are mainly) of Kṣatriya origin.

12. Bhūtoṛīyā takes this version from Rāmlāljī's *Mahājan Vaṃś Muktāvalī,* which is dated 1910.

13. The theme of the ascetic who has difficulty obtaining alms would seem to be recurrent. Bhandarkar (1912: 100) reports a local tradition that Osiyā was originally known as Melpur Paṭṭan. An ascetic named Dhundli Mall once sent his disciple into the village for alms, but without success. He cursed the village, which became "*ḍaṭṭan*" (buried), and was only repopulated when Utpaldev came with his followers.

14. Which Bhūtoṛīyā takes from the *Upkeś Gacch Paṭṭāvalī* (and to which he assigns the date 1345) (1988: 156). I discover some discrepancies between Bhūtoṛīyā's version and Hoernle's translated version of the *Paṭṭāvalī*.

15. That is, she was prepared to die on her husband's funeral pyre.

16. For a general discussion of lineage goddesses in a rural context, see Mayer 1965: 184–88.

17. The story also illustrates an interesting aspect of lineage goddess traditions, namely, that even though these are goddesses associated with agnatic ties, the traditions of their worship are passed down by women who enter these lineages by means of marriage. My friend's mother heard the story, of course, from her mother-in-law. On these issues, see Harlan 1992: Ch. 3.

18. A major Hindu festival falling in the lunar month of Āśvin (September/October).

19. This is an issue on which I do not have good material. A systematic survey of lineage goddesses would reveal much about the migratory past of Osvāl and Śrīmāl clans and lineages.

20. One couple whom I met casually reported that their lineage goddess is a goddess who appears to be a parochial Saciyā Mātā. Her temple is at a place called Baḍlī (in Jodhpur District), and they insisted that she is not the same as the goddess at Osiyā.

21. *Navrātrī* means "nine nights." The term refers to a festival occurring twice yearly—in the lunar moths of Caitra (March/April) and Āśvin (September/October)—and dedicated to the goddess. With regard to food offerings, the *pujārī* told me that while there is no strict rule about taking the goddess's *prasād* away from Osiyā, it is nevertheless the case that if you come here for some special purpose and give the goddess a food offering, you should not take it outside Osiyā. Otherwise some mistfortune will occur. "We've seen this with our very eyes," he told me. This parallels the rule at Nākoṛā.

22. On the role of the goddess in Jainism, on Jain *kuldevi*s, and on the conversion of non-Jain goddesses into Jain goddesses, see Cort 1987; also Granoff 1989b.

23. This story comes from the *Upkeś Gacch Paṭṭāvalī*. However, I was told the same basic tale by the *pujārī*s of the Saciyā Mātā temple at Osiyā. According to a version given by Handa (1984: 14), Saciyā Mātā was the tutelary deity of the Sāṃkhalā Parmārs, and Utpaldev built her temple after he founded Osiyā.

24. Handa (1984: 17) speculates (I believe plausibly) that the goddess's name derives from the word *sāttvik*, meaning "pure," and in this context refering to her new vegetarian purity. On the other hand, a parallel etymology might link the word to *satī*, a woman who has immolated herself on her husband's funeral pyre. Past *satī*s are widely venerated in Rajasthan, and Saciyā Mātā may represent a Jain echo of this theme.

25. These details about the Bahī Bhāṭs are drawn from Bhūtoṛīyā (1988: 109).

26. In a niche at the Mahāvīr temple at Osiyā are two coiled snakes. One of

the *pujārīs* at the Saciyā Mātā temple informed me that these are the snakes in the story. (In one version of the story there are two snakes: one to put the poison in, the other to suck it out.)

27. This story is clearly part of a *gotra* origin myth. It concludes by telling how Bhagvān Singh's son, Lābhrāj, acquired the reputation of a healer, which is why his descendants became known as the Vaidya *gotra* (Bhūtoṛīyā 1988: 111–12).

28. This is evidently from the *Upkeś Gacch Paṭṭāvalī.*

29. A story of milk falling spontaneously on the ground where an image of a deity is buried is common in mythologies of temple origin in India.

30. Bhandarkar (1912: 100–101) reports a slightly different version. Utpaldev (Uppaladeva in this telling) built the temple of Saciyā Mātā, who was in fact the clan goddess of the Sāmkhlā Paramāras. When Ratanprabh (Ratnaprabhsūri) came he failed to convert anyone, and finally hit on the snake scheme. When the king and his subjects became Jains, Saciyā Mātā was infuriated because they would no longer give her living sacrifices, so she cursed the people and made them leave the town. But as a result of their prayers she relented to the extent of allowing them (the Osvāls) to make offerings to her after marriages, as is in fact done today. But no Osvāl should pass the night in the city lest she retaliate with a misfortune. I believe this is the version identified as a Brāhmaṇ version by Dhaky (1967: 63–64).

31. That is, they were worshipers of Viṣṇu. In this connection it is of great interest that Dhaky (1967: esp. pp. 66–67) has argued convincingly that the temple of Saciyā Mātā (as opposed to the Mahāvīr temple) replaced an original shrine that was dedicated to a goddess who, though nonvegetarian, was a Vaiṣṇava goddess.

32. On Vaiṣṇo Devī, see Erndl 1993.

33. According to Harlan's persuasive analysis, the *satī* tradition acts, in part, to resolve contradictions involved in these images. When a warrior dies he has been sacrificed by his lineage goddess on the battlefield, but at the same time this represents a failure of the lineage goddess in her role as domestic protectress and also a failure of the wife as the lineage goddess's emulator, who protects her husband by means of the self-sacrifice expected of all *pativrat*s. Resolution is achieved when the wife becomes a *satī:* "Symmetry is reestablished only through a further sacrifice, that of the wife on behalf of her husband" (1992: 224).

34. Harlan points out that some men participate with women in fasting on such occasions as Navrātrī (1992: 88).

35. There are inconsistencies between these bodies of legend with regard to particular clans. See, for example, the references to the Bhaṇḍārī *gotra* in Bhūtoṛiyā (1988: 175, 181) and Bhansālī (1982: 163).

36. For an excellent discussion of these myths, and wonderful retellings of some of them, see Granoff 1989b.

37. Within the universe of these tales, Jindattsūri was responsible for more conversions than any other ascetic.

38. Winner of the famous debate with the Caityavāsīs. See Chapter Three.

39. An extremely important early Khartar Gacch *ācārya,* though not revered as a Dādāguru.

40. Bhansālī identifies this mendicant as belonging to the Saṇḍer Gacch (1982: 219). I have no additional information about this gacch.

41. As Granoff also points out, the same theme is expressed in the story of Jindattsūri's subduing of sixty-four *yoginīs* (1989b: 206).

42. In general usage, a *brahm* is the malevolent ghost of a Brāhmaṇ who died in an unsatisfied state. See Parry 1994: 231–32.

43. It seems possible that the category of *vyantar* supernaturals arose, in part perhaps, as a reservoir for the assimilation of such beings to the Jain cosmos. See Granoff 1989b: 202–3, n. 13.

44. As Granoff points out (1989a: 369–70), this tale parallels the story, apparently dating from the fourteenth century, of Hemacandra's miracle at Someśvara in which he instructs King Kumārapāla to worship the *linga* (while he himself is in meditation). When the king does, a minute image of Śiva emerges and instructs the king on the superiority of Jainism. The conquest of Śiva by the ascetic's power is also a theme in biographies of Siddhasena and Samantabhadra (ibid.: 365–68). Here, however, it is the Tīrthankar, not Śiva, who appears because of the ascetic's powers. As Granoff points out, these tales play off numerous Śaiva accounts of miraculous appearances by Śiva at or out of *lingas*.

45. The claim is common in northern India. It is made by many castes, including non-Jain business castes such as the Hindu Maheśvarīs. It should be noted, moreover, that the patterns seen in the accounts of Osvāl origin reviewed here are not necessarily generalizable to other Jains, especially in other regions. This chapter is written within a Rajasthani frame of reference. Here the Rājpūts loom large as the regionally dominant caste. Whether or to what degree a similar symbolism underlies Osvāl identity in such areas as Gujarat, where the impact of Rājpūt culture is much less, is an interesting question that needs further investigation. During my relatively brief stay in Ahmedabad I did not collect relevant data. John Cort (personal communication) suggests that although the Gujarati Jains have similar origin myths, they accord much less importance to the Rājpūt connection than do the Jains of Rajasthan. See also Cort 1989: 80, n. 18.

46. This ambiguity seems to parallel the ambiguity of kingship itself in the wider Jain tradition. How is one to be a Jain king? There have indeed been such, but the institution of kingship is finally suspect; thus, legendary kings (including Ṛṣabh himself) renounce kingship in the end in favor of the spiritual heroism of the ascetic. See Dundas 1991.

47. I should reiterate that this is not, of course, to accept the historicity of clan origin mythology. But the clans exist.

## CHAPTER FIVE

1. I should add that this comparison is commonly made by Jaipur Jains. For example, they will often say that ritual usages they regard as un-Jain "must have come from the Vaiṣṇavas."

2. That is, Kṛṣṇa holding the mountain over the heads of the people of Braj whom he is protecting from a storm. Kṛṣṇa had persuaded the people of Braj to discontinue Indra's worship, and the storm was Indra's furious response.

3. In an echo of this theme, Divālī is also regarded as an appropriate occasion for good eating by the Jains, and this is consonant with the festival's emphasis on

wealth, success, and well-being among Jains and Hindus alike. But, predictably, asceticism prevails in the end in the Jains' Divālī; for them, Divālī also marks the anniversary of Mahāvīr's liberation, the culmination of his renunciation of the world. At this point, Mahāvīr ceases eating permanently (according to the Śvetāmbar view; the Digambars hold that he had already given up food entirely). See Laidlaw (1995: Ch. 17) for a description and analysis of the complex relationship between auspiciousness and asceticism in Divālī as celebrated by Jaipur Śvetāmbar Jains.

4. According to Barz (1976: 92), a fifth, the *śānta bhāv,* is not stressed in the Puṣṭimārg.

5. "I now," says the devotee, "do dedicate . . . my bodily faculties, my life, my soul, and its belongings, with my wife, my house, my children, my whole substance, and my own self" (Barz 1976: 85).

6. Similar ideas can be found in other Vaiṣṇava traditions. See Hayley 1980.

7. The Puṣṭimārgī initiate is, of course, also a renouncer. But the initiate then recovers what he renounced, which has now become sanctified by Kṛṣṇa.

8. There are other inversions as well. Among the Jains, as my friend pointed out, God is possessionless. This gives rise to the additional reflection that it is not he but his worshipers who are rich: rich in their ritual personae as vastly wealthy deities, and also often rich in their lay identities as wealthy businessmen who, in imitation of the largess of the gods of heaven, bestow wealth on Jain temples. In the Puṣṭimārg it is precisely Kṛṣṇa's worshipers who are possessionless, because in fact they have given everything—mind, body, and wealth—to Kṛṣṇa. He in turn is rich, for he possesses everything. Of course many Puṣṭimārgī initiates are rich businessmen too, and as Bennett (1983: 322) points out, these ideas have the effect of sanctifying wealth and the gaining of wealth; the businessman "renounces all yet gives up nothing."

On the face of things, it seems rather mysterious that these two traditions should be so radically opposed. But given the fact that Śvetāmbar Jainism and the Puṣṭimārg have nearly identical lay constituencies, namely business castes, its seems likely that this opposition in fact expresses a close relationship. It may be that a very similar sociocultural context requires a radical difference in religious orientation in the interest of clarity of boundaries. The materials I have at hand, however, do not permit me to go beyond mere speculation.

9. Tīrthankars-to-be are also regally generous, but obviously not after they renounce the world, at which point they no longer have anything to give. The shift from redistributive kingship to kingship on another plane seems to be signaled by the year of gift giving that occurs before a Tīrthankar's initiation.

10. The nonreturnability of offerings in Śaiva worship is also discussed in Stevenson 1971: 388–92.

11. Digambar Jains use the same term for the remnants of worship.

12. The Śaivas also believe, as do the Jains, that worship can generate material benefits (Davis 1991: 154). The mechanism seems to be karmic amelioration.

13. It is interesting to note a much stronger assertion of what seems to be the same theme in the Kāpālika sect, a now-extinct, disreputable cousin of mainstream Śaivism. The Kāpālikas propitiated Bhairava, a fierce form of Śiva, by means of sacrificc. Though thc victim (apparently sometimes human) needed to be pure and

auspicious, he was regarded "as a scapegoat, the repository of the transgressions of the sacrificers" (Lorenzen 1972: 85). Whether such offerings were then consumed by the offerers is not clear from Lorenzen's account. Among the Kāpālikas, too, the theme of emulation was very strong; the idea of sacrifice found an echo in the notion of self-sacrificial penance. At the center of Kāpālika praxis was the *mahāvrata,* which required the votary to imitate Śiva's penance (as Bhairava) for the sin of Brahmanicide (ibid.: 73–82). But it must also be said that, in contradistinction to what seems to be the Śaiva Siddhānta pattern, the idea of actual consubstantiation with Śiva seems to have played an important role in the Kāpālikas' tantric rituals (ibid.: 88–93).

14. For a comparison of the transactional aspects of Hindu and Sinhalese Buddhist rituals, see Gombrich 1971: 120–24,

15. Between Parry and Raheja there are some differences of interpretation (see Parry 1994: 135–39), especially regarding the role of impurity (as opposed to inauspiciousness) in *dān* transactions and also the relationship between such transactions and the status differences of givers and receivers. These differences, which seem likely to reflect significantly different ethnographic contexts, need not, I think, detain us here.

16. One informant tells Raheja that Kālī is a killer and a blood-drinker. Sweepers, he goes on to say, are the most violent and meat-eating of castes, and for this reason *pujāpā* of Kālī should go to members of the Sweeper caste (Raheja 1988: 201). Raheja notes that the *pujāpā* of a deity named Guggā is given to a recipient who has been possessed by this deity in the past. "When offerings are made to these recipients, Guggā is said to receive them, while the inauspiciousness of the *bāgharvālā* (Guggā, "the one from Bāghar") is assimilated by the *pātra,* the recipient of the *pujāpā*" (ibid.: 202).

17. A small example is as follows: If a child's first tooth erupts in the upper jaw, this is believed to lead to difficulties for the child's mother's brother. The mother's brother ties an offering made of wheat flour and sugar in a red cloth, which he then throws over the wall of his sister's conjugal house. This offering is then passed onward as *dān* to a Dakaut.

18. The mendicant author Hemprabhāśrījī states precisely that one obtains the spiritual benefit of *dān* (*dān dharm*) from performing the offering (*arpan*) of material things (*dravya*) in *pūjā* (1977: 26). Moreover, in the texts surveyed by Williams, *pūjā* is considered to be *dāna* "in the largest sense," and the giving of *dāna* to mendicants, in turn, "is regarded as a *pūjā* of the *atithi* [the ascetic guest]" (Williams 1963: 119, 216).

19. On the other hand, we must note that the Puṣṭimārg maintains that one who eats food *not* first offered to Kṛṣṇa partakes of "sin" and "digests" his own selfishness (Bennett 1990: 192).

20. Marriott links the minimalist transactional mode with the Vaiśya *varṇa,* suggesting that at the social level this general stance is "plainly that of the trader" (1976: 127). Of course (and as we have noted), the Puṣṭimārg's Kṛṣṇa, specializing in what would seem to be a maximal transactional mode, is also associated with traders. Where Jain ritual transactions fall in Marriott's later three-dimensional Indic ethnosocial science (1990) is an intriguing question. The Tīrthankar's transactional isolation clearly exemplifies the quality Marriott calls "unmixing." This

same characteristic would seem to remove the Tīrthankar altogether from Marriott's scale of "marking"/"unmarking," although the Tīthankars certainly "marked" lay worshipers through the subtle medium of their teachings when they lived (as do living ascetics today). The absolute coherence of the Tīrthankars' omniscience suggests their location on the extreme "matching" end of Marriott's "matching"/"unmatching" axis.

# Glossary

| | |
|---|---|
| *abhiṣek* | anointing or bathing an image |
| *ācārya* | religious preceptor; ascetic leader; leader of an ascetic lineage |
| *agra pūjā* | worship performed in front of and at a distance from the image (as opposed to *ang pūjā*); the latter parts of the *aṣṭprakārī pūjā* in which offerings are made outside the inner shrine |
| Agravāl | a merchant caste of northern India |
| *ahiṃsā* | nonharming |
| *akṣat pūjā* | the sixth part of the *aṣṭprakārī pūjā* in which a diagram is formed with grains of rice |
| *ang pūjā* | the opening phases of the *aṣṭprakārī pūjā* involving physical contact with the image (as opposed to *agra puja*) |
| *aparigraha* | nonpossession |
| *āratī* | a lamp offering in which the lamp is moved in a circular fashion before the image |
| *aṣṭprakārī pūjā* | the "eightfold worship"; the principal rite of worship among Jains |
| Baniyā | a merchant; a member of one of the trading castes |
| Bhairav (Bhairava) | a deity who protects Jain temples, often said to be a fierce form of the Hindu deity Śiva |
| *bhakti* | devotion |
| *bhāv pūjā* | mental or internal worship (as opposed to *dravya pūjā*) |
| *bhogbhūmi* | the land of enjoyment; those areas of the terrestrial zone whose inhabitants suffer no hardships and exist in a state of perpetual pleasure, and where liberation is not possible |
| Brāhmaṇ | the ancient social class of teachers and priests |

| | |
|---|---|
| *caitya vandan* | a rite of worship involving the recitation of praise-verses in coordination with certain physical postures |
| Caityavāsī | temple-dwelling monks |
| *cakravartin* | universal emperor |
| Cāmuṇḍā | a meat-eating Hindu goddess |
| *candan pūjā* | the second part of the *aṣṭprakārī pūjā* in which the image is anointed with sandalwood paste; also called *kesar pūjā* or *kesar-barās pūjā* |
| *cāturmās* | the four-month rainy season retreat for monks and nuns |
| *caturvidh sangh* | the fourfold order of Jain society: monks, nuns, laymen, laywomen |
| Chagansāgar | a distinguished Khartar Gacch monk (1839–1909) |
| *chatrī* | an umbrella; a cenotaph |
| *cyavan* | the death of a deity or hell being |
| *dādābāṛī* | "garden of the *dādā*"; a shrine where the Dādāgurus are worshiped |
| Dādāguru (or Dādāgurudev) | one of four greatly venerated monks of the past belonging to the Khartar Gacch |
| *dān* (*dāna*) | alms; a charitable gift; a merit-generating gift |
| *darśan* | sight; vision; seeing an august personage or the image of a deity |
| Devcandrajī | a distinguised Khartar Gacch monk (1689–1755) who authored the text of the *snātra pūjā* used in the Khartar Gacch tradition |
| *dharm* (*dharma*) | sacred duty; righteousness; religion |
| *dhūp pūjā* | the fourth part of the *aṣṭprakārī pūjā* in which the image is worshiped with incense |
| Digambar | "sky clad"; the Jain sect whose monks are nude |
| *dīkṣā* | initiation |
| *dīpak pūjā* | the fifth part of the *aṣṭprakārī pūjā* in which the image is worshiped with a lamp |
| Divālī | the "festival of lights" associated with Lakṣmī, the goddess of prosperity; celebrated by Jains and Hindus |
| *dravya pūjā* | worship with material things (as opposed to *bhāv pūjā*) |
| Durgā | the "Inaccessible One"; a meat-eating, martial goddess |
| eightfold worship | see *aṣṭprakārī pūjā* |
| five-*kalyāṇak pūjā* | see *panc kalyāṇak pūjā* |
| *gacch* | a lineage of ascetics based on the principle of disciplic descent |
| *gaṇdhar* | one among a Tīrthankar's foremost disciples |
| *gati* | destiny; one of the four birth categories of hell-beings, gods, humans, and animals and plants |
| Gautam Svāmī (Gautama) | Mahāvīr's foremost disciple |

| | |
|---|---|
| *gotra* | exogamous patriclan |
| *guṇasthān* | one of the fourteen stages of spiritual advancement toward liberation |
| *hiṃsā* | violence; harm (as opposed to *ahiṃsā*) |
| Indra | the king(s) of the gods, of which there are sixty-four |
| Indrāṇī | the consort of an Indra |
| *jal pūjā* | the first part of the *aṣṭprakārī pūjā* in which the image is bathed |
| Jambūdvīp | the vast circular continent at the base of Mount Meru |
| *janam* | birth |
| Jina | a victor; one who has defeated all desires and aversions; synonym for a Tīrthankar |
| Jincandrasūri II | the fourth Dādāguru (1541–1613) |
| Jincandrasūri "Maṇidharī" | the second Dādāguru (1140–1166) |
| Jindattsūri | the first Dādāguru (1075–1154) |
| Jinkuśalsūri | the third Dādāguru (1280–1332) |
| *jīv* | a soul |
| *kalyāṇak* | one of the five auspicious and welfare-producing events that occur in the last lifetime of every Tīrthankar: descent into a human womb, birth, initation, attainment of omniscience, and final liberation |
| Kamaṭh | Pārśvanāth's antagonist who followed him through many births |
| *karm* (*karma*) | action that affects the subsequent destiny of the actor; in Jain doctrine, material particles that are drawn to the soul by action and stick to the soul as a consequence of desire and aversion |
| *karmbhūmī* | the land of endeavor; those areas of the terrestrial zone where suffering takes place, where humans must work for subsistence, and where liberation is possible |
| *kevaljñān* | omniscience |
| Khaṇḍelvāl | a merchant caste of northern India |
| Khartar Gacch | an ascetic lineage among Śvetāmbar Jains |
| Kṛṣṇa | a Hindu deity; a form of Viśṇu |
| Kṣatriya | the ancient social class (*varṇa*) of warriors and rulers |
| *kuldevī* | lineage goddess |
| Mahāvideh | a terrestrial zone where Tīrthankars are always active and liberation is therefore always possible |
| Mahāvīr (Mahāvīra) | the twenty-fourth and last Tīrthankar of our continent and era |
| Maheśvarī | a Hindu merchant caste of northern India |
| Mandirmārgī | Śvetāmbar Jains who worship images in temples |

| | |
|---|---|
| *mantra* | a sacred or power-filled verbal formula |
| Meru | a mountain at the center of the terrestrial world |
| *mokṣ* (*mokṣa*) | liberation |
| *mokṣ mārg* | the path of liberation |
| *muni* | a generic term for a male Jain ascetic |
| Mūrtipūjak | Śvetāmbar Jains who worship images in temples |
| *naivedya pūjā* | the seventh part of the *aṣṭprakārī pūjā* in which food is offered |
| *namaskār mantra* | the most frequently uttered prayer and sacred formula in Jainism; an expression of homage to the five worship-worthy beings: the Tīrthankars, the liberated souls, the ascetic leaders, the ascetic preceptors, and ordinary ascetics |
| Nandīśvar | a continent lying outside the zone in which humans can live; a place where the gods and goddesses worship eternal images of the Tīrthankars |
| Navrātrī | "nine nights"; two periods of the year dedicated to the worship of the goddess |
| *nigod* | the smallest and lowest form of life |
| *nirvāṇa* | In Jainism the death and liberation of an omniscient being |
| *nisīhi* | a word uttered by worshipers in Śvetāmbar temples signifying the passage from one ritual state to another |
| Osiyā | a town, north of Jodhpur, that is an important pilgrimage site for Osvāls; the site of Saciyā Mātā's temple |
| Osvāl | a merchant caste of northern India prominent among Śvetāmbar Jains; there are also Hindu Osvāls |
| *pañc kalyāṇak pūjā* | a major rite of worship celebrating the five *kalyāṇak*s of a particular Tīrthankar |
| *pāp* | sin; "bad" karma |
| Pārśvanāth | the twenty-third Tīrthankar of our place and era |
| Paryuṣaṇ | a period of religious observances taking place during the rainy season |
| *pativrat* | a dutiful and virtuous wife |
| Pauṣ Daśmī | an annual festival held in honor of Pārśvanāth's birthday |
| *phal pūjā* | the eighth and final part of the *aṣṭprakārī pūjā* in which fruit is offered |
| *pratikramaṇ* | a ritual of confession and expiation |
| *prasād* | blessing; grace; food that has been offered to a deity or august personage; objects sanctified by contact with a deity or august personage |
| *pūjā* | worship, homage |
| *pujārī* | among Hindus a temple priest; among Jains a menial temple servant |
| *puṇya* | merit; "good" karma |

| | |
|---|---|
| *puṣpā pūjā* (also *phul pūjā*) | the third part of the *aṣṭprakārī pūjā* in which flowers are offered |
| Puṣṭimārg | a Kṛṣṇa-worshiping Hindu sect founded by Vallabhācārya in the fifteenth century |
| Rājpūt | a caste or caste cluster; the martial asristocracy of Rajasthan and other areas of northern and central India |
| Ṛṣabh | the first Tīrthankar of our continent and era |
| Saciyā Mātā | lineage goddess of many Osvāls |
| *sādhu* | a male ascetic |
| *sādhvī* | a female ascetic |
| Śaiva | a worshiper of the Hindu deity Śiva |
| Śaiva Siddhānta | a Śaiva sect |
| *sāmāyik* | a ritual of meditation |
| *saṃsār* (*saṃsāra*) | the cycle of rebirth; the world of transmigrating beings |
| *samudāy* | an ascetic sublineage |
| *samvasaraṇ* | the universal assembly of deities, humans, and animals who have come to hear a Tīrthankar's teaching |
| *sangh* | the Jain community |
| Śatruñjaya | a holy mountain (in Gujarat) that is one of the principal pilgrimage sites for Śvetāmbar Jains |
| *siddh* (*siddha*) | a liberated soul |
| *siddhcakra* | a sacred figure portraying nine essential elements of Jainism |
| *snātra pūjā* | a rite of worship focused on the bathing of a Tīrthankar-image |
| *śrāvak* | a "listener"; a Jain layman |
| *śrāvikā* | a Jain laywoman |
| Śrīmāl | a merchant caste of northern India prominent among Śvetāmbar Jains |
| Sthānakvāsī | a reformist Śvetāmbar sect that opposes the worship of images |
| *sthāpnā* | a rite that invokes the presence of a deity at a place of worship |
| *svastik* | a swastika; also called *sāthiyā* |
| Śvetāmbar | "white clad"; the Jain sect whose monks and nuns dress in white |
| Tapā Gacch | an ascetic lineage among Śvetāmbar Jains |
| Terāpanth | a reformist Śvetāmbar sect that opposes the worship of images |
| Tīrthankar | "fordmaker"; an omniscient teacher who promulgates Jainism |
| *tīrthankar nām karm* | the *karma* that will bring about later attainment of Tīrthankar status |
| *tyāg* | abandoning; renunciation |

| | |
|---|---|
| *upvās* | a fast |
| Utpaldev | a Rājpūt prince who is believed to have founded the town of Osiyā; also Upaldev |
| Vaiṣṇava | a worshiper of the Hindu deity Viṣṇu or one of his forms |
| Vaiśya | the social class (*varṇa*) of merchants |
| Vallabhācārya | the founder of the Puṣṭimārg |
| *varṇa* | the four classes of Hindu society: Brāhmaṇ, Kṣatriya, Vaiśya, Śūdra |
| *vāskṣep* | a yellow powder used by Jain ascetics to confer blessings |
| *vrat* | a restraint; a vow; in common Hindu usage, a votive fast |
| *vyantar* | a lower class of Jain deities |
| *yati* | a male Śvetāmbar ascetic whose vows are less onerous than those of full ascetics |
| *yojan* | a measure of distance; about 8 miles |
| *yugpradhān* | the foremost spiritual leader of the age |

# Bibliography

Agrawala, R. C. n.d. "Iconography of the Jain Goddess Saccika." *The Jaina Antiquary* 21 (No. 1): 13–20.

Ames, M. M. 1966. "Ritual Prestations and the Structure of the Sinhalese Pantheon." In M. Nash et al., eds., *Anthropological Studies in Theravada Buddhism,* pp. 27–50. New Haven, Conn.: Yale University Southeast Asia Studies.

Aruṇvijayjī Mahārāj, Pū. Munirāj. n.d. *Karm kī Gati Nyārī, Cāturmāsik Ravivāsriya Sacitra Vyākhyānmālā.* Jaipur: Śrī Jain Śvetāmbar Tapāgacch Sangh.

Babb, Lawrence A. 1975. *The Divine Hierarchy: Popular Hinduism in Central India.* New York: Columbia University Press.

———. 1986. *Redemptive Encounters: Three Modern Styles in the Hindu Tradition.* Berkeley: University of California Press.

———. 1988. "Giving and Giving Up: The Eightfold Worship among Śvetāmbar Mūrtipūjak Jains." *Journal of Anthropological Research* 44: 67–85.

———. 1993. "Monks and Miracles: Religious Symbols and Images of Origin among Osvāl Jains. *Journal of Asian Studies* 52: 3–21.

———. 1994. "The Great Choice: Worldly Values in a Jain Ritual Culture." *History of Religions* 34: 15–38.

Banks, Marcus. 1992. *Organizing Jainism in India and England.* Oxford: Clarendon Press.

Barz, Richard. 1976. *The Bhakti Sect of Vallabhācāryā.* Faridabad: Thompson Press.

Bennett, Peter. 1983. "Temple Organisation and Worship among the Pustimārgiya-Vaiṣṇavas of Ujjain." Ph.D. diss., University of London.

———. 1990. "In Nanda Baba's House: The Devotional Experience in Pusti Marg Temples." In O. Lynch, ed., *Divine Passions: The Social Construction of Emotion in India,* pp. 182–211. Berkeley: University of California Press.

Bhadrabāhu Vijay. 1989. *Jindarśan*. Mahsāṇā: Śrī Viśvakalyāṇ Prakāśan Ṭrasṭ.
Bhandarkar, D. R. 1912. "The Temples of Osiā." Pp. 100–115 of *Archaeological Survey of India, Annual Report, 1908–1909*. Calcutta.
Bhansālī, Sohanrāj. 1982. *Osvāl Vaṃś, Anusandhān ke Ālok mẽ*. Jodhpur: Kuśalam Jain Granthālaya.
Bhatnagar, V. S. 1974. "Akbar and Jainism." *Jijnasa* 1 (3/4): 52–59.
Bhūtoṛiyā, Māngīlāl. 1988. *Osvāl Itihās kī Amar Bel*. Calcutta: Priyadarśī Prakāśan.
Caillat, Collette, and Ravi Kumar. 1981. *The Jain Cosmology*. English rendering by R. Norman. New York: Navin Kumar, Inc.
Carrithers, Michael. 1987. "Passions of Nation and Community in the Bahubali Affair." *Modern Asian Studies* 22: 815–44.
———. 1989. "Naked Ascetics in Southern Digambar Jainism." *Man* (n.s.) 24: 219–35.
———. 1990. "Jainism and Buddhism as Enduring Historical Streams." *Journal of the Anthropological Society of Oxford* 21: 141–63.
Cort, John E. 1986. "Recent Descriptive Accounts of the Contemporary Jainas: A Review Essay." *Man in India* 66: 180–87.
———. 1987. "Medieval Jaina Goddess Traditions." *Numen* 34: 235–55.
———. 1989. "Liberation and Wellbeing: A Study of the Śvetāmbar Mūrtipūjak Jains of North Gujarat." Ph.D. diss., Harvard University.
———. 1991a. "Śvetāmbar Mūrtipūjak Jain Scripture in a Performative Context." In Jeffrey R. Timm, ed., *Texts in Context: Traditional Hermeneutics in South Asia*, pp. 171–93. Albany: SUNY Press.
———. 1991b. "The Śvetāmbar Mūrtipūjak Jain Mendicant." *Man* (n.s.) 26: 549–69.
———. 1991c. "Two Ideals of the Śvetāmbar Mūrtipūjak Jain Layman." *Journal of Indian Philosophy* 19: 391–420.
Crooke, William. 1978. *The Popular Religion and Folk-Lore of Northern India*. 2 vols. Reprint of 2d ed. (1896). New Delhi: Munshiram Manoharlal.
Davis, Richard H. 1991. *Ritual in an Oscillating Universe: Worshiping Śiva in Medieval India*. Princeton, N. J.: Princeton University Press.
Dhaky, M. A. 1967. "The Iconography of Sacciya Devi." In *Bābū Choṭelāl Jain Smṛti Granth* (Part 4, English Section), pp. 63–69. Calcutta: Bābū Choṭelāl Jain Abhinandan Samiti.
———. 1968. "Some Early Jaina Temples in Western India." In *Shri Mahavir Jaina Vidyalaya Golden Jubilee Volume* (Part I), pp. 290–347. Bombay: Shri Mahavira Jaina Vidyalaya.
Dundas, Paul. 1985. "Food and Freedom: The Jaina Sectarian Debate on the Nature of the Kevalin." *Religion* 15: 161–98.
———. 1987–88. "The Tenth Wonder: Domestication and Reform in Medieval Śvetāmbara Jainism." *Indologica Taurinensia* 16: 181–94.
———. 1991. "The Digambara Jain Warrior." In M. Carrithers and C. Humphrey, eds., *The Assembly of Listeners: Jains in Society*, pp. 169–86. Cambridge: Cambridge University Press.
———. 1992. *The Jains*. London: Routledge.
———. 1993. "The Marginal Monk and the True *Tīrtha*." In R. Smet and U. Watanabe, *Jain Studies in Honour of Josezf Deleu*, pp. 237–59. Tokyo: Honno-Tomasha.

Eck, Diana. 1981. *Darśan: Seeing the Divine Image in India.* Chambersburg, Pa.: Anima Books.
Ellis, Christine M. Cottam. 1991. "The Jain Merchant Castes of Rajasthan: Some Aspects of the Management of Social Identity in a Market Town." In M. Carrithers and C. Humphrey, eds., *The Assembly of Listeners: Jains in Society,* pp. 75–107. Cambridge: Cambridge University Press.
Erndl, Kathleen M. 1993. *Victory to the Mother: The Hindu Goddess of Northwest India in Myth, Ritual, and Symbol.* New York: Oxford University Press.
Fisher, Eberhard, and Jyotindra Jain. 1977. *Art and Rituals: 2500 Years of Jainism in India.* New Delhi: Sterling Publishers.
Folkert, Kendall W. 1993. *Scripture and Community: Collected Essays on the Jains.* Edited by John E. Cort. Atlanta: Scholars Press.
Geertz, Clifford. 1973a. "Religion as a Cultural System." In C. Geertz, *The Interpretation of Cultures,* pp. 87–125. New York: Basic Books.
——. 1973b. "Ritual and Social Change: A Javanese Example." In C. Geertz, *The Interpretation of Cultures,* pp. 142–69. New York: Basic Books.
Gombrich, R. 1966. "The Consecration of a Buddhist Image." *Journal of Asian Studies* 26: 23–36.
——. 1971. *Precept and Practice: Traditional Buddhism in the Rural Highlands of Ceylon.* London: Oxford University Press.
Gopāljī. n.d. *Śrī Dādā Guru Guṇ Iktīsā.* Jaypur: Pārasmal Singhī.
Granoff, Phyllis. 1989a. "The Biographies of Siddhasena: A Study in the Texture of Allusion and the Weaving of a Group Image." Part One. *Journal of Indian Philosophy* 17: 329–84.
——. 1989b. "Religious Biography and Clan History among the Śvetāmbara Jains in North India." *East and West* 39 (Nos. 1–4): 195–215.
——. 1990a. "The Biographies of Siddhasena: A Study in the Texture of Allusion and the Weaving of a Group Image." Part Two. *Journal of Indian Philosophy* 18: 261–304.
——. 1990b. *The Clever Adulteress and Other Stories: A Treasury of Jain Literature.* Edited by Phyllis Granoff. Oakville, Ont.: Mosaic Press.
——. 1992. "Worship as Commemoration: Pilgrimage, Death and Dying in Medieval Jainism." *Bulletin d'Etudes Indiennes* 10: 181–202.
——. 1993. *Speaking of Monks: Religious Biography in India and China.* Oakville, Ont.: Mosaic Press.
Guṇārthī, Rameścandra. 1987. *Rājasthāni Jātiyõ kī Khoj.* Ajmer: Arya Brothers Bookseller.
Handa, Devendra. 1984. *Osian: History, Archaeology, Art & Architecture.* Delhi: Sandeep Prakashan.
Harlan, Lindsey. 1992. *Religion and Rajput Women.* Berkeley: University of California Press.
Hastīmaljī Mahārāj, Ācāryaśrī. 1988. *Jain Dharm kā Maulik Itihās* (Pratham Bhāg, Tīrthankar Khaṇḍ). Jaipur: Jain Itihās Samiti.
Hayley, Audrey. 1980. "A Commensal Relationship with God: The Nature of the Offering in Assamese Vaishnavism." In M. F. C. Bourdillon and M. Fortes, eds., *Sacrifice,* pp. 107–25. New York: Academic Press.
Hemprabhāśrījī Mahārāj. 1977. *Śrī Jain Dharm Praveśikā.* Calcutta; Hīrālāl Lūṇiyā.

Hoernle, A. F. Rudolf. 1890. "The Paṭṭāvali or List of the Upkeśa-Gacchha." *Indian Antiquary* 19 (August 1890): 233–42.

Humphrey, Caroline. 1991. "Fairs and Miracles: At the Boundaries of the Jain Community in Rajasthan." In M. Carrithers and C. Humphrey, eds., *The Assembly of Listeners: Jains in Society*, pp. 201–25. Cambridge: Cambridge University Press.

Humphrey, Caroline, and James Laidlaw. 1994. *The Archetypal Actions of Ritual: A Theory of Ritual Illustrated by the Jain Rite of Worship*. Oxford: Oxford University Press.

Jain, Bābulāl (ed.). 1990. *Srī Samagr Jain Cāturmās Sūcī*. Bombay: Samagr Jain Cāturmās Sūcī Prakāśan Pariṣad.

Jain, Hīrālāl. See Śāntisūri

Jain, Kailash Chand. 1963. *Jainism in Rajasthan*. Sholapur: Gulabchand Hirachand Doshi (Jaina Samskrti Samrakshaka Sangha).

Jain, Manjul Vinaysāgar. 1989. "Khartargacch kī Sanvign Sādhu Paramparā kā Paricay." In Sādhvī Śrī Śaśiprabhā Śrī Jī, *Śramaṇī (Ācārya Śrī Jinudaysāgar Jī kī Ājñānuvartī Pravartinī Sajjan Śrī Jī Mahārāj kī Svarg-Jayantī ke Upalakṣya par Abhinandan-Granth)*, Part 3, pp. 44–58. Jaipur: Śrī Jain Svetāmbar Khartargacch Sangh.

Jaini, J. L. 1918. *Jaina Gem Dictionary*. Arrah: (Kumar Devendra Prasad Jaina) The Central Jain Publishing House.

———. 1974. *Tattvarthadhigama Sutra* by Umasvami Acharya. Edited with introduction, translation, notes and commentary in English by J. L. Jaini. Reprint of 1920 ed. issued as Vol. 2 of the Sacred Books of the Jainas. New York: AMS Press, Inc.

Jaini, Padmanabh S. 1979. *The Jaina Path of Purification*. Berkeley: University of California Press.

———. 1985. "The Pure and the Auspicious in the Jaina Tradition." *Journal of Developing Societies* 1: 84–93.

———. 1991a. *Gender and Salvation: Jaina Debates on the Spiritual Liberation of Women*. Berkeley: University of California Press.

———. 1991b. "Is There a Popular Jainism?" In M. Carrithers and C. Humphrey, eds., *The Assembly of Listeners: Jains in Society*, pp. 187–99. Cambridge: Cambridge University Press.

Jargaḍ, Umrāvcand. 1959a. "Śrīmad Devcandrajī kā Jīvan Caritra." In Umrāvcand Jargaḍ, ed., *Śrī Devcandrajī Kṛt Snātra Pūjā Sārth (Jīvan Caritra Sahit)*. Jaipur: Umrāvcand Jargaḍ.

———. 1959b. *Śrīmad Devcandrajī Kṛt Snātra Pūjā (Pariśiṣṭ Sahit)*. Edited by Umrāvcand Jargaḍ. Jaipur: Umrāvcand Jargaḍ.

Jinharisāgarsūri. 1948. *Mahātapasvī Jīvan-Caritra*. Lohāvaṭ: Pārakh Indracand Jain.

Jitendravijayjī. 1986. *Vividh Pūjā Sangrah (Hindi Vidhiõ Sahit)*. Sivānā. Tapāgacch Jain Sangh.

Johnson, Helen M. (trans.). 1931. *Triṣaṣṭiśalākāpuruṣacarita* [of Hemacandra]. Vol. I, *Ādīśvaracarita*. Baroda: Oriental Institute (Gaekwad's Oriental Series).

Jośī, Madanlāl (ed.). 1962. *Dādāvāṛī-Digdarśan*. Bombay: Pratāpmal Sethiyā (Śrījindattsūri Sevā Sangh).

Kāntisāgar. n.d. *Śrī Jin Guru Guṇ Sacitra Puṣp Mālā*. Nāmor (Rājāsthān): Srī Kānti Darśan Jñān Mandir.

Kāslīvāl, Kastūrcand. 1989. *Khaṇḍelvāl Jain Samāj kā Vṛhad Itihās*. Jaipur: Jain Itihās Prakāśan Sansthān.

Kavīndrasagar, Śrımajjin. 1964. *Śrī Pārśvanāth Panckalyāṇak Pūjā*. Jaipur: Śrī Puṇya Suvarṇ Jñān Pīṭh.

Kinsley, David R. 1975. *The Sword and the Flute: Kālī and Kṛṣṇa, Dark Visions of the Terrible and the Sublime in Hindu Mythology*. Berkeley: University of California Press.

Kothari, M. M. 1982. *The Saint of Mt. Abu: Yogiraj Shantivijayji*. Jodhpur: Hopes Books.

Laidlaw, James. 1985. "Profit, Salvation and Profitable Saints." *Cambridge Anthropology* 9 (3): 50–70.

——. 1995. *Riches and Renunciation: Religion, Economy, and Society among the Jains*. Oxford: Oxford University Press.

Lalvānī, Gaṇeś. 1985. *Jain Dharm va Darśan*. Jaipur: Prākṛt Bhāratī akādamī.

Lath, Mukund. 1981. *Half a Tale: A Study in the Interrelationship between Autobiography and History. (The Ardhakathanaka translated, introduced and annotated by Mukund Lath)*. Jaipur: Rajasthan Prakrit Bharati Sansthan.

Lorenzen, David N. 1972. *The Kapalikas and Kalamukhas: Two Lost Saivite Sects*. Berkeley: University of California Press.

Madan, T. N. 1987. *Non-Renunciation: Themes and Interpetations of Hindu Culture*. Delhi: Oxford University Press.

Marriott, McKim. 1976. "Hindu Transactions: Diversity without Dualism." In B. Kapferer, ed., *Transaction and Meaning: Directions in the Anthropology of Exchange and Symbolic Behavior*, pp. 109–42. Philadelphia: Ishi.

——. 1984. "A Description of *Samsara:* A Simulation of Rural Hindu Life." Mimeographed. University of Chicago: Civilizations Course Materials Project (Social Sciences Collegiate Division).

——. 1990. "Constructing an Indian Ethnosociology." In McKim Marriott, ed., *India through Hindu Categories*, pp. 1–39. New Delhi: Sage Publications.

Mauss, Marcel. 1967. *The Gift: Forms and Functions of Exchange in Archaic Societies*. New York: W. W. Norton & Company.

Mayer, Adrian C. 1965. *Caste and Kinship in Central India: A Village and its Region*. Berkeley: University of California Press.

Meister, Michael W. 1989. "Temples, Tirthas, and Pilgrimage: The Case of Osian." In Devendra Handa and Ashvini Agrawal, eds., *Ratna-Chandrika: Panorama of Oriental Studies*, pp. 275–81. New Delhi: Harman Publishing House.

——. 1993. "Sweetmeats or Corpses: Community, Conversion, and Sacred Places." Paper presented at workshop on Jains in Indian History and Culture, Amherst College, June 1993.

Mishra, Ratan Lal. 1991. *The Mortuary Monuments in Ancient and Medieval India*. Delhi: B. R. Publishing Corporation.

Muktiprabhvijay, Muni. n.d. *Śrāvak ko Kyā Karnā cahiye?* Translated into Hindi by R. C. Sāh. Vaḍhvāṇ Śahar: Kalyāṇ Sāhitya Prakāśan.

Nāhṭā, Agarcand (presumed author). 1988. *Dādā Guru Caritra (Cārõ Dādā Sāhab kā Sankṣipt Jīvan)*. Ajmer: Śrī Jindattsūri Maṇḍal.

Nāhṭā, Agarcand and Bhanvarlāl. 1939. *Dādā Śrī Jinkuśalsūri.* Calcutta: Śankardān Śubhairāj Nāhṭā (New Rajasthan Press).

———. 1978. *Jainācārya Pratibhodit Gotra evam Jātiyā̃.* Pālītāṇā: Śrī Jinharisāgarsūri Jñān Bhaṇḍār.

Nāhṭā, Agarcand and Bhanvarlāl (eds.). 1971. *Maṇidhārī Śrījincandrasūri Aṣṭam Śatābdī Smṛti-Granth (s. 1223–2027).* Delhi: Maṇidhārī Śrījincandrasūri Aṣṭam Śatābdī Samāroh Samiti.

Nyāyatīrth, Anupcand (chief editor). 1990. *Jaipur Digambar Jain Mandir Paricay.* Jaipur: Śrī Digambar Jain Mandir Mahāsangh.

Obeyesekere, G. 1966. "The Buddhist Pantheon in Ceylon and Its Extensions." In M. Nash et al., eds., *Anthropological Studies in Theravada Buddhism,* pp. 1–26. New Haven, Conn.: Yale University Southeast Asia Studies.

Pal, Pratapaditya. 1994. *The Peaceful Liberators: Jain Art from India.* Los Angeles and New York: Los Angeles County Museum of Art and Thames and Hudson, Inc.

Parry, Jonathan P. 1986. "The Gift: The Indian Gift and the 'Indian Gift.' " *Man* (n.s.) 21: 453–73.

———. 1994. *Death in Banaras.* Cambridge: Cambridge University Press.

Parsons, Talcott, and Edward A. Shils (eds.). 1962 (orig. 1951). *Toward a General Theory of Action: Theoretical Foundations for the Social Sciences.* New York: Harper & Row.

Raheja, Gloria G. 1988. *The Poison in the Gift: Ritual, Prestation, and the Dominant Caste in a North Indian Village.* Chicago: University of Chicago Press.

Ratnasenvijay, Muni. 1995. "The Rite of Veneration of the Jina Image (*Caitya-vandan*)" Translated by John E. Cort. In Donald S. Lopez, ed., *Religions of India in Practice,* pp. 326–32. Princeton, N. J.: Princeton University Press.

"Ṛddhisār." 1962. *Śrī Dādā Gurudev kī Pūjā.* Calcutta: Śrī Jain Upāśray Committee.

Reynell, Josephine. 1985. "Honor, Nurture and Festivity: Aspects of Female Religiosity Amongst Jain Women in Jaipur." Ph.D. diss., Cambridge University.

———. 1987. "Prestige, Honour and the Family: Laywomen's Religiosity amongst the Svetambar Murtipujak Jains in Jaipur." *Bulletin d' Etudes Indiennes* 5 (1987): 313–59.

———. 1991. "Women and the Reproduction of the Jain Community." In M. Carrithers and C. Humphrey, eds., *The Assembly of Listeners: Jains in Society,* pp. 41–65. Cambridge: Cambridge University Press.

Sangave, Vilas A. 1980. *Jaina Community: A Social Survey.* Rev. 2d ed. Bombay: Popular Prakashan.

Śānti Sevā Sangh (pub.). n.d. *Śrī Vijay Śāntisūriśvarjī Jīvan Jhalak.* Māṇḍolīnagar (Jālor Dist.): Śrī Śānti Sevā Sangh.

Śāntisūri. 1949. *Jīvvicār Prakaraṇ (sārth-savivecan).* Edited by Hīrālāl (Dūgaṛ) Jain. Madras: Śrī Jain Mārg Prabhāvak Sabhā.

Schechner, Richard. 1988. *Performance Theory* (revised and expanded edition). New York and London: Routledge.

Seneviratne, H. L. 1978. *Rituals of the Kandyan State.* Cambridge: Cambridge University Press.

Sharma, J. P. 1989. *Jaina Yakshas.* Meerut: Kusamanjali Prakashan.

Singer, Milton. 1972. *When a Great Tradition Modernizes: An Anthropological Approach to Indian Civilization.* New York: Praeger.

Singh, Munshi Hardyal. 1990. *The Castes of Marwar.* Reprint of 1894 ed. Jodhpur: Books Treasure.

Singhi, N. K. 1991. "A Study of Jains in a Rajasthan Town." In M. Carrithers and C. Humphrey, eds., *The Assembly of Listeners: Jains in Society,* pp. 139–61. Cambridge: Cambridge University Press.

Smith, Brian K. 1989. *Reflections on Resemblance, Ritual, and Religion.* New York: Oxford University Press.

Smith, Frederick M. 1987. *The Vedic Sacrifice in Transition: A Translation and Study of the Trikandamandana of Bhaskara Misra.* Poona: Bhandarkar Oriental Research Institute.

Smith, Vincent A. 1917. "The Jain Teachers of Akbar." In *Commemorative Essays Presented to Sri Ramakrishna Gopal Bhandarkar.* Poona: Bhandarkar Oriental Research Institute.

*Snātra Pūjā.* 1979. *Śrī Devcandrajī Kṛt Vidhi Sahit Snātra Pūjā.* Ajmer: Cāndmal Sipāṇī (Śrī Jindattsūri Maṇḍal, Dādābāṛī).

——. n.d. *Snātra Pūjā.* With explanatory material by Śrī Vicakṣaṇ Śrījī Mahārāj Sāhab. Calcutta: Śrī Vijñānśrījī Vicakṣaṇśrījī Jñān Bhaṇḍār.

Śrīmāl, Rājendra K. n.d. *Śrīmāl Jāti (Ek Paricay).* Jaipur: Śrī Lābhcand Pustakālaya.

Śrīśrīmāl, Saubhāgyamal (chief editor). 1984. *Jaypur Jain Śvetāmbar Samāj Ḍayrekṭrī.* Edited by C. S. Barlā, N. Bhānāvat, and S. Bhānāvat. Jaipur: Sanyojak Prakāśan Samiti.

Stevenson, Mrs. Sinclair. 1971. *The Rites of the Twice Born.* Reprint of 1920 (Oxford University Press) original. New Delhi: Oriental Books.

——. 1984. *The Heart of Jainism.* Reprint of 1915 (Oxford University Press) original. New Delhi: Munshiram Manoharlal.

Sūryamall, Yati. 1941. *Jain Ratnasār.* Calcutta: Surana Printing Works.

Tambiah, S. J. 1976. *World Conqueror and World Renouncer: A Study of Buddhism and Polity in Thailand against a Historical Background.* Cambridge: Cambridge University Press.

Toomey, Paul M. 1990. "Krishna's Consuming Passions: Food as Metaphor and Metonym for Emotion at Mount Govardhan." In O. Lynch, ed., *Divine Passions: The Social Construction of Emotion in India,* pp. 157–81. Berkeley: University of California Press.

Trautmann, Thomas R. 1981. *Dravidian Kinship.* Cambridge: Cambridge University Press.

Upādhye, Svāmī A. N., and Pt. P. Siddhāntśāstrī (eds.). 1982. *Jñānpīṭh-Pūjāñjali.* New Delhi: Bharatiya Jnanpith.

Van Gennep, Arnold. 1960. *The Rites of Passage.* Translated by M. B. Vizedom and G. L. Caffee. Chicago: University of Chicago Press.

Vidyut Prabhā Śrī. 1980. *Camakte Sitāre.* Barmer: Śrī Kuśalsūri Bhakti Jain Maṇḍal.

Vinaya Sagar, Mahopadhyaya (ed. and Hindi trans.). 1984. *Kalpasūtra.* English translation by Mukund Lath. Jaipur: Prakrit Bharati.

Vinaysāgar, Mahopādhyāy. 1989. "Khartar Gacch kā Sankṣipt Paricay." In Sādhvī Śrī Śaśiprabhā Śrī Jī, *Śramaṇī (Ācārya Śrī Jinudaysāgar Jī kī Ājñānuvartī*

*Pravartinī Sajjan Śrī Jī Mahārāj kī Svarg-Jayantī ke Upalakṣya par Abhinandan-Granth)*, pp. 1–35, Part 3. Jaipur: Śrī Jain Svetāmbar Khartargacch Sangh.

Vinaysāgar, Mahopādhyāy (ed.). 1959. *Kartargacch kā Itihās, Pratham Kaṇḍ*. Bhūmikā lekhak, Agarcand Nāhṭā. Ajmer: Dādā Jindattsūri aṣṭam śatābdī mahotsav svāgatkāriṇī samiti.

Williams, R. 1963. *Jaina Yoga: A Survey of the Mediaeval Śrāvakācāras*. London: Oxford University Press.

# Index

Titles, Hindi terms, and page numbers for illustrations are in italics.


Abhaydevsūri, 124
*Abhiṣek*, 33, 70, 74, 85; defined, 217. *See also* Bathing: of sacred images
Abortion, 51
Abu, Mount, 107, 148, 210n. 7
Acal Gacch, 54
*Ācārya*, 22, 54, 119–20, 140, 142, 169; Caityavāsī, 117; defined, 217; Khartar Gacch, 111; Upkes Gacch, 143. *See also specific names*
Acyutendra, 74
*Addhāpalyas*, 42
*Adhiṣṭhāyak devs*, 79, 133, 208n. 54
*Adhiṣṭhāyak pīrs*, 118
*Adho lok*, 200n. 26
Ādināth, 200n. 29
Agni, 180
Agra, 125
*Agra pūjā*, 87–88, 90, 94, 98, 202n. 57; defined, 217
Agravāls, 4, 139; defined, 217; Hindu, 210n. 1
Agrawala, R. C., 157
Ahaṛ, 152
*Āhāra*, 87. *See also* Food
*Ahiṃsā*, 2, 56–57, 138, 170; defined, 217. *See also* Nonviolence
Ahmedabad, 17, 18 (map); ascetics in, 52, 54–55; *pujārīs*, 68, 202n. 3; rituals of worship in, 27, 79, 85–86, 88; temples, 65–66, 69, 145; *vāskṣep* powder in, 61
Airāvat, 40, 41, 72
Ajmer, 111, 117, 111–21, 209n. 71
*Akbar pratibodhak*, 124
Akbar the Great, 124–25
*Akṣat*, 88. *See also* Rice
*Akṣat pūjā*, 88, *89*, 127; defined, 217
*Akṣay tṛtīyā*, 43. *See also* Calendrical festivals
Ambaḍ, 119
Ambar, 166
Ambārgaṛh, 167
Ambikā Devī, 119
Ames, Michael, 185, 186
Añcal, 140
*Ang pūjā*, 87–88, 98; defined, 217
Animal sacrifices, 141, 147, 150, 157, 159, 160, 168
Animals and plants, 45, 46, 88–89. See also *Tiryanc*
Animal welfare organizations, 2, 138
Annakūṭa, 179
*Antarāy nivāraṇ pūjā*, 27
Antardvīps, 200n. 24
Anthropomorphic images, 111, 112, 127, 128
*Anuttars*, 47
*Aparigraha*, 57–58; defined, 217. *See also* Nonpossession
*Aparyāpt*, 201n. 41

*Apkāy,* 45
*Āratī,* 36, 68, 76; defined, 217. *See also* Lamp offerings
*Arhats,* 22, 23, 34, 185
Arṇorāj, 117
Aruṇvijay Mahārāj, Pu, 49–51, 201nn. 38, 39
*Āryikās,* 53–54
Asceticism, 2, 8–10, 47, 59–60, 106, 169–71, 176, 179; Aruṇvijay and, 51; in the cosmos, 40, 42; Dādāgurus and, 131, 134; goal of, 81; laity and, 83–84, 106; liberation and, 78, 195; miracles and, 117; objects of worship and, 15, 65, 174–75, 177, 183, 191; rewards of, 78; Tīrthankars and, 25–26, 38, 82, 84; *vrats* and, 188; worship and, 93, 99, 107, 160, 183; worship-worthiness and, 134
Ascetic praxis, 19, 110, 175
Ascetics, 5, 9–10, 50, 78, 100, 115, 198nn. 7, 8; conversion by, 161, 169, 176; Dādāgurus as, 130–34; deceased, 102–36; deities and, 81–82; eating and, 58–60; gifting to, 60; images in Jain temples, 66; initiation of, 117; Khartar Gacch, 114; laity and, 52–53, 57–58, 83, 105, 117; liberation and, 62, 92; lineage, 17, 44, 52–53, 135, 143, 161; living, 52–63; magical power and, 109, 168; mendicancy, 56–58; miracles and, 162, 165; as objects of worship, 10, 23–63, 79, 84, 92, 94, 98, 101–2, 110, 174, 193; organization, 53–56; *pūjā* and, 11; traveling and, 56–57; Upkeś Gacch, 151; vows of, 197n. 5; worship and, 28, 55, 83, 128; worship-worthiness of, 62–63, 79. *See also* Dādāgurus; Mendicants; Monks; Nuns; Tīrthankars; *and specific names*
Āśrampad, 33
*Asteya,* 57
*Aṣṭottrī snātra,* 124
*Aṣṭprakārī pūjā,* 13, 17, 65, 69, 76, 84–91; defined, 217. *See also* Eightfold worship
*Aśubh,* 78. *See also* Inauspiciousness
Aśvasen, King, 32
Atibal, 121
Audience, 15, 29; performers and, 12–13, 85
Auspiciousness, 32, 36, 71, 78, 197n. 7, 214n. 3, 214–15n. 13. *See also* Inauspiciousness
*Avadhi,* 33–34
Ayodhya, 26
Babb, Lawrence A., 158, 198n. 10, 202n. 63
Baḍlī, 211n. 20
Baḍnagar, 118
Bahādur, Ray Badrīdāsjī, 108
Bahī Bhāṭs, 148–51, 156, 160
Banaras, 187
Baniyās, 3, 210n. 11; defined, 217
Banks, Marcus, 198nn. 7, 12, 202n. 55
*Barās,* 86. *See also* Camphor
*Baṛī dīkṣā,* 105. *See also* Initiation
Bārsī, 104
Barz, Richard, 177, 179–81
Bathing: by ascetics, 56, 202n. 57; of infant Tīrthankar, 33, 70, 74, 86; by *pūjā* principles, 28; of sacred images, 32, 75, 85–86, 91, 96–98, 129
Bathing rite, 69. See also *Snātra pūjā*
Bāvelās, 163
Benefit, 60, 92, 106, 202n. 62
Bennett, Peter, 177, 179–81, 214n. 8, 215n. 19
Betel, 115, 167
Bhadrabāhu Vijay, 93
Bhadrasūri, 165
Bhagvānsāgar, 105, 107, 205nn. 8, 10, 12
Bhairav (Bhairava), 80–81, 118, 133, 145, 204n. 35, 209n. 62, 214–15n. 13; Black, 123; defined, 217; Nākoṛā, 79–80, 95–96; White, 123
*Bhakti,* 28, 69, 93; defined, 217
*Bhaṇḍār,* 164; box, 88, 90
Bhaṇḍārīs, 145, 164–65, 212n. 35
Bhandarkar, D. R., 211n. 13, 212n. 30
*Bhaṇḍśāl,* 163, 165
Bhansālī, Sohanrāj, 161–62, 165–66, 212nn. 35, 40
Bhansālis, 163, 165–66
Bhānucandra Upādhyāy, 208n. 53
Bharat, 39–42, 72, 200n. 33, 203n. 12
Bhāṭīs, 163
Bhatnagar, V. S., 208n. 53
*Bhāv,* 28, 60, 84, 93, 99, 180
*Bhavanvāsis,* 47–48
*Bhāv pūjā,* 68, 87, 91, 98–99, 203n. 20; defined, 217
Bhīmjī, 164
Bhīmpallī, 123
Bhīmsen, 141, 163
Bhīnmāl, 141–42, 151, 210n. 7
*Bhog,* 105, 107, 121, 179
*Bhogbhūmi,* 40, 46; defined, 217
Bhuraṭs, 146
*Bhūtāveś,* 107. *See also* Possession (spirit)
Bhūtoṛiya, Māngīlāl, 140, 142, 143, 147,

148, 152, 153, 210nn. 2, 6, 8, 9, 10, 12, 211nn. 14, 25, 212nn. 27, 35
Bikaner, 55, 106, 108, 145
Bīlāḍā, 126
Birth, 45, 46, 48, 49–51. *See also* Rebirth
*Bisā,* 17
*Bīs sthānak tapasya,* 31
Bohitth, King, 167
Boraṛ, King, 167
Boraṛs, 167
Botharās, 145, 167
*Brahmacarya,* 57. *See also* Celibacy
Brahmans, 114, 118–19, 125, 132, 141, 164, 188, 200n. 33, 210n. 11, 212n. 30, 213n. 42; Chagansāgar and, 106; conversion of, 135; defined, 217; gifts and, 190; Mahāvīr and, 199n. 7; Osvāls and, 161; priests, 115, 187; *pujārīs,* 202n. 3
*Brahm rākṣas,* 165. *See also* Possession (spirit)
Braj, 178, 179
Bṛhad, 140
Brooms, 2, 56, 57, 116, 125, 166. See also *Ogha*
Buddha, The, 185, 192, 203n. 19, 206n. 24
Buddhism, 2, 141, 184–86, 200n. 32, 204n. 32

Caillat, Collette, 200n. 22, 201n. 40
*Caitya vandan,* 69, 73, 91; defined, 218
Caityavāsīs, 114–15, 117, 129; defined, 218
*Cakravartin,* 31, 33, 203n. 19; defined, 218. *See also* Universal emperor
Cakreśvarī, 79, 97, 163
Calendrical festivals, 25, 27, 43
*Cāmars,* 72
*Camatkārī,* 109, 132, 204n. 39
*Camatkārs,* 95, 132
Camphor, 78, 86
Cāmuṇḍā (Cāmuṇḍā Devī), 142–43, 147–48, 152, 155, 157, 159; defined, 218
Caṇḍa, 182–84, 189–90, 193
*Candan,* 86. *See also* Sandalwood paste
*Candan pūjā,* 86; defined, 218
Caṇḍikā, 166
Candrasen, 141
Cāndśrījī, 105
Carrithers, Michael, 60
Castes, 4, 17, 54, 137–38, 143, 161, 172, 213n. 45; business, 214n. 8; in Jaipur, 19; untouchable, 202n. 3. *See also specific names*
*Cāturmās,* 35, 52, 56; defined, 218. *See also* Rainy season retreats
*Caturmāsik pratikramaṇ,* 108
*Caturvidh sangh,* 6, 52, 126; defined, 218
Cauhans, 148, 162–64. *See also* Rājpūts
Celibacy, 57, 105–6, 197n. 5
Chagansāgar, 104–10, 112, 117, 126, 130; defined, 218
Chājeṛ, 122
Charisma, 123. See also *Prabhāv*
*Chatrī,* 108, 112, 128; defined, 218
Chogmal, 104–5. *See also* Chagansāgar
*Cintāmaṇi,* 126
Cittauṛ, 116–17, 163
Clairvoyant knowledge, 72–74
Clans, 140–43, 146, 150, 156; histories, 138–39, 168; origin mythology, 160–67, 172. See also *Gotras* and *specific names*
Coconuts: in rituals of worship, 32, 64, 71, 150
Coins: in rituals of worship, 76, 89
*Comāsu.* See *Cāturmās*
Confession, 99–100
Consecrations: of sacred images, 117, 121, 123, 140; of temples, 121–22
Consubstantiation, 180, 191, 215n. 13
Conversions, 143; by Dādāgurus, 116, 121, 135–36; in Khartar Gacch legends, 162–67; Rājpūts to Jains, 138–39, 142, 146–47, 151, 154–55, 159–61, 168, 176; and transformation of converts, 168–73
Cort, John E., 6, 54, 55, 60, 61, 78, 83, 90, 197n. 7, 198n. 12, 201nn. 49–51, 202nn. 53, 55, 60, 4, 203nn. 10, 21, 23, 24, 204nn. 25, 37, 205n. 14, 211n. 22, 213n. 45
Cosmos, 38–52, 62, 76, 213n. 43; asceticism in, 40, 42; biology of, 44–48; deities' role in, 79; liberation in, 40, 42; rules, 48; space in, 38–41; time in, 41–44; Tīrthankars in, 40, 42–44
Crooke, William, 207n. 37
Cures: role in conversions, 163
*Cyavan,* 27; defined, 218
*Cyavan kalyāṇak,* 30–32

*Dādā,* 206n. 21
*Dādābāṛīs,* 69, 108, 111, 122, 124, 127, 130, 132, 144, 207n. 36; defined, 218
*Dādāguru baṛī pūjā,* 128
*Dādāguru Iktīsā,* 127
Dādāgurus (Dādāgurudevs), 19, 27, 55, 63, 96, 102–3, 111–36, 166; asceti-

Dādāgurus (continued).
cism and, 131, 134; as ascetics, 130–34; defined, 218; identity and, 171–73; liberation and, 126–27, 130–31, 209n. 70; and Tīrthankars, 112–13, 131–36, 172; worship of, 127–30; worshipers and, 103, 126, 129–30, 132, 134, 171–72, 175–76, 193. *See also specific names*
Ḍagā, 140
Dakauts, 189, 215n. 17
*Ḍākiṇīs*, 107
*Dān* (*dāna*), 25, 43, 59, 143, 187–91, 193; defined, 218
*Darśan*, 23, 68, 74, 92, 106, 121, 127, 144, 154; defined, 218
*Dasā*, 17
Daśarath, King, 188
*Daśavaikalikasūtra*, 115
Daśehrā, 145–46
Davis, Richard H., 182–84, 189
Deities, 6, 50, 76–82, 88, 97, 208n. 61; ascetics and, 81–82; clan, 165; in the cosmos, 40, 45, 47–48; guardian, 152; Hinduism and, 192; images in Jain temples, 66; lineage, 165; as models, 79–82; as objects of worship, 77, 79; *prasād* and, 96; unliberated, 133–34; *vrat*s and, 188, 192; worshipers and, 96
Delhi, 120–23
*Derāsar*, 66. *See also* Temples
Derāur, 123, 132
Deśnok, 107
*Dev*, 45, 133. *See also* Deities
Devalvāḍā, 167
*Devātmā*, 123, 133
Devcandrajī, 69–70, 76, 172, 206n. 20; defined, 218
*Devdravya*, 93
*Devlok*, 40, 99, 119–20
Devotion, 28, 69, 93
Devrājpur, 123
Dhaky, M. A., 140, 210n. 3, 212nn. 30, 31
*Dhan*, 34, 105, 110, 178
Dhāndhūjī, 148–49
*Dharm* (*dharma*), 51, 60, 105, 110, 168, 209n. 66; defined, 218
Dharmdevjī Upādhyāy, 116
Dharmsāgarjī, 124
Dharṇendra, 33, 34, 35, 201n. 44
Dholkā, 116
Dhundli Mall, 211n. 13
*Dhūp*, 88. *See also* Incense
*Dhūp pūjā*, 88, 127; defined, 218
*Dhvaj pūjā*, 133
Digambars, 4, 17, 53, 66, 137, 199n. 19, 214nn. 3, 11; ascetics, 53–54, 202nn. 58, 59; Dādāgurus and, 208n. 56; defined, 218; female Tīrthankars and, 199n. 4; Jaipur, 65; offerings and, 204n. 33; *prasād* and, 202n. 64; Rājpūts and, 139; self-starvation, 60; *sthāpnā mantras*, 203n. 8
Dikkumārīs, 33, 73
*Dīkṣā*, 27, 33, 56, 199n. 2; defined, 218. *See also* Initiation
*Dīpak pūjā*, 88; defined, 218
Disciplic succession, 17, 44, 54, 97, 175; Chagansāgar's, 109–10; Dādāgurus and, 129, 134–35; Devcandrajī's, 76; Jindattsūri's, 118; Pārśvanāth's, 141
Divālī, 179, 204n. 31; defined, 218
*Doṣ* (*doṣa*), 87, 144, 178, 183. *See also* Fault
*Dravya pūjā*, 68, 87, 91, 93, 99, 107, 203n. 20; defined, 218
Dreams, 33, 37, 104, 149, 153, 158, 167; before birth of a Tīrthankar, 31–33, 57, 72, 82, 109
Duggaṛs, 145–46
*Dukh*, 45
*Dukhamā*, 42
Dundas, Paul, 3, 37, 58, 197n. 5, 202n. 53, 206nn. 22, 26, 27, 207n. 31, 213n. 46
Durgā, 146, 153–54, 157–58; defined, 218
Durlabhrāj, King, 114–15

Eating, 83, 90, 178; ascetics and, 58–60. *See also* Fasting; Food; Vegetarianism
Eightfold worship, 13, 17, 65, 69, 76, 84–91, 98–100, 127–29, 131; liberation and, 130; offerings in, 93–95, 132, 136
Ellis, Christine M. Cottam, 3, 198n. 12
Erndl, Kathleen M., 158, 212n. 32
Ethnographic research, 19–20

Fasting, 24–25, 53, 57–58, 106, 160, 178, 199n. 3, 205n. 11; as asceticism, 83–84, 99, 170; by Chagansāgar, 108; Dādāgurus and, 116, 126; goddesses and, 158; by laity, 106; by Ratnaprabhsūri, 150; by women, 24, 25, 58. *See also* Eating; Food; Vegetarianism
Fatehpur, 145
Fault, 87, 144, 178, 183–84
Fazl, Abū'l, 208n. 53

Felicity, 37, 78, 81, 100–101, 175
Five-*kalyāṇak pūjā*. See *Pañc kalyāṇak pūjā;* Pārśvanāth's five-*kalyāṇak pūjā*
Flags: in rituals of worship, 32–34, 36, 127–28, 131
Flower offerings, 72–74
Flowers: in rituals of worship, 36, 86–87, 128, 133
Folkert, Kendall W., 202n. 55
Food, 45, 190; ascetics and, 58–60; in rituals of worship, 87. *See also* Eating; Fasting; Vegetarianism
Food offerings, 32, 43, 89–90, 94, 96, 121, 132, 145, 178–80, 211n. 21; The Buddha and, 185; Jain, 184; Kṛṣna and, 191; Śaiva Siddhānta and, 182, 184
Foot images, 102, 108, 111, *112*, 127–28, 205nn. 1, 2
Fruit: in rituals of worship, 32
Fruit offerings, 90–91, 127–29, 136

*Gacch*, 54, 139–40; defined, 218. *See also specific types*
Gaṇadhara Copaḍā, 140
*Gaṇādhīśvar,* 105
*Gaṇdhars,* 61; defined, 218
Gāngs, 164
*Garbhaj,* 45–46
Gaṛh Sivānā, 122
Garlands: in rituals of worship, 32–33
*Gatis,* 45, 49–50; defined, 218
Gautam Svāmī (Gautama), 206n. 22; defined, 218
Geertz, Clifford, 198n. 9
Gemstone business, 17, 23
Ghaṇṭā Karṇ Mahāvīr, 95, 204n. 35
*Ghāti karmas,* 34
Girnār, 119, 123
*Gocarī,* 59
Goddesses, 119, 121, 165; clan origins and, 166; conversion of, 147–48, 155, 158–59; guardian, 119; Hindu, 147, 155, 157–58, 166; meat eaters, 142, 147, 155, 157, 166; *mithyādṛṣṭi,* 121; tantric, 118, 142; tutelary, 144; vegetarian, 155, 157, 159. *See also* Lineage goddesses and *specific names*
Golechā, 104
Gombrich, R., 185, 186, 204n. 32, 215n. 14
Gopāljī, 208n. 60
*Gotras,* 129, 139, 143; defined, 219; origin myth, 212n. 27. *See also* Clans
Govardhan, Mount, 178–79
Govardhannāthjī, Śrī, 178
*Graiveyaks,* 47
Granoff, Phyllis, 117, 119, 139, 165, 166, 205n. 3, 206n. 28, 207nn. 32, 35, 38, 208n. 55, 211n. 22, 212n. 36, 213nn. 43, 44
*Gṛhasth dharm,* 106
Gugga, 215n. 16
Gujarat, 2, 17, 18 (map), 54–55, 83, 95, 114, 142, 203n. 25, 213n. 45; Jain temples, 66
Guṇārthī, Rameścandra, 139
*Guṇasthāns*, 8, 34; defined, 219
*Guru bhakti,* 166
Gurudev, 133
*Guru pūjā,* 61
Gurus, 52, 206n. 21
*Guru vandan,* 61

Hagiographies, 36, 103–4, 110, 116–17, 123, 125, 130–31, 135, 206n. 20
Handa, Devendra, 142, 157, 210nn. 8, 11, 211nn. 23, 24
Hanumān, 204n. 36, 208n. 60
Hanumān Cālīsā, 208n. 60
Harisinghācārya, 116
Harlan, Lindsey, 156, 157, 158, 159, 211n. 17, 212n. 33
Hastīmaljī Mahārāj, Ācāryaśrī, 60
Hayley, Audrey, 214n. 6
Heaven, 119. See also *Devlok*
Hell-dwellers, 45–48, 50, 72, 77, 88, 203n. 11
Hemacandara, 213n. 44
Hemprabhāśrījī Mahārāj, 85, 91, 92, 93, 99, 100, 204nn. 27, 29, 215n. 18
*Hiṃsā:* defined, 219. *See also* Violence
*Hiṃsak janams*, 50
Hinduism, 3–4, 78, 84, 98, 134, 146–47, 176–77, 181, 194, 201n. 48, 203nn. 16, 18, 206n. 24, 208n. 60, 210n. 1; castes, 202n. 3; deities and, 123, 192, 204n. 36; goddesses, 147, 155, 157–58, 166; ritual culture and, 94, 186, 192; temples, 68, 145; vegetarianism and, 138
Hīrvijaysūri, 208n. 53
Hoernle, A. F. Rudolf, 210n. 5, 211n. 14
Human beings, 45–48, 51, 61, 77, 88
Humbaḍ, 116
Humphrey, Caroline, 90, 91, 93, 198n. 7, 203n. 24, 204n. 29
Hyderabad, 104

Identity, 169–74
Images. *See* Sacred images
Image-worshipers, 6, 10, 52–53, 103, 171

Inauspiciousness, 78, 88, 188–90, 192. *See also* Auspiciousness
Incense, 32, 88, 127–28, 132
Indra, 33, 47–48, 61, 70, 100, 199n. 7, 206n. 20, 213n. 2; defined, 219; kingship and, 82; as models, 79, 170; in *snātra pūjā,* 72, 74–76; worshipers and, 172, 175–76, 179
Indrāṇī, 48, 79, 82, 100, 170; defined, 219; worshipers and, 172, 175–76, 179
Initiation, 33–34, 56, 105, 135; of ascetics, 117; of Dādāgurus, 116, 120, 122, 124; of nuns, 106. See also *Dīkṣā*
Īśān Devlok, 74

Jahāngīr, 125
Jain, Bābulāl, 53, 54, 55
Jain, Hīrālāl, 200nn. 21, 28, 201nn. 38, 39, 203n. 13
Jain, Kailash Chand, 139, 140, 210n. 4
Jain, Manjul Vinaysāgar, 205nn. 8, 11
Jaini, J. L., 41–42, 200n. 27
Jaini, P. S., 37, 66, 82, 198n. 1, 199n. 4, 205n. 41
*Jain Sampradāy Śikṣā,* 210n. 6
Jaipur, 17, 18 (map), 19, 26, 60, 63, 80, 83, 101–3, 108; ascetics in, 52–58, 202n. 61; *dādābāṛīs,* 111; Jain castes in, 4, 19; Khartar Gacch in, 61, 160–61; lineage goddesses, 144; *pūjārīs,* 68, 202n. 3; rituals of worship in, 27, 79, 85–86, 88; temples, 55, 65–66, 69, 204n. 35
Jaisalmer, 119
*Jajmān,* 188, 189
*Jal pūjā,* 85–86, 203n. 25; defined, 219
Jambūdvīp, 39–41; defined, 219
*Janam,* 27; defined, 219
*Janamābhiṣek,* 70, 71, 77
*Janam kalyāṇak,* 32
*Janmotsav,* 70
Jargaḍ, Umrāvcand, 71, 202n. 5, 203n. 6
Jāṭ, 205n. 10
*Jātis,* 50, 54, 161. *See also* Castes
Jaysen, King, 141
Jina, 5–6, 9, 82, 91, 179, 204n. 25; defined, 219
Jincandrasūri, 122, 124
Jincandrasūri "Maṇidhārī," 111, *113,* 119–22, 124, 164; defined, 219
Jincandrasūri II, 111, 124–26; defined, 219
Jindattsūri, 111, 115–21, 129, 135, *162,* 164–67, 201n. 52, 209n. 66, 213n. 41; defined, 219
Jineśvar (Jineśvarsūri), 114–15, 123, 129, 163, 167, 207n. 40
Jinharisāgarsūri, 104
Jinkuśalsūri, 111, 122–24, 126, 132, 133, 163, 205n. 1; defined, 219
Jinmāṇikyasūri, 124
Jinpatisūri, 122, 123
Jinprabhasūri, 207n. 38, 208n. 55
Jinsenācārya, 139
Jinvallabhsūri, 116, 163, 164, 166, 207n. 31
Jitendravijayjī, 203n. 8
*Jīvs,* 39, 44, 125; defined, 219
*Jñan bājī,* 201n. 43
*Jñānbal,* 120, 209n. 67
*Jñan-darśan-cāritra,* 86
*Jñāns,* 33
Jodhpur, 108, 146, 165, 198n. 11
Jogā Kanvar, 148
Jogīdāsjī, 148
Johnson, Helen M., 201n. 42
Jośī, Madanlāl, 111, 209n. 72
Jūnāgaṛh, 148, 149
*Jyotiṣks,* 47, 48

Kadambri, 34
Kājī, 125
Kakksūri, 153
*Kalaś,* 36
Kālī, 158, 215n. 16
Kālkācāryajī, 108
*Kalpasūtra,* 57
*Kalpātīt,* 47
*Kalpopapans,* 47
*Kalptaru,* 119, 126
*Kalyāṇ,* 6, 27, 44, 135
*Kalyāṇaks,* 27–28, 34–35, 37, 44, 47, 70, 76, 79, 135, 172, 199n, 7; defined, 219; fifth, 91–92, 110
Kamaṭh, 30–34, 201n. 44; defined, 219
Kāndh Rāv, 148, 150
Kānkarāvat, 163
Kānkariyās, 163
Kāntisāgar, 130, 133
Kāpālikas, 214–15n. 13
*Karm* (*karma*), 7–8, 27, 31–32, 85, 199n. 14; asceticism and, 84; defined, 219; liberation and, 44; of Pārśvanāth, 37; removal of, 60, 78, 92, 99–100. See also *Nirjarā*
Karman, 122. *See also* Jinkuśalsūri
*Karmbhūmī,* 40–42, 46; defined, 219
Karṇ, 167
*Karnā,* 56
Karnataka, 2
*Karvānā,* 56
Kāslīvāl, Kastūrcand, 139, 197n. 2

Kaṭāriyās, 162
*Kathā*, 188
Kavīndrasāgar, 28, 69
*Kesar*, 86. *See also* Saffron
*Kesar-barās pujā*, 86
Kesariyānāthji Temple, 199n. 6
*Kevaljñān*, 8, 27, 34, 35, 199n. 16; defined, 219
Khaṇḍelā, 139
Khaṇḍelvāls, 4, 139; defined, 219
*Khartar*, 115
Khartar Gacch, 17–19, 54–56, 70, 103, 124, 135, 139, 175; clans and, 140; defined, 219; hagiography, 103–4; history of, 114–15, 129, 209n. 66; legends, 160–67; monks, 28, 52, 209–10n. 75; nuns, 92, 102, 105, 116; *prasād* and, 96; *snātra pūjā* and, 69; *vāskṣep* and, 61. *See also* Dādāgurus
Khednagar, 167
Khetsar (Khetāsar), 124
Khīcand, 105
Khīmjī, 163–64
Khīmsarās, 163–64
Kingship, 5, 82–84, 137–38, 147, 156–57, 168–73; Kṛṣna and, 181; Tīrthankars and, 175–76, 181
Kinsley, David, 158
Kiraṇveg, 31
Kolāyatjī, 106
*Koṛākoṛī*, 41
Koranṭak, 140
Kṛpācandrajī, 55
Kṛṣna, 15, 178–81, 184, 191–92; defined, 219
Kṣatriyas, 82, 137, 139, 141, 148, 151, 161, 166, 199n. 7; conversion to Jains, 135, 142, 169, 176; defined, 219. *See also* Rājpūts
*Kuldevī*, 140, 144, 154, 157, 211n. 22; defined, 219. *See also* Lineage goddesses
*Kulkars*, 43
*Kuls*, 43, 144, 156
Kumār, Sultān, 124
Kumārapāla, 213n. 44
Kuśalkīrti, 122. *See also* Jinkuśalsūri
*Kusamāñjalī*, 72. *See also* Flower offerings

*Lābh*, 60, 92, 106, 202n. 62
Lābhrāj, 212n. 27
Lahore, 124
Laidlaw, James, 3, 25, 55, 59, 60, 70, 83, 84, 99–100, 197n. 6, 197–98n. 7, 198n. 8, 201n. 49, 202n. 55, 203nn. 21, 22, 205n. 42, 206nn. 21, 22, 208n. 59, 214n. 3
Laity, 10–11, 43, 51, 56, 198n. 7; asceticism and, 83–84, 106; ascetics and, 52–53, 57–58, 83, 105, 117; ritual role of, 11–12; worship by, 83
Lākhan, Rāv, 164
Lakṣmī, 158
Lalvānī, Gaṇeś, 43, 200n. 31
Lamp offerings, 32–33, 36, 64, 68, 73, 76, 128
Lamps: in rituals of worship, 88, 127–28
Lath, Mukund, 210n. 2
Laymen. *See* Laity
Liberation, 5–9, 24–25, 36–38, 47, 51, 64, 81, 94, 167, 175–76, 181, 183, 201n. 48; asceticism and, 78, 195; ascetics and, 62, 92; *bhāv pūjā* and, 99; in the cosmos, 40, 42–44, 49, 200n. 34; Dādāgurus and, 126–27, 130–31, 209n. 70; deities and, 78, 119; of Devcandrajī, 70; in eightfold worship, 89–90, 130, 136; of Pārśvanāth, 141; Śiva and, 193; Tīrthankars and, 25–26, 37, 76, 91–92, 100, 110; worship and, 91
Lineage. *See* Ascetics: lineage; Disciplic succession
Lineage goddessses, 118, 140, 143–60; fluid imagery and, 159–60; Osvāls and, 144–48, 156; protection and, 156–57; Rājpūts and, 144, 156, 158–60. See also *Kuldevī*
*Linga*, 167, 182–83, 213n. 44
Lodravā, 163, 165
Lohāvaṭ, 105, 107–9
Lorengen, David N., 214–15n. 13
Lūṇiyā, 140

Madan, T. N., 78
Madanpāl, King, 121
*Madhya lok*, 200n. 23
Madhya Pradesh, 2, 55, 111
Magical powers, 107, 110, 117, 120–21, 130–31, 152; ascetics and, 109, 168. *See also* Miracles
*Mahābhārata*, 207n. 37
Mahādev, 152
Mahājan, 3
*Mahājan vaṃś*, 153
*Mahājan Vaṃś Muktāvalī*, 210nn. 7, 12
*Mahāmantra*, 22
*Mahāpūjā*, 27
Maharashtra, 2, 55
Mahātapasvījī, 106
Mahatīyān, 120

Mahāvideh, 39–40, 42, 70, 72, 119, 200n. 34; defined, 219
Mahāvīr (Mahāvīra), 2, 6–7, 31–32, 42–44, 54, 57, 67, 72, 141, 172, 199n. 7, 204n. 31, 206nn. 22, 25; defined, 219; disciplic succession and, 109, 118, 129, 134–35; image of, 155, 160; liberation of, 142, 214n. 3; temple, 140, 151–53, 159–60, 211–12n. 26, 212n. 31; *vāskṣep* powder and, 61
Mahāvīr Jayantī, 4, 104
*Mahāvrats*, 56. *See also* Vows
Maheśvarīs, 106, 135, 161, 213n. 45; defined, 219
Mahiṣāsur, 147, 157
Mahish, 157
Mahuḍī, 95–96
*Mala,* 183
Maldhārī, 140
Mālī, 87, 202n. 3
Mallināth, 199n. 4
Mālpurā, 24, 111, 124, 132, 145
*Man* (mind), 56, 178
*Mandir,* 66. *See also* Temples
Mandirmārgī, 4, 198n. 11; defined, 219
Maṇḍor, 142
Maṇek Cauk, 122
*Mangal dīp,* 36, 76. *See also* Lamp offerings
*Maṇi,* 120, 207n. 46
Maṇidhārī. *See* Jincandrasūri "Maṇidhārī"
*Manokāmnā,* 126, 207n. 43
Mantra, 97, 163; defined, 220
Manus, 200n. 31
*Manuṣya,* 45. *See also* Human beings
*Mānuṣya lok,* 200n. 23
*Mardānā,* 160
Marriage, 43, 54, 144–46, 153, 155, 158, 164, 178, 212n. 30; caste differences and, 4; intermarriage, 17
Marriott, McKim, 16, 192–93, 201n. 43
Martial values, 5, 82, 169. *See also* Kingship
Marubhūti, 30–34
Marwar, 116
*Mās-madirā,* 141, 168
*Mati,* 33
Maulvī, 125
Mauss, Marcel, 16
Mayer, Adrian C., 211n. 16
Meat eaters, 9, 141, 168, 215n. 16; goddesses as, 147, 155, 157, 166; Rājpūts as, 138, 159
Meditation, 83, 107, 109, 116. See also *Sāmāyik*
Meḍtā, 106
Meghmālin, 33–34
Mehraulī, 111, 122, 209n. 71
Meister, Michael W., 140, 210n. 3
Melpur Paṭṭan, 211n. 13
Men: fasting by, 212n. 34; lineage goddesses and, 158; rituals of worship and, 25, 30
Mendicancy, 56–58
Mendicants, 2, 4, 10, 83, 114, 121, 124, 162, 201n. 49, 203n. 21; *dān* and, 190; lineage, 17. *See also* Ascetics; Monks; Nuns
Merit, 25, 50, 78, 84, 87, 92, 99, 187, 190, 204n. 38; deities and, 77; feeding ascetics and, 59–60; worship and, 97, 100. See also *Puṇya*
Meru, Mount, 33, 38–40, 70–71, 74, 86, 203n. 12, 206n. 20; defined, 220
Milk, 75, 152–54, 159, 178
Miracles, 107, 109, 117–18, 121–22, 124–25, 129–30, 132, 151; artwork depicting, 130; ascetics and, 162, 165; in Khartar Gacch legends, 162–65; in Ṛddhisār's *pūjā,* 135. *See also* Magical powers
Mishra, Ratan Lal, 206n. 17
Modha Singhī Solankī, 148
Mohan Bāṛī, 26, 30, 55, 56, 102–3, 111–13
Mohanlāljī, 55
Mohīpur, 164
*Mokṣ* (*mokṣa*), 8, 24, 78, 99, 167, 209n. 70; defined, 220. *See also* Liberation
*Mokṣ mārg,* 24–25, 170, 175, 195; defined, 220
Monks, 2, 6, 10, 18, 43, 52–57, 102, 123, 139, 161, 199n. 2, 201n. 45, 209n. 75; asceticism and, 170; conversion miracles and, 165; deceased, 112; lineage of, 17; ritual role of, 12. *See also* Dādāgurus; *Sādhus*
Mortuary cults, 103, 110–11
Mouth-cloth, 2, 56–57, 66, 71, 116, 119; and *puja,* 29, 202n. 54
Mughals, 145
*Mukpattī,* 56, 206n. 23. *See also* Mouth-cloth
*Mukt,* 44, 131
Muktiprabhvijay, M., 85–91, 204n. 29
*Mūl nāyak,* 68
*Muṇḍan,* 144. *See also* Tonsure ceremony
*Muni,* 53; defined, 220
Mūrtipūjak, 4–5, 10; defined, 220
Muslims, 118, 125, 145, 207n. 37, 208n. 56

Nābhi, 43
Nāḍol, 164
Nāgaur, 107
Nāgdev, 119
Nāg Pañcmī, 178
Nagpur, 116–17
Nāhṭā, Agarcand, 120, 122, 139, 161, 165–66, 168, 207n. 32, 208n. 54
*Naivedya,* 90. *See also* Food
*Naivedya pūjā,* 89–90; defined, 220. *See also* Food offerings
Nākoṛā (temple complex), 80, 95–96, 211n. 21
Nākoṛā Bhairav. *See* Bhairav; Nākoṛā
*Namaskār mantra,* 22–23, 33, 53, 71, 112, 164; defined, 220; text of, 198n. 1
*Namutthunam Sūtra,* 73
Nandīśvar (Nandīśvar Dvīp), 31, 34, 76; defined, 220
*Narak,* 41
*Nāraki,* 45. *See also* Hell-dwellers
Nārāyaṇsingh, 164
Nāthdvāra, 178
*Navkār mantra,* 22
Navnidhisāgarjī, 106
*Navpad olī,* 57. *See also* Fasting
Navrātrī, 121, 144, 147, 157, 159–60, 212n. 34; defined, 220
Nemināth, 33, 72
*Nigods,* 45, 49–50, 201n. 39; defined, 220
*Nirjarā,* 60, 78, 84, 92, 99. See also *Karm (karma)*
*Nirmālya,* 182–83, 204n. 33
*Nirvān,* 8, 27, 34, 167, 206n. 25; defined, 220
*Nirvāṇa,* 185
*Nirvāṇ kalyāṇak,* 34
*Nisīhi,* 67, 85, 91; defined, 220
Nonpossession, 58, 83, 214n. 8. See also *Aparigraha*
Nonvegetarians, 202n. 3, 212n. 31. *See also* Meat eaters; Vegetarianism
Nonviolence, 2, 5, 8–9, 138; eating and, 58–59. See also *Ahiṃsā*
Nuns, 2, 6, 10, 18, 43, 52–57, 102, 105, 123, 145, 199n. 2, 201n. 52, 205n. 11, 206n. 19; asceticism and, 170; Digambar, 53–54; initiation of, 106; lineage of, 17, 54; writings by, 12. See also *Sādhvīs*
Nyāyatīrth, Anupcand, 65

Obeyesekere, G., 185
Objects of worship, 13–15, 22–63, 186, 193; asceticism and, 15, 65, 174–77, 183, 191; ascetics as, 10, 23–63, 79, 84, 92, 94, 98, 101–2, 110, 174, 193; The Buddha as, 185; Dādāgurus as, 102, 112–13, 128; deities as, 77, 79; Kṛṣna as, 185; Tīrthankars as, 10–11, 19, 23–27, 66, 77, 79, 81, 92, 94, 99, 103, 111, 185, 193; worshipers and, 94, 131, 174, 178
Offerings, 32, 62, 93, 149, 188; The Buddha and, 185; Dādāgurus and, 127, 131–32; in eightfold worship, 76, 88–91, 98; formulas, 128–29; *pujārī* and, 93; Puṣṭimārg and, 191; Śaiva Siddhānta and, 182–84, 189; in *snātra pūjā,* 72; Tīrthankars and, 194; unreturned, 93–96, 182–84, 190–91; *vrats* and, 188–89. *See also specific types*
*Oghā,* 56, 166, 206n. 23. *See also* Brooms
Omniscience, 8, 27, 34, 199n. 16. See also *Kevaljñān*
Orthopraxy, 59, 84
Osiyā, 139–43, 149–51, 153, 155, 159–60, 211n. 21; defined, 220
*Oslā,* 142
Osvāls, 4, 17, 68–69, 104, 137, 151, 164–65, 197n. 2, 198n. 11, 207nn. 47, 51, 209n. 65, 210n. 2; clans, 140–43, 150, 153, 161; defined, 220; genealogies of, 148; Hindu, 210n. 1; lineage goddesses and, 144–48, 156; Mahāvīr and, 155; origin mythology of, 19, 139–43, 147, 150, 152, 159–61, 169–70; Osiyā and, 140; Rājpūts and, 138–39, 168–69
Osvaṃśīya, 153

Padmāvatī, 27, 33–34, *35,* 79, 97, 167
Pal, Pratapaditya, 201n. 43
Pālī, 107
Pallivāl, 140
*Palyas,* 42
*Pañcācār,* 86
*Pañcam kāl,* 42
*Pañcāmṛt,* 75
*Pañcendriy,* 45
*Pañc kalyāṇak pūjā,* 27–37, 55, 62; defined, 220. *See also* Pārśvanāth's five-*kalyāṇak pūjā*
*Pāṇḍavas,* 207n. 37
Pāṇḍuk Grove, 74
*Pāp,* 31, 78, 87, 201n. 46; defined, 220. *See also* Sin
*Parameṣṭhins,* 22, 108, 199n. 12
*Paramparā,* 135
*Parcā,* 149
Paṛihārs, 148

*Parivārs*, 54
Parmārs, 148, 164, 210n. 7, 211n. 23
Parry, Jonathan, 16, 185, 187, 190, 213n. 42
Parsons, Talcott, 198n. 9
Pārśvacandra Gacch, 54
Pārśvanāth, 2, 26, 43, 72, 80, 141–42, 197n. 4, 199n. 9, 201n. 44; defined, 220; temples, 97, 121
Pārśvanāth's five-*kalyāṇak pūjā*, 27–38, 51, 58, 172, 203n. 7; coconuts in, 64; as congregational worship, 85; eightfold worship and, 98; Ṛddhisār's *pūjā* and, 128–29, 134–35; *snātra pūjā* and, 69–71; unreturned offerings in, 62, 93. See also *Pañc kalyāṇak pūjā*
Paryuṣaṇ, 24, 57, 82–84, 108; defined, 220
Pāṭaṇ, 114, 119, 122–23, 166
*Pativrat*, 158, 160; defined, 220
*Pātra*, 122, 188–89
Pauṣ Daśmī, 26–28; defined, 220
Pāvāpuri, 206n. 25
Performances, 12–16, 85; audience and, 85; dramatic, 71; ritual, 64, 174
Performers, 13–14; audience and, 12–13
*Phal*, 7, 90. *See also* Fruit
Phalodī, 104–8
*Phal pūjā*, 90, 136; defined, 220. *See also* Fruit offerings
Pholmaljī, 107
Phophliyās, 167
*Phul pūjā*. See *Puṣpā pūjā*
Pilgrimage, 24, 144–47, 167; centers, 95, 140; cosmos as, 49–52; parties, 105, 122–23
Pīpad, 107
*Pīrs*, 118, 207n. 37, 208n. 54
*Poṣadh*, 83
Possession (spirit), 107, 165, 215n. 16
Possessionless. *See* Nonpossession
*Prabhāv*, 106, 123
Prabhāvatī, 33
Prabhāvit, 106–7, 121, 168
*Prabhāvnā*, 95, 110, 150
*Prakṣāl pūjā*, 85
*Prasād*, 61–62, 94–96, 177, 179–80, 209n. 70, 211n. 21; Buddha and, 185; defined, 220
*Prātihāryas*, 34
*Pratikramaṇ*, 24, 57, 83, 108, 119; defined, 220
*Pratyek*, 45
*Pratyek vanaspati*, 49
*Prithvīkāy*, 45
Protection: and lineage goddesses, 156–57
*Pūjā*, 28, 79, 81, 90–93, 100, 124, 190, 198n. 7; Dādāgurus and, 55, 132–35, 172; defined, 220; Digambars and, 204n. 33; of lineage goddesses, 144–45, 150; liquids in, 64–65; mouthcloths and, 29, 202n. 54; participants, 128; of Tīrthankars, 135, 167; Vaiṣṇava influence on, 177. *See also specific types*
*Pūjā* principals, 28–29, 32, 128
*Pujārī* (*pujārīs*), 29, 68, 91–94, 118, 132, 140, 152, 190, 204n. 35, 205n. 2, 211n. 23; defined, 220; of Saciyā Mātā temple, 153–55, 157, 160
*Pungīphal*, 167. *See also* Betel
Puñja, 210n. 8
*Puṇya*, 25, 31–32, 59–60, 77–78, 84, 87, 92, 97, 99, 204n. 38; defined, 220. *See also* Merit
*Puṇya bandh*, 92
*Purāṇa*, 183
*Puṣpā pūjā*, 86; defined, 221
Puṣṭimārg, 177–85, 192–94; defined, 221; offerings, 191

Raheja, Gloria, 16, 187–92, 194
Rainy season retreats, 53–57, 106–8, 120–22, 126, 201n. 45, 205n. 13; of Aruṇvijay, 49; of Jindattsūri, 116, 162; of Pārśvanāth, 35; of Ratnaprabhsūri, 142, 150
Rajasthan, 2, 18 (map), 26, 83, 95, 137, 148, 169, 195, 198n. 11, 211n. 24, 213n. 45; Dādāgurus and, 103, 111–12; Khartar Gacch in, 55; kingship and, 176; Vaiṣṇavas, 177
Rājpūts, 108, 137–39, 141, 146–47, 151, 161, 164–65, 170, 202n. 3, 210n. 7; clans, 143; conversion to Jains, 146–47, 151, 154–55, 159–61, 168–69; defined, 221; lineage goddesses and, 144, 156, 158–60. *See also* Cauhāns
Rāma, Lord, 26
Rāmdev, 120
Rāmlāljī, Yati, 210nn. 7, 12
Rānkā, 166–67
Rānkā-Vānkās, 166
Rāsal, Śreṣṭhī, 120
Ratanpur, 162
Ratanpurās, 162
Rāṭhors, 150
Ratnaprabhsūri, 142–43, 147, 150–54, 212n. 30
Ratnasenvijay, Muni, 202n. 4
Raypati, 122–23
Ṛddhisār, 55, 128–36, 172

Rebirth, 7, 48, 51, 78, 84, 100
Redemption, 181
Reflexivity, 91–93, 183, 186, 193
Religious donations, 25. See also *Dān*
Religious identity: of Jains, 2–4, 11
Religious traditions, 4, 16; Jain, 5; non-Vedic, 2; South Asian, 7, 14
Reproduction, 45–46
Reynell, Josephine, 25, 55, 144, 198n. 12
Rice, 32, 36, 72, 88, 89, 128, 131
Rihaḍ, 124
Ritual culture, 11–16, 38, 79, 94, 170–71, 186–89, 194–95; Buddhist, 184–86, 189–90; Jain, 37, 91–92, 99, 176–78, 182, 186, 189–90; Puṣṭimārg, 177–81, 192; Śaiva, 181–84, 189, 194; South Asian, 176, 190; Vaiṣṇava, 177–81, 189
Ritual gifting, 16, 187–91
Ritual roles, 11–16, 110, 186, 194–95
Rituals of worship, 10–11, 13–16, 18–19, 25–37, 53, 64–101, 110, 174; Dādāgurus and, 128; men and, 25; wealth and, 25–26; women and, 25; worldly benefits of, 64. *See also* Worship; *specific rites*
Ṛṣabh, 42–43, 72, 97, 102, 112–13, 199n. 9, 213n. 46; defined, 221
Rudrapallī, 121

*Saccī devī*, 147
Saciyā Mātā (Sacciyā Mātā, Saciyā Devī), 140, 142, 145–50, 159–60, 165; defined, 221; Durgā and, 157; temple, 149, 152, 212n. 23
Sacred images, 28–30, 64, 97–98; annointing of, 208n. 61; bathing of, 32, 75, 85–86, 91, 96–98, 129; consecrations of, 117, 121, 123, 140, 152, 154; of Dādāgurus, 133; in Jain temples, 66, 68; of lineage goddesses, 144; of Tīrthankars, 66–69, 78, 80, 98, 127, 152; *vāskṣep* powder and, 61
Sacrifice, 81, 87, 154, 159–60, 214–15n. 13; *dān* and, 187; Vedic, 81, 187. *See also* Animal sacrifices
*Sādhāraṇ*, 45, 201n. 38
Sādhu, King, 142
*Sādhus*, 6, 22, 52–54, 59, 115, 199n. 2; defined, 221. *See also* Monks
*Sādhvīs*, 6, 52–53, 199n. 2; defined, 221. *See also* Nuns
Saffron, 75, 86, 133, 149
*Sāgar* (*sāgaropam*), 41, 50
Sāgar, King, 149, 163, 165
Śaivas, 118–19, 123, 125, 181–84, 189, 193, 213n. 44; defined, 221
Śaiva Siddhānta, 181–84; defined, 221
Sajjanśrī, 55, 102
*Śakra-stava*, 73
Śākta, 123, 125
*Śakti*, 156
Salīm, 124
*Sallekhanā*, 2, 60
Samantabhadra, 213n. 44
*Samarpaṇa*, 189
*Sāmāyik*, 24, 83; defined, 221. *See also* Meditation
Samaysundarjī, 123
*Sammūrchim*, 45–46
*Saṃsār* (*saṃsāra*), 48–49, 90, 104, 172; defined, 221
*Samsara*, 201n. 43
*Saṃsārī*, 44
*Saṃsār sāgar*, 123
*Saṃsār yātra*, 49
*Samudāys*, 51–55, 105, 107; defined, 221
*Samvasaraṇ*, 34, 66, 71; defined, 221
*Saṃvatsarī*, 108
Sandalwood paste, 30, 32, 72, 85–86, 91, 127–28
Saṇḍer Gacch, 212n. 40
Sāṇḍvā, 150
Sangave, Vilas A., 198n. 12
*Sangh* (*sangha*), 76, 116, 122, 141, 185; defined, 221. *See also* Pilgrimage: parties
Śani, 188
*Sankaṭ*, 109
*Sankaṭ mocan*, 208n. 60
*Śānta bhāv*, 214n. 4
*Santhārā*, 60
*Śānti kalaś*, 64
Śantināth, 72, 199n. 9
Śāntisūri, 39, 200nn. 21, 22, 201nn. 39, 40, 203n. 13
Śānti Vijay, 102, 205n. 1
Sānt Rāv, 148
Sarāvgīs, 4
Sarvadevgaṇi, 116
*Śāstrārth*, 121, 124
*Śāstras*, 115
*Śāśvat niyam*, 48
*Sāthiyā*. See *Svastiks*
Satī, 143, 145, 150, 211n. 24, 212n. 33
Satīmatā, 145–46
Śatruñjaya, 123, 167, 208n. 53; defined, 221
*Satya*, 57
Saubhāgya Devī, 143
Saudharma Devlok, 119
Saudharmā Munipati, 129
Saurashtra, 166

Schechner, Richard, 12–14
Self-starvation, 2, 60
Seneviratne, H. L., 185–86
*Sevā,* 178
Sexual relations: of deities, 47
Sharma, J. P., 199n. 17
*Siddh (siddha),* 8, 22, 182; defined, 221
Siddhasena, 207n. 35, 213n. 44
*Siddhcakra,* 30, 57, 71, 75; defined, 221
*Siddhis,* 107. *See also* Magical powers
*Siddh śilā,* 8, 38
Sīmandar Svāmī, 119, 200n. 34
Sin, 50–51, 78, 87, 187, 190, 215n. 19; eating and, 58. See also *Pāp*
Sindh, 123
Singer, Milton, 12
Singh, Bhagvān, 150, 212n. 27
Singh, Munshi Hardyal, 139
Singhi, N. K., 198n. 12
Śiva, 118, 141, 150, 152, 167, 182–84, 193, 213n. 44
Smith, Brian K., 81
Smith, Frederick M., 81
Smith, Vincent A., 208n. 53
Snakebite, 142–43, 150–51, 154; in Khartar Gacch legends, 162
Snakes, 166, 178
*Snātra pūjā,* 65, 69–76, 82, 86, 98, 129, 153, 172, 199n. 13, 209n. 64; defined, 221
Social identity: of Jains, 2–3, 11, 169, 171–72; of worshiper, 15–16, 176
Social order, 44, 52, 135, 140
Sociocultural identity, 214n. 8; of lay Jains, 170
Solankīs, 148
Somcandra, 166. *See also* Jindattsūri
Someśvara, 213n. 44
Songs, 28, 34, 58, 65, 109; in Dādāgurus' worship, 127–29; in *snātra pūjā,* 69, 71–72
Soteriology, 8, 10, 16, 43–44, 64, 86, 91, 103, 130–31, 137, 174, 181, 189, 195
Soul, 7–8, 45, 49–51, 82, 91; eating and, 58; unliberated, 172
South Asia: religious traditions, 7, 14, 21, 61, 71, 86, 123, 158, 176, 194, 201n. 48, 208n. 57; ritual cultures, 176–77, 182, 190
Spirit, 28, 60, 84. See also *Bhāv*
Spiritual succession. *See* Disciplic succession
*Śrāvak dharm,* 106, 164
*Śrāvaks,* 6, 163, 166, 197n. 1; defined, 221
*Śrāvikās,* 6; defined, 221
Śrī, 33
Sri Lanka, 186
Śrīmāl (city), 139, 141
Śrīmāl, Rājendra K., 139
Śrīmāls, 4, 17, 111, 122, 139, 141, 151, 169, 209n. 65; defined, 221
Śrīpālcandrajī, 210n. 6
*Śrīphal,* 32. *See also* Coconuts
*Śrut,* 33
Stevenson, Mrs. Sinclair, 214n. 10
Sthānakvāsī, 4, 56, 60, 126, 198n. 11; ascetics, 53; defined, 221; *vāskṣep* and, 61
Sthānsāgar, 105, 109
*Sthāpanācārya,* 57
*Sthāpnā,* 71, 129, 131; defined, 221
*Sthāvar,* 44–45
*Stotra,* 164
*Śubh,* 78. *See also* Auspiciousness
Śubh (Śubhdatt), 34
*Śuddh,* 78
*Śuddhādvaita,* 181
Sudharmā, 54, 109, 129
Śūdra, 183
Suhaṛ, 141–42
*Sukhamā,* 42
Sukhsāgar (Sukhsāgarjī), 55, 105, 107
*Sukṣam,* 45, 201n. 38
Supernatural beings: conversion and, 165–67
Sūrācārya, 114
Sūryakumār, 120. *See also* Jincandrasūri "Maṇidhārī"
Sūryamall, Yati, 119
*Svarga loka,* 81
Svarṇbāhu, 31
*Svarṇsiddhi,* 166
*Svastiks,* 30, 32, 64, 71, 73, 88–90, 144; defined, 221
Svayamprabhsūri, 139, 141–42
Śvetāmbars, 4, 17–19, 61, 103, 137, 199n. 19; ascetics, 53–63; Dādāgurus and, 126; defined, 221; disciplic succession, 109; Jaipur, 65; Paus Daśmī and, 26; Rājpūts and, 139; rituals, 10, 25, 27, 30, 65; self-starvation, 60; temples, 65–69, 88; *vāskṣep* powder and, 61
Sweepers, 215n. 16
Sweets, 95; in rituals of worship, 32, 89, 128, 132, 147, 150, 154–55

Tambiah, S. J., 200n. 32, 203n. 19
Tantrics, 141–42
Tapā Gacch, 17, 52, 54–55, 124, 203n. 15, 209n. 75; Dādāgurus and, 205n. 4; defined, 221; mendicants, 208n.

53; *snātra pūjā* and, 203n. 8; *vāskṣep* and, 61
*Tapas,* 190, 204n. 28
*Tapobal,* 131, 150
Temple priest, 68
Temples, 97, 123, 145–47, 204n. 35; Ahmedabad, 65–66; anniversaries of, 25, 27, 127; Buddha, 185; consecrations of, 121–22; Jain, 3, 65–69, 154, 214n. 8; Jaipur, 55, 65–66; of lineage goddesses, 144; of Mahāvīr, 151–53, 212n. 31; Osiyā, 140, 211n. 26; of Pārśvanāth, 121; of Saciyā Mātā, 149, 152, 212n. 31; Svetambar, 65–66; Vaiṣṇava, 154, 205n. 40
Terāpanthi, 4, 52–53, 56, 61, 106–7, 126, 198n. 11; defined, 221
*Teukāy* (*tejkāy*), 45
*Tīrth,* 5
*Tīrthankar nām karm,* 31, 72, 135, defined, 221
Tīrthankars, 5–8, 22, 27, 32, 52, 104, 109–10, 139, 169, 177, 190–92; ascetic garb of, 199n. 19; asceticism of, 25–26, 38, 82, 84; bathing of image, 96–98; bathing of infant, 33, 70, 74, 86, 179, 206n. 20; in the cosmos, 40–44; Dādāgurus and, 112–13, 131–32, 134–36, 172; defined, 221; dreams before birth of, 31–33, 57, 72, 76, 82, 109; eightfold worship and, 89–91; female, 199n. 4; images of, 66–69, 78, 80, 98, 102, 111, 127, 152, 192, 208n. 61; initiation of, 214n. 9; *kalyānaks* and, 135; kingship and, 175; liberation and, 25–26, 37, 76, 91–92, 100, 110; as objects of worship, 10–11, 19, 23, 25–27, 66, 77, 79, 81, 92, 94, 99, 103, 111, 185, 193; offerings and, 93–94, 96, 209n. 70; omniscience, 7; Puṣṭimārg and, 178–81; rebirth as a, 199n. 14; in *snātra pūjā,* 70, 72, 76, 203n. 12; worship-worthiness of, 36, 53, 62–63, 79, 134; worshipers and, 6, 91–92, 94, 96, 98, 131, 171, 177, 179, 184
*Tiryañc,* 45–46, 48, 50. *See also* Animals and plants
Tonsure ceremony, 144–46, 154
Toomey, Paul M., 179–80
Transmigratory context, 36–38, 135
*Tras,* 44–45
*Tras nāḍī,* 38, 39, 40
Trautmann, Thomas, 16, 190–91
Trilok Singh, 143
Tristuti Gacch, 54
Tughluq, Ghiyasuddin, 122–23
*Tyag,* 90, 101, 131, 184; defined, 221

Udaipur, 198n. 11
*Uddhārapalyas,* 42
Udyotansūri, 114
Uhaṛ, 141–42, 152
Ujjain, 118
Universal emperor, 33, 37, 82. See also *Cakravartin*
*Upādhyāyas,* 22
Upaldev. *See* Utpaldev
*Upāśray,* 55, 60
Updrav, 152, 166, 207n. 39
Upkeś, 140
Upkeś Gacch, 141, 143, 151, 153
*Upkeś Gacch Caritra,* 210n. 9
*Upkeś Gacch Paṭṭāvali,* 210nn. 5, 6, 211nn. 14, 23, 212n. 28
Upkeśīya, 153
Upkeśpur, 142, 147
*Upvās,* 83; defined, 222. *See also* Fasting
*Ūrdhva lok,* 200n. 25
Utpaldev (Upaldev), 141–42, 144, 147–50, 153, 155, 210n. 7, 211n. 23, 212n. 30; defined, 222

*Vacan,* 56
Vaidyas, 212n. 27
*Vaimāniks,* 47
Vaiṣṇavas, 106, 146, 154, 157, 177–81, 184; defined, 222; temples, 154, 205n. 40
Vaiṣṇo Devī, 157–58
Vaiśya, 137, 215n. 20; defined, 222
Vajnābh, 31
Vajrasvāmi, 117
Vallabhācārya, 178, 180–81; defined, 222
Vāmā, Queen, 32, 37
*Vammārgī,* 141–42
*Vaṃs,* 156
*Vanaspatikāy,* 45
Van Gennep, Arnold, 95
Vānkā, 166–67
Vardhmānsūri, 114–15, 128
*Varṇas,* 43, 82, 137, 139, 142, 151, 215n. 20; defined, 222
*Vāskṣep,* 61, 62, 107, 119; defined, 222
*Vāyukāy,* 45
Vedas, 183
Vedic sacrifice. *See* Sacrifice: Vedic
Vegetarianism, 2–3, 23, 45, 47, 138, 146–47, 170, 211n. 24; goddesses and, 155, 157–59. *See also* Eating; Food; Meat eaters
Vicakṣaṇ Bhavan, 55

Vicakṣaṇśrī, 55, 102, 205n. 2
*Vidhimārg,* 115
Vidyut Prabhā Śrī, 119, 207nn. 32, 47, 50, 51
Vijaysensūri, 208n. 53
*Viklendriy,* 45
Vikrampur, 120, 135
Vimal Gacch, 54
Vinaya Sagar, Mahopadhyaya, 57
Vinaysāgar, Mahopādhyāy, 123, 206nn. 26, 29, 207nn. 30, 32, 40, 44, 48, 49, 209n. 66
Violence, 168, 170
*Vīrs,* 204n. 36
*Virya,* 204n. 28
Viṣṇu, 177, 199n. 5, 212n. 31
Vorsidān, 121
Vows: of ascetics, 56–58, 197n. 5
*Vrat*s, 160, 188–89, 192; defined, 222
*Vṛhat Pūjā-Sangrah,* 199n. 9
*Vyantar*s, 47–48, 77, 165–66; defined, 222
*Vyavahārapalya*s, 42

Wealth: and rituals of worship, 25–26
Williams, R., 81, 87, 215n. 18
Women, 24, 54, 84, 160; fasting by, 24–25, 58, 212n. 34; lineage goddesses and, 144, 158, 211n. 17; rituals and, 25, 30
World renunciation, 131, 175, 190
Worship, 24–25, 68, 93; asceticism and, 93, 99, 107, 160; of ascetics, 10, 23–63, 79, 84, 92, 193; congregational, 27, 84–85; of Dādāgurus, 127–30; internal, 91; materials used in, 91; physical, 91, 98; of Tīrthankars, 10–11, 19, 23–26, 110, 193; transformative, 192–93; worldly benefits of, 91–92, 97, 99–101, 126, 128, 133–34, 171, 214n. 12. See also Objects of worship; *Pūjā;* Rituals of worship
Worshipers, 93–94, 100, 171, 183; ascetics and, 61, 68; Dādāgurus and, 103, 126, 129–34, 171–76, 193; deities and, 81, 96, 179; deities as, 79; identity, 174–76; objects of worship and, 94, 131, 174, 178–86; role of, 29–30, 77, 79, 83, 100–101; Tīrthankars and, 6, 91–92, 94, 98, 129–30
Worship-worthiness, 36, 53, 62–63, 77, 79, 134

Yaśobhadrasūri, 164
Yaśodā, 180
*Yati*s, 55, 128, 145; defined, 222
*Yogbal,* 117, 131
Yoginīpur-Delhi, 120
*Yoginī*s, 118, 213n. 41
*Yojan,* 38; defined, 222
*Yugpradhān,* 119, 124; defined, 222

*Zanānā,* 160

Compositor: Jarrett Engineering
Text: 10/13 Sabon
Display: Sabon
Printer: Thomson-Shore, Inc.
Binder: Thomson-Shore, Inc.